# FORTH

LE FORT NE SE SOUMETTRA JAMAIS

DEUS ARMA MINISTRAT

The Armorial Bearings of
**Nathaniel Parker Forth**
( born 1744, died 1809),
granted by William Hawkins, Ulster King of Arms,
on 13th April 1698, to his grandfather Samuel Forth,
Captain in Wolseley's Regiment of Horse,
High Sheriff of Longford in 1704.

# FORTH

## Marion Ward

## Phillimore

1982

Published by
PHILLIMORE & CO. LTD.
London and Chichester

*Head Office*: Shopwyke Hall,
Chichester, Sussex, England

ISBN 0 85033 439 X

Printed and bound in Great Britain by
BILLING & SONS LIMITED
Guildford, London, Oxford, Worcester

# CONTENTS

## I. SPECIAL ENVOY

Chapter 1    The Half-Commission Man    1

2    Paris and Versailles    12

3    Fontainebleau    26

4    The Blackmailer    38

5    The Ladder of Promotion    50

6    End of a Mission    65

7    The Portsmen    79

## II. DUKE'S AGENT

8    In Search of Two Foundlings    93

9    Duties of an Agent    103

## III. PRINCE'S CREDITOR

10    Raising the Wind    121

11    Watershed    137

12    The Du Barry Affair    147

13    Reaping a Whirlwind    157

## IV. ELIZA'S HUSBAND

14    The Revenant    177

15    Husband and Wife    187

16    Eclipse    200

Postscript    212

Notes    213

Index    232

# LIST OF ILLUSTRATIONS

*Frontispiece*: The Armorial Bearings of Nathaniel Parker Forth

(*between pages 78 and 79*)

1. Nathaniel Parker Forth in middle age. Artist unknown
2. Forth aged 59. Artist unknown
3. Eliza Forth, *c*. 1809, by Baron Gérard
4. John Petrie, by Andrew Plimer
5. Frederick Henry Alexander Forth. Artist unknown
6. Sophie Elie Alexandre, Baron Forth Rouen, by Novak
7. William Murray, 1st Earl of Mansfield, 1779, by Nollekens
8. David Murray, 7th Viscount Stormont. Engraving, artist unknown
9. Louis Philippe Joseph, Duke de Chartres by Angelica Kauffmann
10. Pamela with the Countess de Genlis and Mademoiselle d'Orléans. Engraving by Mauzaisse after Giroust
11. Jean Frédéric Phélypeaux, Count de Maurepas. Engraving by Dupin

## ACKNOWLEDGEMENTS FOR PLATES

Plates 1, 2, 4 and 5 are from private collections; plate 3 by courtesy of the late Comte Charles Gerrard de Rohan Chabot; plate 6 by courtesy of the Viscomte François de l'Escale; plates 7 and 8 by courtesy of the Greater London Council as Trustees of the Iveagh Bequest, Kenwood; plate 9 by courtesy of Bibliotèque Nationale, Paris; plates 10 and 11, photos by Giraudon.

*To my Parents*

STEPHEN AND MARION WARD

# PREFACE

NATHANIEL PARKER FORTH, my great-great-grandfather, who is the subject of this biography by Miss Marion Ward, was previously an almost unknown historical figure, but has come prominently into the limelight of recent years.

In 1967 Miss Ward's first book, *The Du Barry Inheritance* was published, in which he was an important character. In that year also, I was approached by Mr. Philip Laski, who was at that time writing *The Trial and Execution of Madame Du Barry*.

He found many references to Nathaniel Parker Forth's diaries in his researches, but could not trace the original diaries which had been handed to me by my father, and which were in my possession.

He was eventually put into touch with me, and I placed the diaries at his disposal, and allowed him to quote those parts which referred to Nathaniel Parker Forth's association with the Comtesse Du Barry.

The 18th century was one of the most interesting epochs of our history. England was ruled over by a monarch who was respected and well beloved by his people, despite his long periods of ill-health.

It was George III who said, when addressing Parliament for the first time '. . . I glory in the name of Briton', and perhaps it was the inspiration of a king who spoke these words which urged my great-great-grandfather in his endeavours to give of a tradition which he inherited from his father, and from his grandfather, the first Captain Samuel Forth, High Sheriff of County Longford, that tough old cavalry soldier of Wolseley's Regiment of Horse, who was in the thick of the fighting in the

Enniskillen, Boyne, and Aughrim campaigns, and who was aide-de-camp to Marshal Duke of Schomberg. On looking back on his exploits, one is reminded of the words of Macaulay's *Armada*:

> With his white hair unbonnetted,
> See the grand old Sheriff comes,
> Behind him march the halbardiers,
> Before him sound the drums.

Since our childhood days in Ireland, my sisters and I seem to have grown up with our ancestor, listening to our father's stories of his activities amidst the glittering splendour of the Court of Versailles, the dangerous role of his diplomatic endeavours, or the exciting pleasures of horse-racing, and the Chasse à Courre, making him a part of our lives. Often we would beg him to tell us more about 'Old Nat', as he was always affectionately called within our family circle.

Whatever Nathaniel Parker Forth's failings and mistakes, and despite his great disappointment at the treatment which he received in later years from the Royal Princes, it is true to say that he always remained a staunch Royalist, eager and proud to be of service.

I have read Miss Ward's book with tremendous pleasure, and I have only one regret—it is that my father, the late Lieut-Colonel Willoughby Forth, 1st Battalion (88th) Connaught Rangers, and H.M. Indian Army, is not alive to read her book.

To him must go the credit for preserving safely in his turn, the diaries, memoirs and documents of his great-grandfather, and for the painstaking research he carried out to add to these.

My father would wish me to pay a special tribute to the late Madame Denyse le Marchand (grand-daughter of Nathaniel Parker Forth) his cousin and greatest friend, who collaborated with him in collecting documents and papers, all of which I placed at Miss Ward's disposal.

Who knows what additional historical information might have come to light had not a bomb demolished the family house of Monsieur Edgard le Marchand, Minister Plenipotentiary to the Pyrenees, husband of my cousin Denyse, at Vernon in Normandie, during the Second World War. In this house was a precious parchment box containing further Forth papers.

I wish also to include among the members of my family who have helped me in gathering information, my cousin the late Lieut-Colonel N. B. de Lancey Forth, D.S.O. and Bar, M.C., the Manchester Regiment, who after my father's death, enthusiastically assisted me in the checking of certain documents at the College of Arms.

I feel a strong sense of personal gratitude to Miss Ward for having portrayed my ancestor so vividly, and for the further very extensive research which she has carried out over the past six years, in order to present a full and accurate account of the life and services of Nathaniel Parker Forth.

N. de ROUEN FORTH

# FOREWORD

WHO IS Nathaniel Parker Forth, and what interest can there be in the life of a minor character in another century?

To the many who like travelling backwards in time there is much to recommend the pursuit of just such a character. Most men or women do not find themselves ruling a country or influencing the lives of thousands. The problems of those who do are, and always have been, exceptional. The average man with his bread to earn and a family to support is bound by other circumstances. These change greatly from one period to another, and in so doing highlight the differences between the present and the past.

By following Forth's career there are many insights to be gained about life in England and France in the mid-18th century and at the time of the French Revolution.Through his eyes, while envoy of the British Government during the War of American Independence, one can take part in crucial negotiations in Paris; oblige the French Court by outwitting a blackmailer of Marie Antoinette; become indispensable to a French Prince of the Blood; and organize an intelligence network. At a later date Forth can be seen making a success in international finance; unwisely lending money to the future Prince Regent of England; helping Madame Du Barry to recover her stolen jewels; and precariously ending his career in France under the surveillance of Napoleon's police.

Forth was a sharp observer with an ear for dialogue. His life is not only entertaining on its own account, but his encounters with other, better-known historical characters show them in an unfamiliar situation: Beaumarchais, the creator of Figaro, combining diplomacy and blackmail, with the Chevalier d'Eon as his victim; Vergennes, the French Foreign Minister, venturing

financial speculations on the outcome of peace or war; and the
generally maligned Philippe Egalité in a more sympathetic light.

History is uncovered at many levels: this portrait of a
Gentleman Unknown is also very much a picture of a period.

# ACKNOWLEDGEMENTS

ONE OF THE pleasures of finishing a book is the chance to acknowledge the kindness of many people who so generously gave their time and their knowledge while work was in progress. Among these, my first very warm thanks must go to Captain Nevill de Rouen Forth, T.D. He not only lent me his great-great-grandfather's papers during the preparation of this book, and allowed me to quote from them, he also gave me the greatest help on all the many questions that arose over the Forth family history. I am glad to have this opportunity to acknowledge gratefully my debt to him and to the other members of his family who also contributed information. Another debt of gratitude is due to three people on whose special skills I depended heavily, my brother Mr. S. G. P. Ward, Mr. John Brooke and Mr. Hugh Murray Baillie. They suggested many fruitful lines of investigation, prevented me from making many mistakes, and added to their kindness by reading the book in manuscript. I am also extremely grateful to the present Viscount Mansfield for allowing me to consult his ancestor's papers at Scone, and to Lady Mansfield for her hospitality. Further thanks are due for help from Mr. J. Imrie of the Scottish Record Office, and to Mr. J. K. Bates and Mrs. Auld of the National Register of Archives (Scotland); to Father Francis Edwards, S.J., who helped me with the Archives at Simancas, and to Mr. and Mrs. José Luis Medina who translated for me; also to Mrs. Stollard and Mrs. Clausen who gave me useful information about their ancestor Lyon de Symons; to the Reverend G. Fitzgerald for information about la belle Paméla, and to Mr. Peter Noble of Messrs. Christopher, wine merchants. Much appreciated help also came from the Salop County Archivist; the Archivist of Barclays Bank Ltd.; and the staffs of the British Library, the London Library and the Public Record Office; with special thanks to the staff of the Royal Commission on Historical Manuscripts. Crown copyright material appears by permission of the Controller of H.M. Stationery Office.

In France I owe much to the help of Monsieur Denis Lambin and his father the late Monsieur Georges Lambin. I am also grateful to Madame d'Huart and Monsieur Géraudel of the Archives Nationales; to Mademoiselle Fleury of the Minutier Centrale; to Maître P. Champenois, Notary of Paris, who allowed me to quote from his firm's archives; to Maître Tricou, Notary and érudit of Lyon: to the Archivists of the Archives Départementales at Lyons and Versailles; to the staff of the Bureau des Cimetières de la Préfecture de la Seine; and to the staff of the Archives Diplomatiques of the Ministère des Affaires Etrangères. I acknowledge permission granted by the Conservateur en Chef to quote from these archives.

# I. SPECIAL ENVOY

## Chapter One

# THE HALF-COMMISSION MAN

IN THE DAYS when King George III reigned in England, and the *ancien régime* was still the established, and very powerful government of France, a man made a fortune and a career for himself in both countries. He did so at a time when this was not easy for someone without great inherited wealth or powerful connexions. Though he receives no mention in the *Dictionary of National Biography*, he played a part in history and was the confidant and intimate friend of men who made it. His name was Nathaniel Parker Forth.

It was a name that was causing a good deal of interest in the early days of the year 1777. Several Foreign Ministers were asking their ambassadors in London who was Mr. Forth, and receiving some very varied replies. He was an Irishman; a stock jobber; a spy with an indiscreet mistress; an intimate of the Earl of Mansfield; he was attached to the British Embassy at Paris. They might have added that he was a bold rider who helped to introduce the English form of horse-racing to France, and a musician who never travelled without taking his violin with him, and sometimes a viola as well.

1

Forth was born at Ludlow Castle in Shropshire on 29 July 1744. When he was eight the Gregorian calendar replaced the Julian in England, and from that time Forth celebrated his birthday on 9 August. He was a man who enjoyed anniversaries so that the change was probably as unwelcome to him as it was to others who clamoured for the return of their eleven lost days.

The Forths were Anglo-Irish gentry settled for several generations on estates in the County of Longford in Leinster.

Forth's father Samuel held a position as Sovereign of Longford, an office that combined the functions of mayor and military governor. Forth's mother Eleanor Bray, Samuel's second wife, was related to the Parkers, a family which in Elizabethan times had produced an Archbishop of Canterbury, and nearer to Forth's day included Lord Chancellor Macclesfield and his grandson General Lane Parker. It was from the Parker family that Forth derived his second name.[1]

From his schooling, which he probably received at a private school near his home, Forth retained a working knowledge of Latin, together with a number of quotations to store in his excellent memory. He also acquired a good head for figures. In his holidays he rode whenever and whatever he could, becoming in the process a daring and knowledgeable horseman.

It had always been clear that Forth would have to earn his living. His family was prosperous, with a town house in Dublin as well as the Ballymacormic estate, but Nat was a younger son and it was his elder brother Sam who would inherit. Two married sisters, one living in Radnorshire and the other in Hanover, would also have expectations under their father's Will. Forth's income would depend mainly on his own efforts.

Of the two professions in which his family usually engaged, the Army and the Law, Forth's first choice was the Law. But after a little Forth found that he preferred a more active life. It was probably in 1761 or '62, when he was 17 or 18, that General Lane Parker brought Forth to the notice of the great William Pitt in the hope that he might find an opening for his young relation. Nothing came of the introduction. The intervention of another family connexion was more effective. Through a cousin also named Samuel Forth, an extremely wealthy brewer, Forth found employment in the wine trade in the Iberian Peninsula. There he made contact with the banker Robert Herries.[2]

A man with many financial interests, Herries was head of merchant banks in London, Edinburgh and Barcelona (where he was known as Don Roberto). Another Herries bank operated at Antwerp under the direction of one of Herries's relations. But his enterprises were not limited to banking. Robert Herries had trading interests that extended throughout Europe to North

America and India; he issued insurance policies, and pioneered a form of traveller's cheque. Above all he was determined to acquire a large stake in the highly profitable contracts between English and Scottish banks and the French Farmers General for the North American tobacco imports. Here he was in competition with powerful rivals, in particular the London bank of Bourdieu and Chollet.

Forth received his first lessons in international finance under Herries's direction. In the early 1760's England was at war with France. Payment of the armies and navies fighting on the European Continent, in North America, India and on the High Seas was an immensely complicated business. The ships that returned to the British Isles from North America via the Iberian Peninsula with cotton, fish or tobacco also carried Portuguese gold and Spanish silver piastres to pay the troops. The Herries subsidiary at Antwerp, connected with the powerful Hope bank of Amsterdam, and able to rely on a network of exchange facilities all over Europe, was a powerful link in the chain of distribution.

The French on their side were faced with similar problems. Agents of the French financiers who were responsible for raising money to pay the French forces were also in Spain negotiating for supplies of bullion and piastres. One of them was a man whom Forth was to meet at various stages of his career, the playwright Caron de Beaumarchais.

## 2

In 1764, when Forth was twenty, two important events occurred: he inherited £1,000 from his father, and he paid his first visit to France, the country in which he was to spend so much of his life.

It was probably his association with Robert Herries that decided Forth to make a living in France. It was a logical choice for someone connected with the wine trade, but the prospect also offered favourable opportunities for finance and commerce. Herries was still working hard to obtain the French tobacco contracts; at the same time he was engaged with other bankers and merchants in a plan to establish a discount bank in Paris. He was equally involved in securing a share in the French East Indian trade which, now that the British had captured so many of the French possessions in India, could not easily be financed without the help of foreign capital.

Forth could be of considerable help to Herries, particularly in the search for capital. He was all the more able to suggest where this was to be found because he had begun to supplement his earnings as a wine merchant with money derived from stockbroking. The Stock Exchange, which was then at a very early stage in its development, included a certain number of outside dealers who bought and sold for clients on commission. They were allowed a half per cent on each transaction, and were called half-commission men. It was as one of these that Forth now began to operate and to acquire a group of clients in France and England.

There were only a small number of securities, mainly English, in which Forth's clients could invest: Government Stock and loans; and South Sea or East India Company Stock. Englishmen and Dutchmen had invested, and on occasion, gambled in all these for many years, but Frenchmen had been suspicious of credit transactions since the days of John Law and the Mississippi Company. But there were many Frenchmen who had made money in the war that had just ended. Not all of them wanted to invest their profits in the traditional purchase of land; some of them were inclined to try something more speculative. Forth took advantage of the new demand.

At least some of Forth's clients were men who did not want it known that they were speculating. There was no rule that broker's and client's accounts should be kept separately. Forth made investments in his own name, passed all the money arising from the transaction through his own bank account, later on settling with the client. A separate secret ledger showed the state of the client's account. In this ledger each client had a code name.

With characteristic energy and ingenuity Forth developed another way of making himself useful to Robert Herries and his associates. With so many interests in insurance and trading ventures of different kinds it was vital for Herries to have fast, reliable information about the arrival and departure of ships and their cargoes. Forth organized an intelligence network to collect and distribute precisely this kind of information. He had agents in the main French seaports to pass on news of shipping movements; he also derived intelligence from the captains of vessels. In a letter which he wrote later in his life he remarked that captains of packet vessels would go to great lengths for money. No doubt it was when he was setting up his network that he discovered this useful fact.

Forth's life was by no means only spent working. He had a wide circle of friends and acquaintances both in London and Paris, and was able to build up a useful clientèle as wine merchant and as stockbroker. He enjoyed giving and receiving hospitality, and was himself very good company. France as it happened was full of Irishmen. Many of them were descendants of the Wild Geese who followed the fortunes of the Stuart kings, afterwards making careers for themselves in France. Some of them entered the foreign regiments of the French army, Forth's friends, the brothers O'Toole among them. Others, like the Fitzgeralds, became bankers. There were also shipowners such as Walsh de Serrant and the Boyds; wine merchants, such as the Lynches and O'Gormans; or financiers and industrialists like Thomas Sutton, Count Clonard. Although Forth was of the Protestant ascendancy and a loyal subject of King George III he thought of himself as an Irishman; when mentioning a dinner party in his Diary he wrote: "13 to dinner, all Irish",

With a compatriot, young Lord Forbes, son of the Earl of Granard whose estates lay near Forth's family home in County Longford, Forth first briefly caught the public eye in February 1766. The occasion was a horse race on the Plaine des Sablons in the Bois de Boulogne. It was organized by the Count de Lauraguais, a slightly eccentric, anglophile French nobleman, part of whose considerable wealth was invested in some of Herries's enterprises. Lauraguais had a passion for horses, and was now proposing to stage races on English lines with bets on the result. In the first race on 28 February Lauraguais himself rode against Lord Forbes; in a later race Forth on a horse named *Lifeline* was to compete with the Prince of Nassau on *Noir et tout Noir*. Feeling ran high. Forbes won his race, but in the evening Lauraguais's horse was found poisoned. Horace Walpole writing from Paris to his friends in England told them that an English groom in Lauraguais's stables was suspected: 'as if poison was as common as oats and beans in the stables at Newmarket'. The outcry was such that the King at first forbad the running of the second race. Later he relented, but interest had died down, and Walpole was not there to report whether Forth won or lost.[3]

It was not until 1775, nine years later, that the new King of France's young brother, the Count d'Artois, revived an interest in racing. Once again Forth played a leading part.

### 3

During the interval Forth prospered. He concentrated on stockbroking and almost ceased to deal in wine. He acquired some influential clients in France and England, and many useful contacts with bankers and businessmen in both countries. Other contacts were less respectable. Forth's commercial intelligence service, which he continued to operate, brought him into strange company: smugglers, waterfront loiterers, and any other doubtful character who was ready to sell information for money. In this half-world Forth himself was under observation by Herries's business rivals and his own.

In 1776 Forth was in his early thirties, at the height of his powers, good looking and well made, though this might not have been apparent from the description on his passport: 'height, 5 feet 9 inches; eyes, blue; face and nose, long'. His surviving portraits, painted late in his life, when he was already a sick man, nevertheless suggest the self-confidence of someone who knows that he has the power to please.

Forth's temperament was active; physical exercises, especially riding and hunting, were important to him. But he was also a man of some culture who read for pleasure as well as information. When he moved house his books were usually the first of his possessions to be arranged. On his shelves there were works of topical interest such as the *Letters of Junius*, and it was said by one of his contemporaries that Forth was one of the very few to know who Junius really was.[4] There were also poetry and plays, the poets being those with whose works he was familiar in his youth, Swift, Pope and Gay. By no means all his books were English. Forth was a good linguist who spoke French, Spanish and Italian, and at least some German.

Among the few books in Forth's library still in the possession of his descendants are some works of devotion. One of them, *The Week's Preparation for the Worthy Receiving of the Lord's Supper*, shows several passages where Forth has made alterations in pencil to adapt the meditations to his circumstances. Another, *The Christian's Pattern*, acquired in 1773 and used as a means of identification on a mission to Madrid, has been similarly adapted, and prayers have been inserted.[5] Forth's beliefs were sincere and clearly defined, formed in the moderate climate of the earlier eighteenth century; neither scepticism, nor the newer forms of evangelism had touched them.

It was music that stirred Forth's emotions most strongly. In him the love of music ran very deep, and was the foundation of many of his friendships. Born with a good ear and an agreeable singing voice, he had also learnt to play the violin and the viola. At least one of these instruments accompanied Forth on his many journeys, and when he was ill and in pain he turned to his violin for comfort.

In houses and possessions Forth's taste was for the new and fashionable; the antiquarian or the gothic were not at all his style. In London he had a house in Somerset Street in the newly developing quarter of St. Marylebone; in Paris he chose the equally new quarter that was gradually being built on the lower slopes of the hill of Montmartre. He bought china and jasper ware from Wedgwood; handsome wall mirrors and furniture from Poirier and Daguerre. His apartment, which he himself described as richly furnished, certainly contained pieces which were bright with inlay and ormolu. But if Forth liked comfort and luxury, and enjoyed entertaining his friends, he did not live beyond his means. He kept careful accounts of income and expenditure, paid his bills promptly, and gave his household servants their wages regularly every Sunday. He was equally methodical in writing up his diary daily for 36 years.

At the age of 32 Forth was still unmarried. It would have been natural for a man of his time, with its view of marriage

as an alliance rather than a partnership, to choose a wife with
money or useful family connexions to help him in making a
career. Forth did nothing so prudent. In 1776 he took as his
mistress a young girl of 17, pretty and well educated, but
penniless. Her name was Elizabeth Dorothea Child; Forth called
her Betsy.

For reasons that will appear, very little is known about
Betsy. According to a tradition in the Forth family she is said
to have been related to Childs the bankers. If so, her parents
may have been Josiah Child and his wife Henrietta Knight.
Josiah, a Lieutenant of Dragoons, was a younger son of the
extremely rich Earl of Tylney; Henrietta's father, Lord Luxborough, later Earl of Catherlough, came of a landed
Warwickshire family, and her mother was a step-sister of the
famous Viscount Bolingbroke. A less reputable relation, her
grandfather Robert Knight, had been cashier to the South Sea
Company, and only escaped prosecution by fleeing to Paris
where he set up as a banker. Henrietta was married to another
man when Josiah ran away with her in 1751, and it was not
until 1754 that her legal husband eventually divorced her and
she was free to remarry. By that time she and Josiah had at
least one child. After their marriage the couple lived gaily and
extravagantly in Paris, or elsewhere on the Continent when
war or their own lack of funds made it necessary to move. In
1760 Josiah died of consumption at Lyons, leaving his wife
and children very hard pressed for money. Not long afterwards
Henrietta married for the third time, and died in 1763. It is
not clear how many children there were by this time, or what
became of them. The elder boy was brought up in England by
his grandfather, Lord Luxborough; another much younger
child seems to have been left with foster parents. If Betsy, who
was born on 19 January 1759, was one of Henrietta's children,
she would have been four at her mother's death, and might also
have been left in charge of foster parents. It seems certain that
by the time Forth met her, probably through one of the
Knights who was an agent in his intelligence system, she was
badly in need of a protector.[6]

Forth took Betsy under his protection because he was very
much in love with her. But he nevertheless acted chivalrously.

He was generous to her, acknowledged the children that she bore him, treated her as his wife, and expected his friends to do the same. In Betsy's case there were no obstacles of birth or breeding to make this difficult; she could take her place as Mrs. Forth in the highest society. Nevertheless her situation caused complications at a period when, because the phrase 'living in sin' was not merely a figure of speech but the expression of the accepted point of view, it was considered improper for a 'respectably married' woman to meet a man's mistress. It would have been a great deal easier for everyone if Forth had married Betsy. The fact that he did not suggests that there was some obstacle. Perhaps she had been early and unhappily married to a man who was known to be still alive. Whatever the explanation, the fact remains that although for many years Forth was happy with Betsy, this marriage which was no marriage was something of a handicap.

4

In 1777, the year after Forth set up house with Betsy, his life changed decisively. He found himself playing a part in public affairs at a very high level. The change was one result of his friendship with Lord Mansfield.

Lord Chief Justice of England, the 1st Earl of Mansfield was not only a remarkable lawyer, but a man who exercised a great deal of influence in many, sometimes unexpected, places. His first link with Forth was a business one. It is likely that since stock-broking was Forth's profession he invested money for Mansfield. But the relationship soon developed into a close and affectionate friendship. Mansfield called Forth his Mercury because of the speed with which he acted. Forth's name for Mansfield in his Diary (and perhaps in his Ledger), was *Caute*.

It was a great advantage to Forth to be known as a protégé of Lord Mansfield. It certainly eased his relations with the British Ambassador in Paris, Mansfield's nephew and heir, Viscount Stormont. Without Mansfield's friendship it is unlikely that Forth would have seen more of Stormont than any other British resident in a foreign capital sees of his Ambassador. As it was, Stormont came to know Forth well.

Through his intelligence system, especially after the War of
American Independence ·began, Forth was frequently able to
give Stormont useful information. Stormont, for his part, used
Forth on several occasions to make enquiries which he could
not have made himself. He was, Lord Stormont wrote, 'uncom-
monly well acquainted [with France], has numerous connexions with men of different ranks and parties, and from the
address with which he manages these connexions he has often
been able to supply me with such lights as have been the
greatest use to me, and [in order] to do this the more effectu-
ally he has been obliged to assume different shapes, and
sometimes to avoid the appearance of any such connexion.
But he has always acted in secret concert with me . . . ".[7]

The turning point in Forth's life occurred in January 1777
when he was introduced to the French King's Chief Minister,
the Count de Maurepas. How this unlikely meeting came about
remains mysterious. Maurepas said that it was an accident which
seemed like a situation in a dream. Forth's account is not
available as his Diary for this period no longer exists. Afterwards it suited all the parties concerned for it to be supposed
that the introduction took place under Stormont's auspices.
But if, as seems very likely, the idea was Stormont's, at the
time, he pretended to know nothing about it. He was, he told
Maurepas, agreeably surprised to hear of the encounter.[8]

There was some ground for supposing that Maurepas would
find Forth congenial. He possessed the gift of making people
laugh, something that Maurepas always enjoyed. But no one
could have guessed that Maurepas would take so strong a liking
to Forth that he asked if it could be arranged for the British
Government to accredit Forth to him as a Special Envoy. He
was afraid that Stormont might take offence at the suggestion,
so Forth was to keep the plan secret until the British Government had considered it. But Forth's loyalty was to Stormont,
and he reported everything to him.[9]

The proposal that Forth should be made a Special Envoy
was surprising, but Stormont had good reasons for supporting
it. He wrote to the British Prime Minister, Lord North, and to
his own immediate superior, Lord Weymouth, one of the
Secretaries of State, introducing Forth as an English gentleman

of very good family, related to several noble families in England and Ireland, and a man to whose address and abilities he owed much useful information. He left it to Forth to explain Maurepas's proposal, and to present Maurepas's written request to Weymouth and Lord North.

## Chapter 2

# PARIS AND VERSAILLES

## 1

THE APPOINTMENT which Maurepas was proposing for Forth was the outcome of a clash of personalities. At a time of great tension in Anglo-French relations the British Ambassador and the French King's principal Minister were antipathetic.

England was at war with her North American colonies, the colonists had declared themselves independent of the mother country, and a mission which included Benjamin Franklin was at that moment in Paris urging the French to sign a treaty of friendship and commerce. Meanwhile assistance in armaments and provisions were already being supplied privately to the Americans, principally from France, Spain and Holland. England was claiming the right to search ships crossing the Atlantic, and protesting to the French about the use of French ports by American privateers. These were the awkward questions which formed the subjects of Lord Stormont's frequent conversations with the Count de Maurepas.

Both men in their different ways were feeling the strain. Each reacted differently. Lord Stormont's handsome presence and somewhat stiff manner concealed a highly-strung temperament. In moments of agitation, as he himself admitted, he was apt to become excited and talk volubly. In contrast, Maurepas at the age of 78 was superficially frivolous, but his long experience of public service had taught him to mistrust too much zeal. It seemed to him that Lord Stormont was bullying him almost unbearably: he would, he said, prefer a war to being forced to listen to Lord Stormont's inquisition. Both men had exhausted the diplomat's arsenal of polite questions and soft answers. The important factor, as they knew, was the

military situation in North America. If the English armies could
hold their own, the French would probably refrain from open
support; if they were unsuccessful the French would almost
certainly join the colonists, and declare war on England. The
French were all the more ready to do so because they deeply
resented the English conquests in Canada and India during the
last war. Maurepas, who had spent the early part of his official
career at the Ministry of Marine preparing the French Navy to
fight the British, was as likely as any of his compatriots to
welcome the prospect of a fight.[1]

If Forth were appointed to act as intermediary between
Maurepas and Stormont he would remove some of the
friction caused by their personal antipaties. It had been no
help that Stormont, who had many French friends and knew
Paris well, could put his requests into excellent French, or
that Maurepas was one of the comparatively few Frenchmen of his day to know English. Forth's position would be
easier. Because he would not be speaking as the King of
England's official representative, he could on Stormont's
instructions put forward a request or make a demand in
language much blunter than Stormont could appropriately
use. Maurepas could, and did, call him a *fier anglais* without
giving offence.

It would be an additional advantage if Forth had the power
to keep Maurepas amused. It was rumoured that Maurepas's
colleagues kept a supply of jokes ready for just such a purpose. Nor was this unexpected in a Minister who had been
disgraced in the previous reign for an ill-timed (and cruel)
lampoon on Madame de Pompadour, and had commissioned
a collection of satirical verse on all the notables of the day
to entertain him in his exile. Maurepas was himself supposed to
have collaborated with a group of friends in composing a
series of *contes drolatiques*, some related by a Parisian
coachman, and others by a group of housewives shelling peas.
If Forth and Maurepas shared a similar sense of humour it
might be very helpful.

Considerations of this kind were in Lord Stormont's mind
when he recommended his Government to agree to the appointment of Forth as Special Envoy to Maurepas.

2

The Prime Minister, Lord North, discussed the question with
King George III. Both admitted there were objections, some of
them connected with Forth's character. Lord North described
him as 'a very singular man, an adventurer, and a very indiscreet
talker'. The King had heard that he was a stock jobber, a way
of making money that he detested. The King and the Prime
Minister were both influenced by a report which they had
recently received from Lieutenant-Colonel Smith, a government
agent at Le Havre, that Forth had been heard to say that he
could bring about the dismissal of the French Minister of
Marine. 'Some caution', Smith wrote, 'may be necessary with
any man . . . who having things of such importance in contemplation, shall be incautious enough to have put it in the
power of a stranger to attain his secret, or himself be so eager
in his pursuit of information to be suspected in French
company of being a spy to the English ambassador.'[2]

But in spite of these reports the King and his Prime Minister
thought the experiment worth making. Lord North believed
that Forth was 'fair and honest in the business he had now
undertaken'. The King trusted 'that able negotiator' Lord
Stormont to keep Forth on the right lines, and insisted that his
instructions should be drafted in such a way as to give him
little chance of independent action. He was to take Stormont's
instructions before every interview with Maurepas, and report
back to Stormont afterwards; if this was done the King thought
that there were decided advantages in an unofficial envoy.
'There cannot be a doubt,' he wrote of Forth's mission on a
later occasion, 'that through a private hand stronger demands
may be applied for and granted than through an ambassador
it would be either seemly to grant or proper to make.'[3]

On the subject of what Forth was to be paid Lord North
suggested it would be unwise to allow him too much to begin
with: 'as Mr. Forth hopes some time or other to have a permanent position Lord North would propose to give him at present
£1,000. He is extremely poor which he has more than once
signified to Lord North'. The King agreed that Lord North
judged very properly, and added that since Forth would

certainly expect more before his commission is at an end, Lord
North 'would do well to explain to him that this is but an earnest
of what he may expect if he can be of essential service . . .'.[4]

The discussions about Forth's appointment took time, and
although a letter accrediting him as Special Envoy from the
British Government to the Count de Maurepas had been signed
on 23 February by Lord North and the two Secretaries of State
for the Northern and Southern Departments, it was not until
late March that Forth returned to Paris to take up his duties.[5]

3

In weighing the advantages and disadvantages of Forth's
appointment King George III and Lord North very naturally
had regard mainly to the interests of their own country. They
did their best to ensure that lines of communication were
not likely to cross, and that Forth's responsibility should in
no way rival Lord Stormont's. But they did not guess how odd
the appearance of a Special Envoy as well as an ambassador
might look to other governments.

Maurepas's reluctance to discuss business with Stormont
was not entirely due to personal dislike. He also believed that
the Ministers in England were divided, and that Stormont
was not in the confidence of the more influential Ministers.
He hoped that through Forth he might have access to the men
who counted. When, later on, Stormont heard Maurepas's
views he was not unduly worried; sure of his own position, he
supposed that Maurepas had been listening to reports from
Franklin in Paris, or a very anti-British Secretary at the French
Embassy in London.[6]

But Maurepas's doubts were genuine. He discussed them,
together with his views on Forth, with the Spanish ambassador
in Paris. Stormont might have worried more had he known it
because Spain, also ruled by a Bourbon king, was France's
principal ally. Like France, Spain was supplying arms and
other material to the Americans; if France declared war on
England, Spain would follow suit. The Spanish ambassador
had already heard of Forth's appointment, and thoroughly
disapproved. In his view, business should be conducted through
the appropriate channels of ambassador and foreign minister;

the presence of a Special Envoy could only cause complications. Maurepas assured the ambassador that Forth was a favourite of Lord Mansfield, who trusted him more than his nephew Lord Stormont. This should have been good news for the Spanish ambassador since the Spaniards held exaggerated ideas of Lord Mansfield's importance in the British Government, but it did nothing to lessen the ambassador's mistrust of Forth. His informant had told him that Forth drank too much, and frequented bad company. The ambassador expected nothing but trouble; Forth, he wrote to his government, would be like another little bull in the ring.[7]

It might not have occurred to King George III and his Prime Minister that Forth's mission would provoke the disapproval of the Spanish Government, but they certainly assumed that Maurepas would justify it to his own colleague the Count de Vergennes, the Minister for Foreign Affairs. Maurepas, however, told Vergennes nothing. Vergennes was forced to seek information about Forth from the French ambassador in London. Perhaps Maurepas was influenced by his early experience of government in the reign of Louis XV, when a completely separate foreign policy, le Secret du Roi, was administered at the same time as the official one. Whatever his reason, he continued to discuss affairs of state with someone of whose existence Vergennes was officially ignorant.

Vergennes was extremely hostile to England, 'that arrogant Power [which] took satisfaction in humiliating us . . . whose name alone should arouse a feeling of indignation and revenge in the heart of all patriotic Frenchmen'. He hoped that the war in North America would not only give France the opportunity to inflict defeat on the British forces on land and sea, but would also deprive Britain of a large part of her commerce.[8] In these views he was supported by a man who from personal experience could tell him something about Forth, Caron de Beaumarchais.

Imaginative, audacious, malicious and greedy, Beaumarchais was at this time in almost daily correspondence with the Ministry of Foreign Affairs. His witty, informal letters, signed only with the initial B, make a pleasant contrast with the more solid diplimatic material in which they are embedded. It was

Beaumarchais's responsibility to organize the supply of ships, arms and funds to the Americans until the French were ready to do so openly. A credit of one million livres had been made available for the purpose; almost all of it was passing through Beaumarchais's hands. He had set up an agency, Rodriguez Hortales and Company, in offices in the Rue Vieille du Temple to raise loans, build ships and procure munitions and stores. In theory Rodriguez Hortales was no more than a private company, but it was pretty generally known that it was acting with the approval of the French Government.

Beaumarchais was no novice in finance or commerce. His knowledge of the Spanish bullion trade, gained in the first place while acquiring raw material for his father's watch-making business, proved extremely useful in wartime to the financier Pâris Duverney. But after the war was over and Duverney was dead, Beaumarchais became involved in a series of lawsuits with Duverney's heir, and attempted to bribe the wife of one of the lawyers on his opponents' side. By a number of clever, entertaining pamphlets he succeeded in making his opponents look ridiculous, but his conduct was officially censored, and he was deprived of his civil rights. In order to regain them Beaumarchais undertook more than one secret mission on behalf of the French Government; the last of these was the administration of the funds for America, an undertaking which also looked as if it might prove very profitable.

In constant touch with the ports where his ships were built and freighted, and with the bankers from whom he obtained credit, Beaumarchais was moving in the same circles as Forth, and no doubt obtained intelligence from some of Forth's informants. On 16 February Beaumarchais told Vergennes that 'Forstre' employed as courier a man named La Chèvre, 'who runs contraband between Calais and Dover and back ... Forstre's mistress in London [Betsy] rashly confided to someone that this smuggler was a spy in English pay'.[9]

Forth, on his side, was keeping watch on Beaumarchais. Not long after he was appointed Special Envoy he attempted to suborn Beaumarchais's secretary Théveneau de Francy. It would have been extremely useful to Stormont to have an informant in Rodriguez Hortales and Company. Forth knew that Francy's

brother in London, Théveneau de Morande, was a rogue who
would do almost anything for money; he assumed that Francy
was equally open to corruption. On 11 April Beaumarchais sent
Vergennes a description of a situation which might easily have
occurred in one of his plays: 'Mr. Forts, Lord Mansfield's
friend, is back in Paris. He is the bearer of an urgent letter to
my secretary inviting him very politely to allow himself to be
corrupted . . . Very honestly he handed the letter to me. Forts
is due to see him this morning. I propose to show him the
letter that he delivered yesterday unopened, and ask him why
he did not do me the honour of addressing this flattering
invitation to me. I shall be interested to know what he says
when I tease him . . . ".[10]

Perhaps Forth could not be blamed for supposing that
Francy, like his brother, had his price. But looked at from
another point of view this was not quite the sort of business
in which a Special Envoy appeared to advantage. Vergennes
could hardly be blamed for believing that Forth was a man
to be found on the shadier side of diplomacy.

4

In other directions Forth was more successful. He was gradually
making himself familiar with the duties of his new post,
spending much of his time with Lord Stormont at the Embassy,
which was then not a permanent official building but the
Ambassador's private residence where he lived with his young
second wife. The house which Stormont had chosen was the
Hôtel de Deux-Ponts in the Rue Neuve des Augustins. It was
rented from the Countess de Forbach, once the morganatic
wife, and now the widow of the German Duke of Deux-Ponts.
The Countess, who had begun her career as a dancer, liked the
company of artists, musicians and men of letters, especially
the Encyclopaedists, and in her husband's lifetime the Hôtel
de Deux-Ponts had sheltered Gluck while he was rehearsing
the Paris production of *Iphigénie en Aulide*, and composing
*Orphée*. The Hôtel was magnificent, the work of the architect
Hardouin Mansart, redecorated by Pierre Patte for the Deux-
Pont family. It had a vast garden stretching northwards to the

Chaussée d'Antin, beyond which lay cornfields and market gardens sloping up to the windmill-crowned hill of Montmartre.[11]

Forth soon came to know and like most of the members of Stormont's small official 'family', The First Secretary was a newcomer, William Fullarton, a young Scotsman, related to the Adam brothers, and possessed of a great fortune derived from the East India trade. He was a keen horseman who also liked music and paintings: Hogarth's *Rake's Progress*, now in the Soane Museum, was once in his possession. In Paris Fullarton lived in an enchanting Pavilion on the Boulevard de Clichy, the Pavillon Bouëxière (or Boissière); its pièce d'eau. long since filled in, covered much of what is now the Place Adolphe Max. Fullarton liked to entertain at his Pavilion, and Forth was often a guest at his déjeuners dinant and parties with music.

Forth was even more drawn to another of Stormont's secretaries, the Reverend Thomas Jeans, an ex-fellow of New College. Like Forth he was a Freemason, and he also shared his interest in horse-racing. Another friend, Dr. Gem, for many years physician to the Embassy and some of the British residents in Paris, was an important member of Forth's intelligence system. He was considerably older than Fullarton or Jeans, devoted to dogs, a freethinker and an eccentric. Except officially, Forth had little to do with the rest of the Embassy staff, Riddell, another secretary, and Matey, Stormont's chaplain.[12]

While Forth's official appointment considerably increased the pleasures of his life, it was very different for Betsy. She was expecting a child when Forth returned to Paris as special Envoy, but when she rejoined him she was faced with all the difficulties of her ambiguous situation. So long as he had no official position it did not greatly matter if she was Forth's wife or his mistress, but now there were functions which Forth could attend and Betsy could not. She could not be received by Lady Stormont at the Embassy, still less could she be presented at the Court of Versailles. Forth's bachelor friends included Betsy in their invitations, and she was on visiting terms with Lady Barrymore, a somewhat raffish widow, connected by marriage with Forth's business contacts, the

Foleys. Otherwise she spent all too much time waiting in
Forth's carriage while he was with Stormont, or at an inn at
Versailles while he was with Maurepas. It was natural that she
sometimes made scenes. The entries in Forth's Diary, 'returned
home, found Betsy quarrelling with Mr. Jeans', and 'Betsy
broke a saucer . . . very wrong', surely refer to occasions when
her situation seemed intolerable to a girl who was lively, hot-
tempered, and only 18.[13]

The Palace of Versailles, or at any rate that part which contained the Count of Maurepas's quarters, soon became as
familiar to Forth as the British Embassy. Maurepas was lodged
on the second floor of the Palace, immediately above the
King's private apartments, in the suite of small rooms which
had once been occupied by Madame Du Barry. The fact that
these rooms were now allotted to the King's Chief Minister
was one sign of the deliberate break which the young Louis
XVI was making with the policies and associations of the
preceding reign. The King's Council Chamber was below
Maurepas's room, and it sometimes happened that when Forth
was with Maurepas the members of the King's Council
assembled there before descending together for a Council
Meeting. When that happened Forth either awaited Maurepas's
return in his secretary's room, or adjourned to Maurepas's
house, the Hermitage, which had belonged to Madame de
Pompadour.[14]

Forth greatly enjoyed his visits to Maurepas. It was agreeable
to be received at the Palace as His Britannic Majesty's Special
Envoy; to enter by the *vestibule de la Chapelle*, and to be
ushered up the King's staircase to Maurepas's suite, there
to be greeted warmly by Lecler du Brillet, Maurepas's chief
secretary, and shown, a sure sign of favour, straight into the
Minister's presence without waiting in his anteroom. It was
even more flattering when others were denied entrance: '[they]
come to tell him M. de Castries is waiting. Timeo [Forth's
name for Maurepas] furious; "I gave orders that no one should
be admitted except my friend here" '.[15]

There was also the satisfaction of obliging a friend. In the
autumn of 1777, when Robert Herries came to Paris in yet
another bid to obtain the tobacco contract, Forth not only

convinced Maurepas that Herries could manage the business better than his rivals Bourdieu and Chollet, but arranged an interview in which Maurepas was remarkably civil to Herries, and received him before any of the crowd of other suitors waiting in his anteroom.[16]

On a higher level than that of mere self-esteem it was a privilege to be on familiar terms with a man of Maurepas's importance and long experience. If Maurepas was in an expansive mood he would talk to Forth about Louis XVI's attitude to the Ministers of the previous reign, his own views on his predecessor Choiseul and the Noailles family, or the problem of the Bavarian Succession. Plainly Maurepas was enjoying his conversations with the Special Envoy, creating an atmosphere in which Stormont and Maurepas could meet in a more friendly spirit than had been possible for some time.

In March, soon after Forth arrived in Paris with his Commission from the British Government, Stormont thought the moment had come to tell Maurepas that he was aware of Forth's appointment, and felt no resentment. The two men discussed Forth at length, both praising his activity and zeal, and both agreeing that although he was a man with *un caractère à lui*, he was completely frank and open, and incapable of acting dishonorably.[17]

Soon Stormont was telling the Secretary of State that Forth was proving 'of essential use', and Lord North revised his earlier doubts as to Forth's discretion. He told Stormont that in his opinion it would be very difficult for Forth's conversations with Maurepas to go unnoticed in so observing and intriguing a country as France. If there was unfavourable gossip about Forth, it was probably circulated by those whose interests lay in keeping France and Great Britain apart.[18]

## 5

Several times between April and September Forth helped Stormont to keep the peace between England and France while the main issue was being decided on the battlefields of North America.

One of the most contentious issues was naval rearmament. In April Stormont heard that the French had ordered the Brest fleet to be increased from 13 ships to 20, and that the annual sailing of the Newfoundland fishing fleet had been postponed. The orders followed a report from the French Ambassador in London that the English were increasing the number of their ships of the line of battle in preparation for an attack on French ports. Stormont asked Forth to explain the situation to Maurepas, and to convince him that although some extra ships were being sent to Lord Howe's fleet off the coast of America, they were not intended to serve in Europe. Forth was also to suggest that England and France should agree not to arm any more battleships.[19]

At first it looked as if Forth's mission would be a complete success. Maurepas was ready to believe that there was no immediate danger of an English attack on French ports, and that therefore it would be safe to allow the Newfoundland fishing fleet to sail. Forth also satisfied Maurepas that England was not increasing the number of capital ships in European waters; he even persuaded him to agree to halt further naval armament. He drew up two copies of the points which had been agreed, one for Stormont, and the other for Maurepas. Stormont was delighted, and sent Forth to London to report on the success of his negotiations.

Unluckily when Vergennes heard what Maurepas had agreed he was horrified. Maurepas, he said, was weakening France by agreeing to halt naval armament, and he would discourage the Americans who were counting on the help of the French navy; besides it was impossible to enter into any formal agreement about the size of the French navy without informing France's ally Spain. There was no harm in letting the Newfoundland fishing fleet sail, but on the question of naval armament, Stormont should be told that the agreement which Forth had drawn up was no more than a note of points that had been discussed; it was not valid without the French King's signature.

Forth returned to England to find the most important part of the agreement with Maurepas already a dead letter. Maurepas assured Stormont that there was no change of alteration in French sentiments of intentions. But it was obvious that not for

for the first nor the last time a promising attempt to halt an armaments race had foundered on mutual suspicion.

Throughout the summer relations between England and France continued close to breaking-point. Once again comparative naval strength between the two countries was at the root of the trouble. But French assistance to the American privateers was another sore point. In July Maurepas told Forth that the French were sending a senior naval officer and two battleships to the Island of Martinique. 'He asked Mr. Forth,' Stormont wrote, 'what he thought of this, and represented it as a thing that couldn't give us the least jealousy. Mr. Forth with his usual frankness said that he had no doubt some ships of ours would likewise appear on the seas, and offered some very good humoured conversation on the subject. M. de Maurepas left him for a few minutes and went in to the King. At his return he said that they should send only one man of war."[20]

Barely a month later Stormont discovered that in spite of Maurepas's promises, about 4,000 to 5,000 men in transports escorted by several battleships were being sent to Martinique. To Stormont's mind such a flagrant breach of a solemn undertaking meant immediate war. He was on the point of sending off a courier to England when he heard that Maurepas had sent for Forth to come to Versailles to see him, and resolved 'to make one effort more for the preservation of public tranquility'. It had been Maurepas's intention to explain away the orders to embark troops and men of war for Martinique, 'but when he found from the very proper language of [Mr. Forth] whom I had talked to beforehand, that if the resolution was carried into execution a rupture must instantly ensue, he was much affected, and after many marks of the most violent agitation he determined to go to the King ... The Ministers were assembled, and the matter debated for several hours. When [Mr. Forth] who had retired during this interval returned to M. de Maurepas His Excellency declared to him in the most solemn manner that the resolution now taken is that these troops ... shall not go till the month of October, and shall have no ships of the line to convey them, but only two frigates ... which shall ... only replace two other frigates

that shall immediately be sent back to Europe. This he
promised as solemly as a man can promise'.[21]

Peace was secured for the time being. But Stormont did not
count on it. Although the French King assured him that he
earnestly desired to preserve peace, and counter-orders had
gone to the Minister of Marine (whom Stormont considered
a warmonger) the general feeling in France was warlike.
Stormont believed that Maurepas's alarm had been only temporary, once the Newfoundland fishing fleet was safely returned,
his views would change again: 'the unsteadiness of M. de
Maurepas's character or the frailty of his memory, to give
things the softest names, makes him strangely forgetful of the
most solemn promises'. Meanwhile Forth was sent back to
England to give the English Ministers a full report. His valet
Quin was heard ordering posthorses to be brought round at
once because his master was off to England to prevent a war.
One of the many informants who kept an eye on the embassy
and its staff passed this interesting piece of information to the
Spanish Ambassador who was confirmed in his view that
Forth was a most indiscreet emissary.[22]

Happily for Forth King George III and his Ministers had a
higher opinion of his capabilities. He returned to France
entrusted with another mission which the Ministers hoped
would bring French intentions into the open. Forth was
instructed to present Maurepas with five demands to be
accepted or rejected within 24 hours. If the British Ambassador
were to put forward demands in this way it might be regarded
as an ultimatum. Forth's approach could be regarded as
unofficial. He was to make it clear that he was speaking as a
private person who represented public opinion in England, but
was also a friend to France. If the French agreed to the
demands, the English would be reassured and war might be
avoided.

On Friday 22 August Forth saw Maurepas, and presented
the five demands of which the most important were the return
of all ships captured as prizes by the Americans and brought to
French ports; the publication of orders to this effect; and the
issue of orders that American privateers should no longer be
given shelter in French ports. He told Maurepas that Stormont

would attend him the following day to receive a positive reply, and Forth himself would set out at midnight on the 23rd.

Tremendous activity followed. Maurepas saw the King, and called a council meeting for the morning of the 23rd. The Spanish Ambassador, who had just left Versailles after his weekly visit to Vergennes, was hurriedly sent for. The discussions were long and agitated. Maurepas was anxious to give Lord Stormont a reassuring reply within the allotted time; Vergennes was busy evolving ways in which they might avoid carrying out any of their promises; the Spanish Ambassador refused to decide anything without referring to his government. He was not going to be hurried into unconsidered action by any unofficial envoy.

In fact neither France nor Spain were ready for an immediate war. The French needed time to move ships and troops to protect their West Indian possessions; the Spaniards also needed time until the fishing fleet returned from the North Atlantic and the treasure fleet was safely back from Vera Cruz. They decided to temporize, and to use Forth's unofficial status as a pretext for not making too precise a reply. When Stormont came for his answer he was told that orders were being issued to forbid the use of French ports by American privateers. If any other demands were to be considered, they must be made officially by Stormont himself.

Forth carried this answer back with him when he left for Dieppe early on Sunday morning 24 August. He delivered it to a Cabinet meeting which, signal honour, had been delayed on King George III's instructions, until he arrived. Next day the word went round that goods news had come from France; the funds rose, and signs of relief appeared on people's faces. In September news was received in Europe of successful engagements in North America at Brandywine and Ticonderoga. For the time being the prospect of peace in Europe seemed rather more hopeful.

The British Ministers had taken a considerable risk, but largely thanks to Forth it had succeeded. He was becoming a man to be reckoned with. As the French Ambassador in London remarked he was developing from a private person into a public personage.[23]

## Chapter Three

## FONTAINEBLEAU

### 1

FORTH FIRST reaped the benefit of his position as Special Envoy during the French Court's visit to Fontainebleau in October. Of the regular series of *voyages* which punctuated the royal year Fontainebleau was the most lighthearted. Hunting was the main diversion, a sport which King Louis XVI passionately enjoyed. His passion was shared by a large part of the Court; those who did not hunt enjoyed the social occasions which the hunt provided. There was a prevailing atmosphere of holiday and pleasure, due perhaps to the youth of the King and Queen, then 23 and 22 respectively, while the King's brothers and their wives were younger still. For a month Ministers and Court alike exchanged the mists of low-lying Versailles, and the splendid, if sometimes mournful, vistas of its park, for the rocks and forest of Fontainebleau, and its brilliant, almost Italianate, autumn light.

Lord Stormont, with the other foreign ambassadors, followed the French Court: his official 'family' went with him, Forth among them. Hitherto Forth's position had not been clear to the outside world. Accredited to Maurepas, and dealing directly with him, Forth's daily contacts were not with the Ministry of Foreign Affairs, as were those of the Secretaries to the embassy. Vergennes remained wary of Forth, this dubious character, *un personnage amphibie*, whose standing was ambiguous. At Fontainebleau all this was changed. Vergennes might continue to suspect Forth, he could no longer question his standing when he was officially introduced by Lord Stormont, and appeared with him in public at the official entertainments. It was greatly to Forth's advantage that Maurepas liked him, and saw to it that

26

he was invited to hunt with the King, received summons to the Queen's card party, and invitations to attend the other diversions provided for the Court.

It was also lucky for Forth that at Fontainebleau the accent was so strongly on hunting. He was here on familiar ground; his horsemanship and his enviable horses made him a person to be reckoned with on his own account, and brought him the acquaintance of those young princes and aristocrats with whom he shared a passion for horses.

Forth and Betsy set out for Fontainebleau on Thursday 9 October. They lay overnight at Essonne, and arrived at their lodgings in the town at 3.00 the following day. Meanwhile Forth's grooms, with his horses, Mousquetaire, Rouleau, Trimmer and the aptly named, if oddly spelt, Smugler, had come from their stable at Alfort by a different route.

As soon as he had dined Forth rode out with Fullarton. The King's youngest brother, the Count d'Artois, planned to diversify the entertainments of Fontainebleau with race meetings. At Barbeau on the edge of the forest, near the river Seine, a level tract of heathland had been marked out as a race course, and here Forth and Fullarton were summoned to meet Artois to discuss arrangements for the first race meeting. At this encounter Artois, according to Forth, was very gracious. Forth was entering Mousquetaire for the race, and when Artois had gone, he rode off to discuss plans with his grooms.

On Sunday Lord Stormont arrived, and took Forth to Court. He presented Forth to all the ambassadors, and afterwards both men attended a dinner given by Vergennes: 'conversation with him', Forth wrote, 'he is remarkably civil and polite'. In the evening (dinner was at 1.30 or 2.00) Forth saw an *Ordre du Roi* requiring his attendance at the Queen's card party, the *Jeu de la Reine*. The company assembled in the charming *salon de jeu*, its panels newly decorated with arabesques by the Rousseaus. Play was high. This year Marie Antoinette allowed a faro bank to be organized, greatly to the disapproval of her brother, the Austrian Emperor, who told her that her card-room was no better than a gambling hell.[1]

After the card game Forth went to the *Grand Couvert* to watch the King and Queen sup in public, as they did at 7.30, every Sunday, in the Queen's antechamber, the Salle François I.

The following day, in the afternoon, races were run at Barbeau. The meeting was arranged in the English fashion, with handicaps according to weight, and bets on the results. Each race was run in three heats according to the custom at that time. Marie Antoinette watched from a stand erected in the centre of the course. The Austrian Ambassador, who thought it most disrespectful to enter the Queen's presence in riding coat and breeches, looked on with a critical eye:

> I climbed the steps to the Pavilion where I found a large table spread with an ample collation, which a horde of young men, most unsuitably dressed, were engaged in devouring. Amidst these young men were the Queen, Madame, Madame d'Artois, Madame Elisabeth, Monsieur, and the Count d'Artois; the latter was in perpetual motion between the course and the pavilion, chattering all the time, bemoaning his losses, and absurdly elated when he won. He rushed into the crowd below to encourage his grooms or jockeys, and presented the winner of the race to the Queen. I was distressed to watch this spectacle, especially when I observed the embarrassment of Monsieur, Madame, Madame d'Artois and Madame Elisabeth. It must none the less be admitted that in this hurlyburly the Queen preserved a gracious and dignified manner, as she moved about and spoke to everyone . . . [2]

Besides the Count d'Artois and Forth, the Duke de Chartres, the King's cousin, also had a horse running. Forth's stable-lad, Nat, was riding Mousquetaire, and lost. Forth had staked his favourite, Smugler, on a win, and found himself compelled to part with him. The date was the 13th, an unlucky one for Forth. But some days later he was able to buy Smugler back for 35 louis.

Forth's first royal hunt on Wednesday afternoon was a pleasanter experience. Only those expressly invited by the King could take part in the hunt, although many others, Betsy among them, watched the meets, or were present at the kill. Forth, like all those invited, wore a special hunt livery of green and gold, and carried a hunting knife by his side. Wild boar was the quarry in this so-called *chasse noire*. At this first hunt all went well. But two days later, when Forth again hunted with the King, he had a bad fall: 'my head much

cut by my horse falling. The King sends his surgeon and a
chaise, great attention'.[3]

With d'Aillez the surgeon in attendance, Forth was driven
back to his lodging. The surgeon bled him, and put him to bed.
There he remained for a day or two, receiving visits and mes-
sages of sympathy, until he was well enough to go out quietly
for an airing in his carriage. In this he also attended some of
the meets. It was a week before he was once again hunting on
Mousquetaire.

The hunts culminated in those arranged to celebrate the
Feast of St. Hubert. The feast day fell on 3 November, but
celebrations lasted from Monday to Saturday, when the hunts-
men received their customary St. Hubert gratuities. On the
first day, 3 November, there was a stag hunt at which all the
Court were present. At the boarhunt next day, in the presence
of Marie Antoinette and her ladies, Forth, perhaps for a wager,
accomplished a remarkable feat. He undertook that at the
conclusion of the hunt, when the boar was cornered, he would
cut it down, not with a hunting spear, but with his leaded whip.
It was a very dangerous undertaking. Heavy and ferocious, the
boar was at all times a formidable opponent, but never more so
than at the end of the chase: to bring him down with one blow
of a whip—there would have been no chance to repeat the
blow—needed not only courage, but strength and exact timing.
Forth did not want Betsy to be present while he took this risk,
so he sent her home at the beginning of the hunt. In the event
he need not have done so; he killed the boar, and he was
unharmed. His diary entry, laconic as usual, reads: 'St. Hubert
with Betsy. Send her home. Kill a boar with my leaded whip;
all bloody. Come home late'.[4]

Hunting, racing and gambling were not the only amusements
provided at Fontainebleau. There was a masked ball, and there
were concerts and plays. The principal theatrical companies
and the dancers and singers from the Opera followed the
Court from Paris to Fontainebleau to present their best and
newest productions. The entertainments planned for this visit
included ballets by Gardel, *La Chercheuse d'esprit* and *Ninette
à la cour*; *Fèlix*, an opera by Sedaine, set to music by Monsigny,
and *Pomponin* with music by Piccini; *Mustafa*, a tragedy by

Chamfort; and *Matroco*, a parody of all those operas in which
heroes boast of their deeds while doing nothing, heroines lament
their sorrows at interminable length, and villains take fright
at shadows.

Forth saw more than one of these, but remarked only on
two: *Mustafa* on 7 November when all the Court was present,
and the scene was very brilliant, and *Matroco* on which his
comment was 'farcical'. He was more interested in recording
Maurepas's kindness in finding him a seat when the house was
full: 'go to the play; can't get in; meet Timeo who offers
me a place'.[5]

It might seem that with so many distractions there was no time
for public business. In fact work went forward in spite of inter-
ruptions. Stormont, with Forth's help, was able to settle at least
one question which was causing him a good deal of concern.

American privateers had seized some Jamaican merchant
vessels, and were reported to be sailing with them for a French
port. Stormont feared that in spite of their promises the
French would side with the Americans, and allow them to keep
their prize. He asked Forth to raise the matter with Maurepas.
Forth did so, with a most satisfactory result. Maurepas assured
him that his government had no intention of retaining the
vessels. Forth asked if he might write at once to tell Lord
North. Maurepas gave him permission, and Forth wrote in
French in his presence a letter which Maurepas endorsed,
'*J'ai lu la lettre*', and signed it. Lord Stormont immediately
sent off a messenger to England with the news. He had not
long been gone when Maurepas sent to tell Forth that the
vessels were now at Nantes, confiscated to the French King,
and Stormont could have them for the asking. Stormont sent
Forth's courier L'Evesque hurrying in pursuit to supplement
his dispatch with these even better tidings.[5]

On another occasion Forth was able to reassure Lord
Stormont that there was no truth in a report that Admiral La
Motte and six ships of war were sailing for Martinique, and to
quiet Maurepas's fears that 13 warships, said to be commis-
sioning in England, were to be used against France.[6]

On 12 November when Maurepas bade Forth adieu until
their next meeting in Paris, he could look back on the last four

weeks with a good deal of pleasure and satisfaction. On 14
November he too left Fontainebleau.

Although he did not know it, Forth had attended the last
Royal progress to Fontainebleau for some years. It was 1783
before the Court visited it again. When it did so all the arrangements were much less lavish. By that time the King and Queen
had a young family, their interests were more domestic, and
although the King still hunted, the Queen was no longer interested in gambling or horseracing. The prevailing atmosphere
was more staid. Indeed it could be said that in 1777 Forth
witnessed the last Fontainebleau visit of the *ancien régime*.

## 2

His stay at Fontainebleau had considerably improved Forth's
prospects, both public and private.

From this time his relationship with Maurepas became
more personal, and even affectionate. The words 'very
affectionate' now recur regularly in Forth's accounts of his
interviews with Maurepas. From this time too Forth writes to
Maurepas as he would to a friend who is anxious to hear his
news. It is true that Forth was inclined to treat all official
relationships as if they were personal, but in this case there
was evidently a firm foundation of mutual liking. This was
visible at Fontainebleau in the sympathy which Maurepas
showed when Forth was suffering from the effects of his
hunting accident, and when he heard that Forth had to part
with his horse, Smugler. When the two men met for the first
time after the *voyage de Fontainebleau* Forth found Maurepas
amazingly familiar, 'never more civil or more gracious'.

A kind of barometer of Maurepas's feelings for Forth is
the treatment which he received from Madame de Maurepas
and Madame de Flamarens, the niece who often entertained
for Maurepas. The ladies made Forth welcome when he called
officially on Maurepas, and several times he dined with them.
Forth was also on excellent terms with Lecler du Brillet,
Maurepas's chief secretary, the important *premier commis* of
his Department of State, and a man of considerable
culture. A permanent official does not invariably share his

Minister's likings; both Maurepas and Lecler seem to have agreed in liking Forth.

An even more significant development of the Fontainebleau visit was Forth's acquaintance with the Duke de Chartres, the son of the Duke of Orleans, and a Prince of the Blood. Chartres whom posterity knows as Philippe Egalité, was 30 years of age in 1777, the husband of a great heiress, and the father of four children. He was also very close in succession to the French Crown. Volatile, rich and idle, his life was a constant struggle against boredom. The elder branch of the reigning family treated the members of the younger branch with reserve, purposely allowing them to play only a minor part in affairs of state. Louis XVI mistrusted his cousin but for several years the Queen liked him, and it was for her sake that he frequented Versailles. His main interests and distractions however lay elsewhere, on the vast Orleans estates, or in Paris. It was there, at the Palais Royal, that he lived.

Chartres had pursued the pleasures of the senses up to and beyond the point of satiety, and was now very much under the influence of an intellectual (and ambitious) mistress, the Countess de Genlis. He took a superficial interest in science, and later turned to aeronautics: he gambled: he even learnt conjuring from Comus, a famous conjuror (after whom one of Artois's horses was named). At the time when he came to know Forth his mania was horses and horse racing. He longed to visit England, to race at Newmarket and to hunt in the Shires, as his friend the Duke de Lauzun had done, but Louis XVI refused him permission to leave the country.

Forth was introduced to Chartres by the Count d'Artois at one of the race meetings in the Bois de Boulogne. But it was at Fontainebleau that Chartres began to seek Forth's society. The races at Barbeau provided the meeting ground. On two out of these four meetings Artois's horse Comus was successful: at one race Forth expressly noted that there was excessive good running in three heats between Comus and Caddet. If, as is is possible, it was with Forth's help and advice that Artois acquired Comus, the horse's success would enhance Forth's reputation as a judge of horseflesh.[7]

Twice Chartres invited Forth to hunt with him on his estate
at Champagne-sur-Seine, not far from Fontainebleau. At the
conclusion of the second hunt Chartres presented Forth with
the tusks of a huge 21-year-old boar; the tusks alone measured
eight inches. Chartres entertained the hunting-party to an
extremely merry dinner. Forth with his ability to tell an
amusing story, and his enjoyment of good company, was very
much in his element in this masculine society.[8]

Gradually Chartres introduced Forth into his circle of
friends. Among them was the Duke de Lauzun, of whom
Talleyrand said that he was brilliant in every way, handsome,
brave, generous and witty. His countrymen regarded him as
an anglophile, but if he enjoyed English society and had many
English friends, he was none the less eager to raise a regiment
to fight against England in America. There were also the
Chevalier de Durfort, older than Chartres, and his companion
since childhood; the Marquis de Conflans, an eccentric and an
anglophile; the Count de Genlis, the husband of Chartres's
mistress, a soldier and a *bon viveur*. Later on Forth was to act
as agent for the sale of wine from Genlis's estate at Sillery.

Horses and horse-breeding were a common interest for most
of these men, an interest which linked them to others, not of
Chartres's immediate circle, such as the Count of Lauraguais
and the Marquis de Voyer d'Argenson, both of whom imported
bloodstock from England. Lauraguais was the ower of the
famous racehorse, Gimcrack; d'Argenson possessed a stud
wholly furnished by English mares and horses, among them
Marske, Mexico and Topgallant. At a later date Chartres himself
owned Glow-worm, son of Eclipse. Most of these enthusiasts
met every Monday at a club at the Hôtel de la Muette des
Chiens, Conflans being the President. It was a forerunner of
the French Jockey Club.[9]

It was expensive to belong to Chartres's circle. Betting was
high, and Chartres had the reputation of always winning his
bets. At the race on 10 November, when Comus made such
good running, Forth lost 45 guineas beside other bets. Nor
were bets confined to racing: Chartres once laid a· bet with
Lauzun and another friend as to which could walk the fastest
from Paris to Versailles; and on another occasion Genlis bet

Chartres that he would drive to Fontainebleau and back in
the time Chartres could prick 500,000 holes in a piece of paper.
Chartres and his friends also staked heavily on cards and dice;
they played deep, to use the eighteenth-century expression.
Perhaps it was hardly surprising that at the end of four weeks
at Fontainebleau Forth settled debts of £40 and £50 to
Chartres and the others. If he continued to live at this rate,
his £100 a week allowance from the government would be very
much stretched.[10]

Chartres continued to find Forth congenial. He knew where
to buy English staghounds for Chartres's Champagne estate,
he could advise him how to enter for the Selling Plates at
Doncaster; above all he was an agreeable companion. After
Chartres was re-established in Paris, he invited Forth to visit
him at the Palais Royal. At one such visit Forth was greatly
flattered to be singled out from a levée of 500 people waiting
in the antechamber, and passed directly through the crowd
to Chartres's own apartment. On 14 December Chartres paid
Forth the even greater compliment of calling on him at his
own house. By eighteenth-century standards this showed great
condescension from a Prince of the Blood. By any standards
it was an advance in intimacy, a sign that the acquaintance
was not entirely to be carried on at race meetings or out
hunting. Forth describes his own behaviour during the visit
as spirited and respectful. Chartres, on his side, praised Forth,
and assured him that he was anxious to oblige him. Apparently
he did not mind that he had chosen to visit Forth on a day
on which workmen were repairing the stoves. The gesture of
friendship was all the kinder because it came at a moment when
relations between France and England were strained, and
feeling against England was running high.

Doubtless the fact that both Chartres and Forth were
Freemasons made their intercourse easier. Chartres was Grand
Master of the Order in France. Forth, whose name does not
appear in the records of the English or Irish Grand Lodges,
may have been admitted when he first came to France to one
of those Irish or Scottish lodges from which French Masonry
probably developed. By all accounts, masonic practices in the
eighteenth century differed very much from those of today.

Nevertheless Freemasonry at its best stood for the brotherhood, if not precisely the equality, of man, and within its limits put the ideal into practice. Its noblest contemporary expression is surely to be found in the music of the *Magic Flute.*[11]

Forth's relation with Chartres opened up new sources of information, and greatly increased his use as Special Envoy. But flattered as Forth was by Chartres's expressions of interest, and useful as he found the connexion, he had no idea how important their association would become, or where it would lead him.

3

The advantages which Forth gained at Fontainebleau were counterbalanced by a serious disadvantage, the displeasure of Marie Antoinette.

For some time Forth knew nothing of this. He had seen no reason to suppose that the Queen looked on him with disfavour; his impression had been quite the reverse. It was the custom before the *Jeu de la Reine*, at Fontainebleau and elsewhere, for the Queen to make a charitable collection for the poor of the parish. When Marie Antoinette did so during Forth's second attendance at her card-party, he contributed five louis, which she received very graciously. This was not surprising since, knowingly or not, he had given five times the usual amount. But he believed that he had made a good impression, and continued to think so. At the hunts Louis XVI and his brothers were courteous; at two of the meets Forth noticed that the Queen admired Betsy. It was a shock to find that he had been under a false impression.[12]

The first sign that anything was wrong came on 18 November when Forth visited the Embassy for the first time since his return to Paris, and was coolly received by Lady Stormont. Three days later he heard from Jeans that something had happened at the hunt on the day when he had his fall; 'hear of Lady Clermont's and Lady Stormont's treachery. Anecdote of Ladies Spencer and Clermont to the Queen the day I hurt myself'. The cause of the trouble that day, never explicitly mentioned by Forth, was probably Betsy.

Because Betsy was not legally Forth's wife, she could not appear at Court with Lady Stormont and the other English ladies. By encouraging her to attend the King's hunt Forth placed her in a false position. For it is likely that Marie Antoinette, after admiring Betsy on a previous occasion, wanted to offer her sympathies to *la jolie Madame Forth* when Forth was hurt. She would ask Lady Stormont to present Betsy, and learn that she was Mrs. Forth only by courtesy. If this is what happened, the Queen had reason to be displeased, and to consider that Forth had behaved discourteously, even insultingly. It was against all the rules of behaviour in polite society for a man to bring his mistress into the company of married women, as Forth must have known. On a private occasion he might be able to ensure that Betsy was treated as his wife, but he could not reasonably expect to defy convention on a public and royal occasion.

There were other reasons for the Queen's predisposition against Forth. She believed, wrongly as it happened, that he was a friend of General Richard Smith. Smith was a very wealthy, flamboyant East Indian general, who had been fined and imprisoned in England for flagrant bribery at an election. He was now in France with his mistress, Madame Newton, perhaps the 'choice female spirit' against whom William Hickey was once warned, and whom he describes singing one of her best and most convivial songs at a supper at the *Shakespear* tavern. Smith was a heavy gambler and made it clear that he had plenty of money to squander. He had been at Fontainebleau where there had been much talk about his enormous winnings and the casual way in which he had been seen to lean his elbows on the table when he dined with the Count d'Artois and the Duke de Chartres.

The Queen might have been prepared to overlook Smith's reputation and his bad manners, but he also frequented Madame Du Barry's circle, and this was bound to cause offence. Marie Antoinette had never overcome her first dislike and disapproval of Madame Du Barry, and withheld her favour from anyone who was known to move in the ex-favourite's society. Smith, who gambled with Madame Du Barry's young nephew, came into this category; Forth, through his connexion with

Lady Barrymore, who claimed to be related to the Du Barrys', suffered the same disadvantage.

Forth heard on 21 November that 'the Queen's malice forbids the Count d'Artois to receive me or Smith'. At Fontainebleau Forth had not been formally introduced to Smith although he probably met him in company with Chartres or Artois. But now the two men were introduced by a common friend, and because they were both in the Queen's bad graces they were drawn together. Nevertheless, when Smith and his friends abused the Queen, the French nation and Lady Clermont, Forth was silent. He defended himself with warmth and spirit (his own expression) to the ladies he held responsible, Lady Clermont, 'cringing and false', and Lady Dunmore, 'reserved and unfriendly'. He was evidently, from the entries in his Diary, seriously concerned about his position which he discussed at great length with Lord Stormont and even with Maurepas. There was really nothing to be done; he had offended Marie Antoinette, and she did not often change her opinion.

It was unfortunate that just at this time Maurepas asked Forth to undertake a mission which directly concerned the Queen's reputation.

## Chapter Four

# THE BLACKMAILER

### 1

MARIE ANTOINETTE was the subject of gossip throughout her life, especially in the seven years during which her marriage to Louis XVI remained unconsummated and she looked elsewhere for the satisfaction of her emotional needs. Whether her favourites were male or female, and however innocent the relationship, there were always people ready to suspect the worst, and to pass on their suspicions. But the scandalous stories which circulated in France could not be printed there for fear of punishment. The scandalmongers were forced to set up their presses in other countries. London was an easy choice. In that capital a colony of self-exiled French scoundrels made a good living from the publication of scurrilous pamphlets.

In June 1777 the French Government heard that a particularly vicious libel was about to be published. Maurepas asked Forth if he could trace it to its source. Forth was not anxious to take on this task, which he considered below the dignity of a Special Envoy, but he set Quin, his confidential man-servant, to make enquiries in London taverns and coffee-houses.

The field of investigation was a wide one. The French colony included a variety of rogues, many of whom were handy with a pen. There was an army captain who had fled with the regimental funds; a cashier who had run off with the tax receipts of Lyons; an abbé who had eloped with one of his parishioners; and an absconding bankrupt.[1] There were also several professional men of letters who were wanted in their own country for offences including abduction, and living on immoral earnings. A few relatively honest men sometimes

38

found themselves in this dubious company, among them Brissot, the future Girondin.

One possible suspect was Linguet, a clever lawyer who took to journalism when he was dismissed from the Bar. A cutting article on the French Academy made Paris too hot to hold him, and he took refuge in London where he published a literary and political review that earned him many enemies. In 1777 he was writing to Maurepas threatening all kinds of embarrassing revelations about the French Government.[2]

But there was another even more obvious suspect, Charles Théveneau, who called himself without any right to do so, Chevalier de Morande. He was a bully and a blackmailer with an infallible memory. In his early days he used force to extract money from his victims until he found he could achieve the same results more effectively, and less dangerously, with his pen. He was known to have lived on the earnings of prostitutes, whom he threatened with imprisonment when they refused to support him any longer. The Paris police suspected him of other vices, and were glad when he gave them an opportunity to imprison him at For-l'Evêque. He was so troublesome there that he was transferred for corrective detention to the monks of Armentières, which whom he remained for about a year. When he was finally given a certificate of good conduct, and set free, he once again endangered his liberty by writing verses against one of the King's ministers. A *lettre de cachet* was issued against him, and he fled to England.[3]

He arrived in London in 1769 without money, but not without resources: he had discovered a marketable secret which, properly handled, would produce everything that he needed. His intended victim was the Chevalier d'Eon, who was at that time Secretary of the French Embassy in London. D'Eon was a Burgundian, small, quick-tempered, and an outstandingly skilful fencer. He was also, though this was not generally known, a transvestite. Morande knew this, and assuming that he was also homosexual, a crime which carried a capital penalty, he proposed to exploit his knowledge. It was to his advantage that d'Eon's relations with his Ambassador were not good. In the past d'Eon had served as one of the agents of Louis XV's secret diplomacy, which often ran counter to

the policy of the French Ministers from whom the Ambassador
received his instructions. The great days of the *Secret du Roi*
were over, but the mistrust between official and unofficial
diplomats remained, creating an atmosphere which was favourable to Morande's plans.

Some years later d'Eon gave his version of what happened:
'M. de Morande comes from my part of the country, and
claims that he is connected with a branch of my family in
Burgundy. As soon as he came to London, three years ago,
his first act was to write to tell me that he had arrived, that he
was an officer of the Carabiniers, and as my compatriot, wished
to make my acquaintance. Since that time he has knocked on
my door so often that I sometimes allow him to visit me. In
this way I avoid offending a young man with a good heart,
but a turbulent, impetuous nature. In the fever of composition
he is neither to hold, nor to bind, and he ignores rank and
degree . . . If I had not advised him to moderate his writings
and his behaviour, he would by now have been transported
and imprisoned . . . ".

Thanks to his hold on d'Eon, and his own efforts, Morande
soon established himself in London. He married an English
wife, to whom he was devoted, and tried, unsuccessfully,
to persuade d'Eon to stand godfather to one of his children.
But his principal activity was the production of a scandalous paper, which he named the *Gazetier cuirassé*. When
d'Eon was shown a sample of the first issue, he did his
utmost to dissuade Morande from publishing, but Morande
ignored his advice.

The *Gazetier cuirassé* was a profitable venture: some paid
to keep their names from appearing in its pages; others enjoyed
reading its libellous anecdotes. In 1773 Morande went further:
he advertised a pamphlet which would reveal the previous
history of Madame Du Barry, Louis XV's mistress; it was to
be called *Memoirs of a Woman of the Town*. The King gave
orders that the whole edition of the pamphlet should be bought
up and destroyed. The mission was entrusted to the playwright, Beaumarchais, at that time in disgrace with the French
Government; if he successfully prevented publication, he would
be reinstated in his civil rights.

Morande saw exactly how he could make the best of this situation. He made friends with Beaumarchais, and together the two men combined to extort a higher price than Morande could have obtained by himself. Before Beaumarchais's arrival d'Eon, in his official capacity, was responsible for buying up the pamphlet, and he was proposing to offer Morande 800 guineas. He now not only found himself by-passed, but faced with an alliance between Beaumarchais and Morande. Morande had told Beaumarchais d'Eon's secret, which the unholy allies used as a bargaining counter. In the end, d'Eon was compelled to recommend the French Goverment to pay much more than 800 guineas. Morande received a down payment of £1390 sterling, and two annuities worth about £170 and £90 each, one of them settled on his wife. Beaumarchais was not so lucky. He returned to France with his copies of the pamphlet, only to find that Louis XV was dead, Madame du Barry in disgrace, and her reputation of no concern to anyone but herself. As compensation for his wasted efforts he forced Morande to pay him part of his own gains.[4]

The new Queen of France, Marie Antoinette, was Morande's next victim. In the summer he advertised a pamphlet entitled *Important notice to the Spanish branch of the Bourbons concerning its claim to the throne of France*; its subject was the absence of a direct heir to the French throne, and the whole story of the Queen's relations with her husband. Once again Beaumarchais was sent to England to buy up the issue. But on this occasion he told such a far-fetched story about his attempts to gain possession of the pamphlet that Maurepas, who was now Louis XVI's chief minister, did not know what to believe. It was for this reason, that, in June 1777, when Morande once again advertised a pamphlet aimed at Marie Antoinette, Maurepas, who by this time had discovered Beaumarchais's dishonest bargain with Morande, wished for a different emissary and approached Forth.[5]

2

In August 1777 his valet Quin wrote to tell Forth that he had traced the man, who, throughout Forth's correspondence

with Maurepas is always referred to as the Printer, *l'Imprimeur*.
Although he is not mentioned by name, there is little doubt
that *l'Imprimeur* was Morande.

Forth instructed Quin to offer Morande money, and to do
his best to prevent, or at any rate delay, publication of the
pamphlet. Quin lent Morande ten guineas, and entertained him
at the *Green Dragon* inn in the City of London. On three
separate occasions Quin made a present of two guineas to
Morande's wife, and he also provided her with a dress, a cloak,
and some caps. By these attentions Quin managed to delay
publication for a time, but by the end of November Morande
was becoming impatient.[6]

On Monday 1 December, when Forth was at Versailles,
Maurepas showed him a threatening letter which Morande had
sent to the Princess de Lamballe, Marie Antoinette's friend and
the Superintendent of her Household. The full scope of the
Libel was yet to be revealed, but it was evident from the title,
*The Fancy Woman, or the relations of the warm-hearted Queen
with her Superintendent,* what kind of allegations would be
made. In fact, as Forth later discovered, the Libel went a great
deal further. It suggested that Louis XV and Choiseul had
conspired to murder Louis XVI's father, and that Maurepas was
now conspiring to murder Louis XVI; it also found space to
vilify the motives and conduct of almost everyone in the
French Royal Family and their immediate circle.

Throughout December Maurepas tried to persuade Forth to
take an active part in preventing publication of the Libel. By
this time Quin had discovered the whereabouts of a strong-box
containing all the copies of the first printing. Maurepas wanted
Forth to gain possession of the strong-box, and bring it to
Paris. Forth was still reluctant to undertake this distasteful
mission. But Lord Stormont thought it would be useful. Relations between the French and the British Courts were by this
time so strained that Stormont welcomed a chance of obliging
the King and Queen of France over so personal matter. Besides,
Maurepas made it clear that if the Libel appeared he himself
might lose office, perhaps to be replaced by someone less well
disposed to Britain. For both these reasons Stormont believed
that Forth should be encouraged to do what he could to

suppress the Libel. The British Government agreed, and were prepared to help Forth, provided he was discreet.[7] Neither Stormont nor Maurepas wanted the French Ambassador in London to know what Forth was doing, but by sending him to London with dispatches it might be possible to conceal the true object of his journey.

On Sunday 4 January 1778, Forth had a long interview with Maurepas at Versailles. "I am a most unhappy man", Maurepas began, "but there is no help for me. I see that this will be my ruin. The Queen will believe it is a plot hatched between us. Your health prevents you from concerning yourself with my affairs at present". Forth's Diary continues: "Vastly affected, he takes me by the hand . . . then says, "I dread to propose one thing, and yet I must". Here he talks ten minutes of the consequences, and then says, "Nothing but your going there can prevent an event which may distress the King and Queen and others beyond measure. Give any sum of money to stop the Libel, and bring it to me, and I will do everything that you can desire". I then mention my health and the weather, etc. He says, "You did not formerly think of them". "That's true". "What will you do for me?" "*Allons*, I will go, and if possible I will bring you the Libel". Here I speak feelingly of my intentions to oblige him personally. He kisses me, and shakes hands, is very thankful, and says a thousand flattering things to me. We agree to part on Wednesday as I must wait for the courier'.

Later that evening Forth was present at the Queen's card game. Marie Antoinette did not speak to him, although she must by them have been aware that he had undertaken an enterprise which very much concerned her. Maurepas on the other hand showed his gratitude. He entertained Forth to supper after the Queen's game was over, and he placed Forth on his right hand. Afterwards he gave him his passports, and the evening ended with cards. Forth won 78 louis. It was 3.00 in the morning before he returned to Paris and his bed.

The following day Forth made his report to Stormont, and obtained leave to go to London. Two days later he was on his way, arriving in London on Sunday 11 January. Jeans travelled with him.

3

The negotiation which Forth had undertaken was likely to
prove troublesome: it would not be easy to deal with so wily a
scoundrel as Morande, who for the time being seemed to have
gone to ground; if Forth discovered his hiding-place, and he
succeeded in buying up the Libel, there was still no guarantee
that Morande would not pocket the money and produce
something just as bad a few months later, yet Maurepas had
made it clear that Forth's credit largely depended on his
success. It is not surprising that Forth told Le Cler, the Chief
Clerk, that the accursed business of the Libel was driving
him nearly mad.[8]

During the first four days which he spent in London Forth
discussed the Libel with Lord North and Lord Suffolk, both of
whom promised him help. Forth also discussed his plan of
operations with Lord Mansfield. But his chief concern was to
find Morande. In his search Forth hoped to receive help from
Samuel Swinton, a former naval captain, who was now the
proprietor of the *Courier de l'Europe*. This paper was very
different from the *Gazetier cuirassé*, but its contributors came
from the same circle of French exiles.

It was not until he had been in London for five days that
Forth heard from Morande. That Friday morning Forth
received by special messenger a letter signed *Humanity*;
enclosed was a letter over the signature *l'Imprimeur*, and a
handbill advertising the Libel. This was the first advertisement
that Forth had seen: he was horrified by the allegations, and the
number of persons libelled.[9]

Humanity's letter told Forth that he was almost too late to
prevent publication. A Mr. Shaw was offering 500 guineas for
the 1,000 copies which had already been printed; a sale of
two further editions seemed certain, producing a total profit
of 1,500 guineas. Nevertheless, Humanity continued,
*l'Imprimeur* had certain qualms of conscience; he had already
treated with Forth, and he was prepared to sell him the 1,000
copies now in print for 500 guineas, but Forth must reply
before Monday, if he wished to prevent publication taking
place, as proposed, on Tuesday.

*L'Imprimeur's* letter was written in a jargon which was intended to suggest that the writer was either Àlsatian or German, but its meaning was plain: he was raising his price. According to him, his creditor, a Mr. Smith, to whom he owed 300 guineas, had seized copies of the Libel in payment of the debt, and was on the point of publishing. If Forth wanted to stop this, he must be prepared to receive the writer at 7.00 on the morning of Monday 19 January. If Forth was willing to treat, he should apply to Mr. Thomas Smith, at Silver Street, Blackfriars.[10]

The introduction of Mr. Shaw and Mr. Smith into the affair inevitably increased Forth's difficulties; they might have genuine claims, or they might be men of straw, put forward by Morande, but they would certainly make it more expensive to suppress the Libel. Forth thought it necessary to obtain Maurepas's sanction for additional expenditure, and he dispatched the invaluable Quin to Paris with his report; he was to wait and return with Maurepas's reply. Meanwhile Forth worked out a new plan, which he discussed with Lord Mansfield the following day. 'Approves highly of it', Forth wrote in his Diary, 'hopes I shall succeed; no one can but me'.

Forth did not trust Morande to keep the appointment which he had made for Monday morning, he felt that the only way of making certain that he put in an appearance was to bring him to the meeting place, by force, if necessary. He had discovered, perhaps from Swinton, that Morande was at Oxford, and he therefore asked Jeans to go in pursuit. Jeans was a former Fellow of New College, who might carry some weight with the Oxford Justices of the Peace if it should prove necessary, as in the event it did, to call out the constables.[11]

Jeans was successful: on 19 January he brought Morande to Forth's house, where Forth and he cross-examined Morande. It was not an altogether successful interview. Morande insisted that everything depended on his creditor, Mr. Smith; it was Smith who was in possession of the strong-box containing the Libels, and Forth would have to deal with him. Unluckily, Smith was not to be found at his address in Blackfriars. More bribes would be needed before his hiding-place could be discovered.

Meanwhile Forth again discussed the affair with Lord North. It was arranged that Robinson, Joint Secretary of the Treasury, would be present when Morande and Smith finally handed over the strong-box; he would bring with him Hans Stanley, a Member of Parliament and Cofferer to the Household, and two clerks from the Treasury. The presence of so many government officials would impress Morande, and make it easier for Forth to carry out one of the most important parts of his plan. He proposed that Morande should sign a formal undertaking to pay Robinson £1,000 if he published another similar libel.[12] Forth hoped that Morande would hesitate to go back on a legal argument signed before so many influential witnesses.

Friday 30 January, was chosen as the crucial day when Morande and Smith were to bring the strong-box to Forth's house. By that time Forth had received Maurepas's authority to spend whatever was necessary, and Robinson had agreed to advance funds from the Treasury. On 28 January Morande burnt the manuscript copy of the Libel in the presence of Forth and Hans Stanley. In return he received £10 19s. 8d. for a complete suit of new clothes. It now remained to gain possession of the printed copies.

On the appointed day Robinson and the official party arrived as planned at Forth's house, but Morande kept them waiting. When he appeared he announced that Smith was not coming. In his exasperation, Forth beat Morande, and forced him to say where they could find Smith. Jeans was sent off with Quin to fetch him. They were away for some time while Forth fretted exceedingly at the delay. But at last Jeans and Quin returned bringing Smith and the strong-box, and Forth's plan went into operation. Morande signed his undertaking, Smith handed over the box, and they each received 500 and 100 guineas respectively. Later the box was corded and sealed with the Treasury seal, and the seal of all those present. At midnight on the 30th Forth was able to send off a dispatch to let Maurepas know that he had succeeded in his mission.[13]

Forth had a bad journey back to France. For some weeks he had been in great pain from a rheumatic complaint which grew worse as he travelled. After a 14 hour crossing to Calais he was obliged to break his journey for a day at Boulogne before he was fit enough to go further. Near Chantilly, one of the main posting stages on the way to Paris, the trunks broke away from Forth's carriage, an accident that was almost certainly engineered by one of Morande's confederates in a last attempt to gain possession of the Libel. The attempt failed because Forth prudently kept the precious box inside the carriage.

On 6 February Forth was in Paris and able to write to Maurepas's chief clerk, 'here I am, my dear Sir, or rather one half of my body dragging the rest. I have brought everything, and was marvellously successful'. To Maurepas he wrote, 'I rejoice to think that I am actually sitting on a box which contains horrors capable of destroying the peace of mind of so many great and respected persons'.[14]

Maurepas's reply was as grateful as Forth could wish: 'I am delighted, Sir, to know that you have arrived in the country, but distressed at your report of your health. I beseech you to take care of this; I should prefer you to postpone your journey to Versailles, and the pleasure I shall have in seeing you, than to risk adding to your discomfort. I have already informed the King of your achievement. His Majesty is as well satisfied as you can imagine, and very conscious of all the efforts which you have made'. Maurepas went on to make arrangements for disposing of the Libels: 'As to the strong-box containing these choice goods, I do not think it appropriate to send Le Cler to you, nor yet for you to bring it to [Versailles]. I am ordering M. Le Noir, Lieutenant of Police, to collect it from you, but without letting it be known what it is that he is fetching, and to drive it forthwith to the Bastille. That is the safest place for it . . . '.

The Bastille was therefore the final destination of Morande's Libel. Le Noir reported to Maurepas on 7 February that he had carried out his orders, and placed the box, with all its seals intact, in the hands of the Major in command of the fortress.[15]

4

This was not quite the end of the affair. Forth had as yet received neither official thanks nor repayment of his expenses.

He received Maurerpas's acknowledgements at Versailles on 7 February, as well as a very flattering message from the King and Queen. They would, Maurepas said, thank Forth in person in a few days time; the Queen was prepared to be civil. Forth was sceptical, and told Maurepas, 'I will come on Sunday *au jeu de la Reine*, and I will hunt on Monday with the King. If they speak and are civil, *je serai très flatté, s'ils ne me parlent pas, je ne mourrai pas de chagrin*'. To which Maurepas replied, '*Fier anglais!*'[16]

Forth's scepticism was justified. Marie Antoinette could not bring herself to thank Forth. When he attended the Queen's card party on 18 February, the Count d'Artois was gracious, but the Queen, as Forth put it, marched by him three times. She did not bow to him, or acknowledge his bow. Louis XVI, through Maurepas, presented Forth with a gold snuff-box with his portrait on the lid. On instructions from Lord Stormont, Forth refused this; the British Foreign Service did not allow its members to accept a present from a foreign government unless it was accompanied by a letter explaining why the gift was presented. Later Maurepas arranged that such a letter should be forthcoming. In addition, as a token of his own gratitude, Maurepas gave Forth a blue enamelled snuff-box set with diamonds; he made it possible for Forth to accept it by saying it was not for Forth, but for some woman friend.[17]

There remained the question of Forth's expenses. To his surprise and annoyance he found that he was expected to account in detail for all his outgoings. As he wrote to Le Cler: 'There were so many small payments which it was absolutely necessary to make that it is impossible to remember them all. I own frankly that I never expected to make out an account of minor expenses, but as I see that it is the custom of the Court of Versailles to pay all obligations in full, I will comply'.

In the account which Forth so reluctantly drew up the main items of expenditure were the payments of 500 guineas to Morande, and 100 guineas to Smith. There were also Quin's

expenses at the *Green Dragon*, the money given to Madame
Morande, and some £21 which Jeans had spent on his expedition to Oxford in pursuit of Morande. Forth's total expenditure
in connexion with the Libel was £819 5s. 0½d. He particularly
asked not to be paid in cash: he was not accustomed, he said,
to be paid by clerks, and he would like to receive Bills on the
Discount Bank in settlement of payments which he himself
had made in banknotes.[18]

This must have seemed a somewhat odd preference. Most
Frenchmen would greatly have preferred to be paid in specie,
bills on the new Discount Bank, whose paper had only recently
been recognized as legal currency, would have seemed to
many a poor substitute for cash. But Forth was paid on 25
February in the way he wished.

Taking everything into consideration Forth's outgoings
were moderate. When he first embarked on his mission
Maurepas told Forth that the King expected to pay 2,000
louis, the equivalent of 2,000 guineas; Forth acquired the
Libel for less than half this sum. He paid much less than
Morande and Beaumarchais had done for the Libel on Madame
Du Barry. On that occasion Morande received £1,390 and two
annuities on which he and his wife were still living. Quite
apart from the question of expenses, Forth had made it possible
to take legal action against Morande if he published a similar
Libel. In fact he had served the King and Queen of France
very effectively, and above all honestly, at some danger to
himself. It is sad that Marie Antoinette could not bring herself
to accept the obligation more graciously.

*Chapter Five*

# THE LADDER OF PROMOTION

THE SUPPRESSION of Morande's Libel was not the only object of Forth's journey to London in January 1778. He was also concerned about his own future. It was extremely likely that relations between England and France would be broken off and the respective ambassadors recalled. This would mean the end of Forth's special mission; planning ahead was therefore a matter of prudence if not of urgency.

It became plain how urgent it was when the news arrived that General Burgoyne's army had surrendered to General Gates at Saratoga. The surrender took place on 17 October but it was not until the beginning of December that the news reached Europe. Franklin heard it at Passy on 3 December; within hours he had passed it on to Vergennes. The moment was ripe to press the French to conclude a treaty.

Forth first heard what had happened at Saratoga on 5 December at a dinner at old Marshal Biron's town house in the Rue de Varennes. The news was confirmed by the Duke de Chartres whom Forth met at Lady Barrymore's later that evening. Chartres even gave Forth dispatches from Congress describing the surrender, and he asked if Forth thought that the English would now come to terms with the Americans. Forth left as soon as he politely could so that he could carry the unwelcome news to Lord Stormont. Without Forth's friendship with Chartres, the Ambassador would have heard nothing until the following day, when dispatches arrived from England.[1]

Lord Stormont's next object was to discover French reactions to the news. He did not know that Franklin was pressing for a treaty, but he had heard that Vergennes had been deep in conference with the Spanish Ambassador, and he was naturally anxious to know what they had discussed. On 10 December he

sent Forth to Versailles to sound Maurepas. Forth found
Maurepas as friendly as ever, and quite ready to talk. He said
that the Spanish Ambassador had proposed a joint declaration
of war on England; this sermon, as Maurepas called it, was
preached with uncommon warmth and zeal, but without
effect. While Maurepas was talking to Forth he was called in
to the King. He came out assuring Forth that the King had
said, 'I am satisfied all will be well'. Lord Stormont passed on
this somewhat reassuring information in his Dispatch of
11 December.[2]

In spite of Maurepas's assurances, there could be little doubt
that a treaty between the French government and the
Americans was in the offing. On 17 December the King
informed Franklin that under certain conditions he was willing
to recognize American independence, and to enter into a
treaty. On 22 December Forth heard from Chartres that a
treaty had actually been concluded. It was vitally important to
know the terms of the treaty. Lord Stormont sent Forth back
to Chartres for more information, but Chartres had already
said as much or more than could be expected, and Forth
failed to secure an audience. He saw Maurepas on Christmas
Eve, when Maurepas assured him on his word of honour that
there was no treaty in contemplation. Lord Stormont reported
the denial in his next Dispatch, although he was rightly sceptical
how much such a denial was worth. He was convinced that in
helping the Americans, the French government's chief aim was
to undermine the power of Britain. He wrote:

> M. de Maurepas's general characteristics may incline us to believe that
> such an attempt will not be made while he is in power. His professions
> are indeed constantly pacific, and peaceful councils suit his situation
> and natural turn of mind. But I am persuaded he is as hostile to us as
> any of the other French Ministers in his heart . . . as envious of the
> greatness of England, and as desirous to see that greatness impaired . . .
> The general bent of the Nation is more strongly for war than ever it
> has been in my remembrance, and M. de Maurepas may yield to the
> torrent as many other timid Ministers have done before him, may
> plunge into violent measures from mere weakness and irresolution . . .[3]

Not unnaturally Lord Stormont's suspicions of Maurepas
were reflected in their intercourse. Maurepas was also suspicious.
He heard that Lord North was sounding the American

Commissioners about the chances of conciliation: that he had
sent an emissary, Paul Wentworth, to approach Deane, while
a member of parliament, Robert Mayne, had been in touch
with Franklin at Passy. Maurepas believed that conciliation
was extremely likely, and was unconvinced when Lord Stormont
denied it. In fact it was more difficult than ever for the two
men to to preserve the proper diplomatic façade. Both found
Forth useful in this dilemma: he excused Lord Stormont to
Maurepas, and explained Maurepas to Lord Stormont. If he
did not succeed in satisfying either, he at least made it possible
for the two sides to remain in contact. It was partly in the
hope of a détente that Lord Stormont encouraged Forth to
oblige the French Court by acquiring Morande's Libel.

At the interview on 4 January 1778 when Forth finally
promised to go to London in pursuit of Morande he had a
remarkable conversation with Maurepas. Forth knew that he
was putting Maurepas under a considerable obligation, and he
determined to make his own bid to dissuade him from supporting the Americans. He told Maurepas that if he sincerely wished
for peace with England he could ensure it by advising Louis
XVI to send Franklin and Deane out of France.

'And what will you give us?'

'What will you have?'

'Ah! that will require reflection'.

'What will you have? Tell me, and I will communicate it
to Lord North'.

'Non, non, your Opposition would prevent it'.

'The truth is that you are determined to support America,
and only throw that out'.

'Do you think that we can ever imagine that anything guides
these people but the hopes of plunder, *butin, et esprit à révolter,*
and that if France were mad enough, I say *assez folle,* to make
any agreement and treaty with them, that England would not
*à aucun prix* make it up and they both fall on us. What though
now they are *acharné,* yet brothers and sisters must at last be
reconciled, and they will give each other the preference to
French, Spaniards, etc. Time will shew, and prove that we
had more reason to fear you than you to fear us. We are
repairing, improving and putting our Navy in order for fear of
you, and you are constantly augmenting yours in order to

surprise us. But I think we may think more of it. Go to
England. Try to sound there what they would give up of
America, or if the Parliament would agree to it, and I meantime
will sound the King. I think something might be done. Be very
secret, and when you return, we will see.'[4]

If Forth reported him correctly, Maurepas was expressing
some surprising views. Maurepas knew very well that the
American treaty negotiations were far advanced; France·would
have found it difficult to draw back, even if, as Maurepas
seems to be hinting, the British government offered part of
Canada as a bribe. But Congress had still to be consulted,
and the fear of a reconciliation between Anglo-Saxons
was very real to all the French Ministers. Chatham might
return to power. If either or both these things happened
it would be as well to keep negotiations open. Moreover
Maurepas still needed Forth's help over the Libel. He therefore
temporized.

Forth was only too glad to take a hopeful view. He left
Versailles believing that he had opened up great possibilities
of conciliation, which would not only please Lord Stormont,
but impress the government in England. His satisfaction did not
last long. On Wednesday 7 January, Goat (or La Chèvre) the
smuggler told him that a treaty had been signed; the text was
being sent to America on board the *Alfred*. This somewhat
premature report probably had its origin in the events of that
day's Council meeting, when the King approved a Memoir
concerning the treaty, the text of which was then sent to
Congress for approval.

That evening Forth set out for England. Unfriendly eyes
watched his departure, and reported that he left exclaiming that
he had been betrayed. Possibly from the same hostile source
Vergennes heard that Forth had been very indiscreet. He
announced that he was going to England on private business,
but, so Vergennes wrote to the French Ambassador at Madrid,
'during an orgy which preceded his departure, when, following
his praiseworthy habit, he became intoxicated, he read out to
one of his drinking companions two letters from Lord North.
In one the Minister summons him home without further explanation; in the other he urges him to hasten his return, and tells
him that he needs him to convince the doubters . . . '[5]

Drawing his information from Beaumarchais and his circle,
Vergennes held a low opinion of Forth.But he was unjust in
suggesting that Forth was a sot who revealed state secrets while
in his cups. In this case Forth intended to deceive. Both Lord
Stormont and Maurepas wanted to conceal the quest for the
Libel, particularly from Beaumarchais. By committing a calcu-
lated indiscretion Forth kept his real purpose secret: neither
Vergennes nor Beaumarchais knew anything about his transactions with Morande until the Libel was destroyed.

Whether Forth habitually drank too much it is impossible
to say. At a time when hard drinking was the fashion, the
French often criticized the English for excess; similar
criticisms were made of the Duke de Chartres and his
circle. But if Forth drank hard, he also had a strong head.
His daily entries in his Diary often begin, 'Up early', 'Up at 5',
'Up at 6', and very rarely, 'Up at 8', or 'Up at 10'. 'Very merry',
after a supper party at Lady Barrymore's, or a dinner of 12
in his own house, no doubt implied a good deal to drink. But
although a number of evenings finished in this way, many more
ended, 'Chat, tea, to bed'.

A more justifiable criticism could be made of Forth's
gambling acquaintance at this time. In December Forth played
at the Venetian Ambassador's, at the Count de Genlis's, and at
Lady Barrymore's, all houses where large sums were won or
lost. Lady Barrymore introduced Forth to Madame Du Barry,
in whose set play was also high; her young nephew, the
Viscount Du Barry was an inveterate gambler, and the friend
of men who made gambling their profession. Among these
was Major Baggs (also known as a duellist) and that General
Smith who, with Forth, incurred Marie Antoinette's displeasure
at Fontainebleau. Forth was present at Madame Du Barry's
one evening when Smith won 2,000 louis on one card; his
total winnings were 36,000 louis. Forth could not afford to
lose such sums. No doubt he knew this; his gains or losses,
when he records them, are comparatively small. The man who
balanced his accounts and paid his servants once a week was
not the man to stake too much on the turn of a card. But it
was dangerous to move in such circles; General Smith and Major
Baggs were unsuitable acquaintances for a Special Envoy.

2

Untroubled by these considerations, Forth was on his way
to England. He bade an affectionate adieu to Fullarton and
'dear Betsy', and travelled all night to arrive at Dieppe at
8.00 in the evening on 8 January. Finding that only fishing
vessels were leaving from that port, he once again travelled
through the night to Calais. He arrived there at 11.00 next
morning, and sailed on 10 January. Jeans, the parson, embarked
in the same vessel. Like Forth, he was worried about his future
if the British Ambassador were to leave Paris, and he too
planned to put his claims before the Ministers in London.
As travelling companions the two men had John Amyand and
Sir Philip Gibbes, one a banker with a contract to supply the
British troops in North America, the other the owner of
property in the West Indies. Both were likely to be affected
by a war between France and England, and both were anxious
to hear about the situation from a man in touch with events
in Paris. Forth was very willing to oblige: 'Am able, admired,
shine in conversation, listened to with eagerness', he wrote
in his Diary.[6]

At about midnight on Sunday 11 January, the party reached
Westminster. Forth went to leave his Dispatches at Lord North's
house, but finding, not surprisingly, that he was out of town,
he took them to Lord Weymouth's house instead. 'Come home
to bed at 2.00'.

On his first afternoon in London Forth called on Lord North.
He hoped for an opportunity to discuss his future, and it was
in any case his duty to report on the situation in Paris, in
particular his last conversation with Maurepas, and his plans
for obtaining possession of the Libel. But Lord North dismissed
him after a very short interview: 'cold to me, adieu'. In contrast
Lord Suffolk, Secretary of State for the Northern Department,
was 'civil, affectionate and condescendently attentive'. He
examined Forth thoroughly about events in France, and kept
Forth with him for three hours.[7]

Before he left Paris Forth had been suffering from a complaint which he believed to be rheumatic. The journey inflamed
this condition, and Forth was now feeling very ill. He had no

time to take care of himself however; on 15 January he was due once again to see Lord North.

This interview was much more satisfactory. North spent three hours with Forth. He asked about Maurepas's conduct, about the French King and Queen, and the ships which were being equipped to assist the Americans. Forth showed him a Journal of Washington's army, a document which Goat had procured. Lord North found it most illuminating, and kept it to show to Lord Dartmouth, Lord Privy Seal. He praised Forth, 'says the most flattering things, and pays me the greatest compliments'. He also promised to reflect on the notes which Forth had made of his conversation with Maurepas. Forth took advantage of Lord North's favourable mood to put in a good word on behalf of Jeans. All in all Forth was pleased with the way things were going; he felt that he was being appreciated at his true worth. It was pleasant, too, to hear from John Amyand that he was much praised in the City.

The following day Forth had a conversation at the Treasury with John Robinson, Lord North's indispensable man of business. This conversation, as conversations with Forth were apt to do, also lasted three hours. Although Robinson was 'surprisingly civil, polite and attentive', and helpful about plans to circumvent Morande, he was reserved on the subject of Forth's future. Forth was not discouraged, and after another familiar discourse with Lord North (two hours), when Forth gave him a copy of Necker's *Etat des Finances de France*, Forth thought it was time to put his fate to the touch. He asked for a meeting with Lord North and the two Secretaries of State, Lords Suffolk and Weymouth. This was arranged to take place on the evening of Monday, 26 January. Forth seems to have taken it for granted, rightly as it proved, that the three most important Ministers in the government should find time to see him when the country was fighting a long and difficult war in America, and there were many urgent affairs of state to discuss.

From its beginning in Lord North's anteroom the meeting promised badly. After Forth, Lord Weymouth was the first to appear. He had never shown much friendship to Forth; now his behaviour was cool and aloof. He spoke of the state of affairs in France, while Forth listened. Lord Suffolk entered next, 'distantly attentive'. In Lord North's room, John Robinson (who was also present) winked at Forth, but the atmosphere was very formal. The Ministers sat; Forth was kept standing throughout. He had not expected such a chilly reception. He began by reading letters from Maurepas about the Libel and the Libel itself. The Ministers stopped him: the subject of the Libel had already been discussed, and Forth had been promised government support. He was no more successful with the next topic which he raised, the question of *La Grue*, a French merchant ship which had been captured by the British Navy, and taken to Gambia where its cargo had been sold. *La Grue* and her treatment had caused annoyance between France and England for months, and had been the subject of many of Maurepas's conversations with Forth. He would have liked to give Maurepas a satisfactory reply, but the Ministers were afraid of creating an awkward precedent; they preferred the incident to be handled through the French Ambassador and the usual diplomatic channels.

The Ministers reverted to the subject of the Libel, and said if Forth succeeded in suppressing it it would be a good thing for him. Lord Weymouth remarked that he should think himself happy to be employed on it. Forth fired up and exclaimed, 'I never was employed to buy up Libels. If any of you ordered me to do so I would disobey'. At this there were 'cold looks and behaviour', so Forth added, 'if you requested it, I would undertake it with cheerfulness'.

There was a pause. Lord North asked if Forth had anything else to discuss. This was the point at which Forth would have liked to raise the question of his future employment. If the meeting had proceeded as he hoped, the Ministers would by now have acknowledged his merits and his services to his country, and been ready to offer him a permanent official appointment. In spite of everything he decided to put out a feeler:

'*Forth*: M. de Maurepas has offered to give me under another name the Deputy or Lieutenant-Governorship of a Château Royal or some equivalent with a large salary . . . '[*Stopped*].

'We have no diffidence of you, and are sure you will accept nothing from that Court'.

'*Forth*: I will do nothing without your permission'.

'*All*: When do you go back? You can be of more service
there than here . . . '. (*Haughty, Lord North reading*).

'I can now be of little use, but I will go back. What do
you want?'

'No answer.

'Have you no wish, no desire? Tell me any specifick thing,
and I will answer for its success by Lord Stormont's abilities,
Maurepas's timidity, and my intrigue.'

'No answer, and a scornful smile. Stand up all—kept me
standing all the time. If they have anything to trouble me with,
they will let me know. Come home to bed. Jeans comes in.
Tell him some part of this'.

Forth heard what Lord North thought about the meeting
from Jeans when he came back from an interview, also unsuccessful, about his next employment. Lord North told him:
'Forth is not clear. He did not know why he brought us
together. He is a fine piper for that knave Maurepas; he
trumpets forth his praises, and takes his part strenuously'.[8]

None the less things were not quite so bad as Forth feared.
Before he left for France after his successful encounter with
Morande, he not only had encouraging conversations with
Robinson and Lord Suffolk, but with Lord North himself.
'Amazingly polite, attentive and friendly', Lord North told
Forth that he would have liked to oblige Maurepas on the
question of *La Grue*, but the French Ambassador insisted
on keeping the matter in his own hands. He advised Forth
not to press for employment by the government, but to accept
an annuity as an acknowledgement of his services. Forth tried
to persuade him to do something for Jeans: '[Lord North]
takes paper; goes to little house; tell him at best but a shitten
get-off'. Lord North laughed heartily, and they parted on
good terms.[9]

3

While Forth was in London he was able to help his friend and
patron Lord Mansfield out of a dilemma which might have
damaged Forth's own prospects. Lord Mansfield, like Marie
Antoinette, was threatened by a blackmailer.

It might have seemed hard to find a subject for blackmail in the distinguished career of the 1st Earl of Mansfield. It had been said of him that 'in all he said or did there was a happy mixture of good nature, good humour, elegance, ease and dignity; [he was] possessed of a mind nobly gifted by nature and informed with every kind of learning that could serve for use or ornament'.[10] A friend of Alexander Pope and the wits of the last two reigns, he held office as Attorney General and Leader of the House of Commons in the Duke of Newcastle's Ministry; but he gave up politics in 1756 when he was appointed Lord Chief Justice. In this capacity he performed his greatest service to his country, using his formidable intellect and power of lucid expression to clarify the laws concerning trade and commerce.

Nevertheless he was vulnerable in at least one important respect: his family, including his elder brother, Lord Stormont's father, were Jacobites, and Lord Mansfield had himself been accused of Jacobitism. There was even a story that in his youth he had drunk to the health of the Pretender. Such suspicions had bedevilled the early part of his career, and timid by nature, even on his present eminence he still felt insecure.

On the second day after his arrival in England Forth drove out to Highgate to visit Lord Mansfield at Kenwood, the country house which the Adam brothers had remodelled and decorated for him. He received Forth warmly, sent away his hired chaise, and insisted on keeping him at Kenwood overnight. In a great state of agitation he told Forth: 'if you are not an honest man I am ruined; If you are not what I thought you, and still think you, I am overwhelmed in perdition and ruin'. He went on to describe his encounters with an ambiguous character who called himself the Count de Reynach.

Forth knew Reynach already. He was one of those men who made it their business to frequent great men's anterooms in the hope of hearing something useful. They saw who went in and out and who had access to the great man; they picked up much useful gossip which sometimes had a marketable value. Reynach claimed to be a cousin of the Count de Maurepas, and it was in his anteroom that he spent much of his time. He had friends among the stock-jobbers (to whom his ministerial gossip

might be helpful) and his acquaintance included Goat the
smuggler. More important perhaps, he was an associate of
Bourdieu, the head of the bankers Bourdieu and Chollet. A
wish to discredit Forth, the friend of Bourdieu's successful
business rival Robert Herries, was no doubt part of
Reynach's scheme.

When at last Maurepas forbad Reynach admission to his
anteroom Reynach crossed the Channel, and came to visit
Lord Mansfield at his town house in Bloomsbury Square. He
claimed that he had introduced Forth to Maurepas. He had
done so at Forth's own request because Forth told him that he
was a friend of the great Lord Mansfield, the favourite and
confidant of the King of England, the power behind the throne.
According to Reynach, Forth said that Lord Mansfield wished
to treat directly with Maurepas, without the knowledge of the
British Ambassador. On the strength of Lord Mansfield's name
Reynach had done what Forth asked, but received no reward
for his services. All Forth had given him was a *Court Calendar*:
Reynach hoped that Lord Mansfield would be more generous.

Lord Mansfield sent Reynach packing, but he returned more
than once. Sometimes he was humble and apologetic, sometimes he told Lord Mansfield far-fetched stories, but when he
found that Lord Mansfield would not give him money, he
began to threaten. He said he would first write to Maurepas
for confirmation of his assertions, and afterwards he would
make the whole transaction public, and a good deal else besides.

It was this threat that distressed Lord Mansfield. He knew
that many of Reynach's allegations were ridiculous, but they
could cause much mischief. It was by no means the first time
that Lord Mansfield had been presented as the hidden power
behind the throne. Junius, in his *Letters*, made just such an
accusation. Many, including some members of the government, believed him. Lord Mansfield knew this, and was
sensitive about it. He might have been even more worried had
he known that the legend of his powerful influence was current
abroad as well as in England; both the French and the Spanish
Ambassadors in London made a point of reporting to their
governments conversations with Lord Mansfield, or opinions
which he had expressed. It would have seemed completely

credible in France and Spain that Lord Mansfield wished to
have direct access to the chief Minister of France. Indeed
when Forth was appointed Special Envoy this was precisely
what the Spanish Ambassador, encouraged by Maurepas,
had reported.[11]

Forth, unaware of this, was as concerned as Lord Mansfield
to prevent the publication of Reynach's allegations. He did
not want any public discussion of his first introduction to
Maurepas. Moreover he would forfeit the confidence of Lord
North and the Secretaries of State, not to mention his own
chief, Lord Stormont, if they believed that he had claimed to
be Lord Mansfield's personal emissary. It would have been even
more harmful if Reynach were to publish Forth's contacts
among the speculators and their agents. Since Reynach also
moved in that world he was in a position to do so. [12]

It may be that this consideration was also important to
Lord Mansfield. He would not have been involved in 'perdition
and ruin' if Reynach accused him of exercising hidden
influence. The accusation, though unwelcome, was not new.
On the other hand if Lord Mansfield used Forth to make investments on his behalf, the situation would be much more serious.
A report that the Lord Chief Justice was engaged in stock-
jobbing, at a time when the possibility of war with France
made this a highly speculative operation, would have caused a
major scandal. It would greatly have damaged Lord Mansfield
in the eyes of the King; he might even have found it necessary
to resign. Perdition and ruin would aptly describe such a
contingency. Without a doubt Reynach had the power
to disturb the peace of mind of both Lord Mansfield and
Forth.

They discussed the situation until midnight. Forth says
that he calmed Lord Mansfield, comforted him and made him
easy. He himself was in pain, and passed a sleepless night.
At 9.00 breakfast next morning Lord Mansfield and he resumed
their conversation: 'serious discussion until 12'. They planned
that Forth should write to Maurepas about Reynach's activities,
and to ask him, if he would, to send a formal denial of the
allegations about Forth. Meanwhile they would await Reynach's
next move.

On 17 January Lord Mansfield invited Forth to Kenwood for dinner to discuss a new development. Forth went, taking Jeans with him. As soon as they arrived Lord Mansfield took Forth into his cabinet, where they were closeted together for two hours, while Jeans sat with Lady Mansfield and the other guests. Reynach had sent a confederate to see Lord Mansfield, a man named Taaffe. The question was how to handle him. Forth was for taking a firm line. Since he last saw Mansfield he had mentioned Reynach's allegations to Lord North who had made light of them. Encouraged by this, Forth was prepared to confront Reynach's emissary. Lord Mansfield was not so sure: 'differs with me', Forth wrote, 'perfectly satisfied, praises me highly, is calm and easy in my hands . . . come out and shine before Jeans and the women'.

Next morning, Sunday 18, Taaffe came to visit Forth in Somerset Street. 'Taaffe comes, slides in. I ask him who he is. Says, "My name is Taaffe". Shew him into the back parlour. Come to him, ask him to sit, listen.

'*Taaffe*: Sir, I come to you from Lord Mansfield whom I have known intimately these 30 years. I saw his Lordship last Friday, he told me where you lived, and desired I would come to you and consult with you about smothering an affair.

'*Forth*: Sir, I have the honour of knowing Lord Mansfield, and will certainly pay the most respectful attention to every order that comes from him, but every idea that I have formed of him will prevent my giving the least credit to any man who introduces himself by declaring he is come from Lord Mansfield to consult about smothering any transaction. I hear Mr. Jeans, who is Lord Stormont's chaplain, coming downstairs, he is a very honest man and my most intimate friend, and will be able to assist us in anything you have to propose.

'*Taaffe, [greatly agitated]*: Sir, I don't see what Mr. Jeans or any man has to do in any conversation which may pass between you and me.

'*Forth*: I am surprised at your objecting to Mr. Jeans being present. The manner of introducing yourself, the nature of your declaration, my entire ignorance of you and your proposition, the affected, agitated manner in which you speak and act, make it indispensably necessary to have a third person present.

'Seeing him vastly affected and faltering extremely in his speech, I said, "You need not be uneasy at Mr. Jeans's presence, he is a prudent, discreet, confidential man, and very candid". *Enter Jeans.* "Mr. Jeans, this gentleman, who says his name is Mr. Taaffe, has introduced himself by declaring he is come from Lord Mansfield, whom he has known these 30 years, to consult me about *smothering an affair."*

'*Jeans*: I know Mr. Taaffe.'

'*Taaffe*: I did make use of the words *smothering an affair,* I know nothing of it—I will say no more—(*trembling, pallid, faltering)*'.

'*Forth*: Why, Sir, what is the matter? Why not proceed? There is no danger. Sit down; will you drink anything?'

'*Taaffe*: Excuse me, Sir, I'll say no more. I know very little of the matter. Lord Mansfield told me your name was Forte, Ford or Forth . . . '.

'*Forth*: My name is F.O.R.T.H. Forth. I am as candid a man as ever you saw, will listen to you with attention, will take advantage of what you say, and will assist you if you deserve it'.

'*Taaffe*: Sir, do you know Mr. Reynach?'

'*Forth*: What Reynach?'

'*Taaffe*: The gentleman who introduced you to M. de Maurepas'.

'*Forth*: There are four or five Reynachs'.

'*Taaffe*: I won't say another word. Reynach has deceived me'.

'*Jeans*: You had better speak out, Mr. Taaffe'.

'*Taaffe*: I won't say another word. (*Almost fainting*). Goes.'[13]

This was the last that was seen of Taaffe, nor did Reynach make any further attempt to cause trouble. Neither he nor Taaffe had the tenacity or ingenuity of that other blackmailer Morande. A few days later letters arrived from Maurepas, describing his own experiences of Reynach; he confirmed that Forth had been introduced to him by Lord Stormont, and had produced credentials signed by Lord North and the Secretaries of State. The affair was safely buried, as Forth was able to report to Lord Mansfield. He spent more than one evening at Kenwood discussing Reynach, Morande's Libel, Forth's health, and on one occasion, predestination, and was able to return to Paris in the knowledge that his friendship with Lord Mansfield was stronger than ever.

## Chapter Six

## END OF A MISSION

### 1

PARIS WAS FULL of war rumours. Lord Stormont took so gloomy a view of the situation that he was reading the printed dispatches of Lord Bristol, ambassador in Madrid when Spain and England went to war in 1762. He suggested to his Secretary of State that the British government would do well to decide whether to declare war before the French could do so. Forth was one of the few who still believed that peace was possible. He was encouraged in this by the Duke de Chartres, who visited him on the day after his return, and assured him that there would be no war.

Forth did not understand how little Chartres knew of the inner councils of the King and his ministers. On 6 February, the day after Chartres's conversation with Forth, the French government signed treaties of friendship and commerce with America. It was hoped that the Spanish government would soon follow suit. For this reason, and because the treaties needed ratification by Congress, they were to remain secret for the time being.

But so decisive a move could not remain secret for long. Lord Stormont noticed a fermentation in Paris of a kind which he had never seen before. At Versailles there were signs of tremendous bustle and agitation; Maurepas's anteroom was full of officers hoping for employment. Maurepas's manner when he received Lord Stormont was so reserved that the Ambassador was convinced that war would soon be declared.

If this was the case Forth must ensure that his intelligence network was in running order. During the following weeks he was extremely active. Using Goat as his intermediary, he passed instructions to Knight whose task it was to station

observers in the French ports, Lorient, St. Malo, Nantes, Brest
and Le Havre. Suggestions about the kind of information which
these observers should supply no doubt owed something to a
conversation which Forth had on 8 February with Vice-Admiral
Sir George Rodney.

Debts in England had forced Admiral Rodney to settle in
Paris. Forth had met him more than once at the Embassy, or
at the house of Marshal Biron, with whom Rodney was
acquainted. Rodney held strong views on the value of accurate
naval intelligence; when he was stationed at Jamaica he had
been criticized by the Admiralty for overspending on this
account. He knew that intelligence was Forth's business, and
now he came to see him. Forth's network had never been tested in
wartime; it was useful to hear the views of a senior and successful
naval officer on the kind of reports that would be useful. Among
other things Rodney told Forth that if the French were planning
to invade England they would do so from Le Havre and Dunkirk.
Movements of shipping in the port of Brest could be intended only
for the West Indies. Rodney spoke of Marshal Saxe's unsuccessful attempt to make a landing at Gravesend in 1744 (before the
Jacobite rising of 1745), when 3,000 men had been drowned.[1]

However bleak the international situation might appear,
Forth's own life at this time was extremely agreeable. He was
enjoying a considerable success. Although Marie Antoinette
refused to show any gratitude to the man who had worked
so hard to save her reputation, her ministers were not so
grudging. Le Noir, head of police, who had been accused by
one of his own inspectors of retaining 1,200 copies of
Morande's Libel, was 'amazingly civil and attentive' to Forth.
He surprised everyone by escorting Forth to the door of his
coach. Necker, Director General of Finance, came up to Forth
at one of Lord Stormont's diplomatic receptions, and congratulated him on managing the affair so successfully.

News of Forth's achievement spread outside official circles,
ensuring a welcome for him in many of the great houses of
Paris. The Duke de Gontaut gave him a splendid edition of
Tasso's *Gerusalemme Liberata* with illustrations by Gravelot.
Voyer d'Argenson praised him greatly, and sent him a present
of game; he also betted against a formal declaration of war

with England before the first of May. Count Creutz, the
Swedish Ambassador, was extremely polite, and invited Forth
to dinner which, in the event, proved very dull. After one of
Marshal Biron's Friday receptions Forth wrote: 'gracious and
most attentive reception; upbraided for not dining there; all
eyes on me; Lady Dunmore [his former detractor] and
daughters roaring to me; greatly fêted ... go to Opera; greatly
admired and followed'.[2]

Betsy could not accompany Forth on these social occasions,
but she now had her nine-month-old son to occupy her. Forth
had brought little Nat back to France. He and his nurse
travelled separately under the escort of Quin, arriving in Paris
two days after Forth: 'I angry, Quin saucy'. Soon Betsy was
proudly showing off her baby to Lady Barrymore. At this
time, too, Betsy was sitting for her portrait, probably in miniature. The painter was Judlin, an artist settled in Paris, but
perhaps of Irish descent. Sometimes Mr. and Mrs. Judlin dined
with Forth and Betsy, and on occasion Goat and Dr. Gem
made up the 'very merry' party.[3]

2

While Lord Stormont dreaded to hear that France had declared
war on England, Maurepas and his colleagues were equally
concerned lest England and the American colonists should
make peace. If this happened, France would lose all the benefit
of recognizing American independence; it also seemed likely
that a re-united England and America might attack the vulnerable French West Indian possessions. The French Ministers
knew that the English government was planning to send a
conciliatory Commission to America, and they anxiously
followed the Parliamentary debates on this subject. They
feared an English approach to Franklin and his colleagues. The
movements of any possible intermediaries, Paul Wentworth,
William Pulteney, Robert Mayne, and even the head of the
Moravian Brethren, were closely watched. Soon Forth was to
add to Maurepas's anxieties.

Late at night on Saturday 21 February, Forth received
news from one of his London correspondents. He was told

that a ship from Philadelphia had arrived in Liverpool with
dispatches from General Howe: the British army had fought a
successful action against Washington, who had been empowered
by Congress to offer most satisfactory terms; the Americans
would not insist on independence if all hostile legislation
since the Stamp Act were revoked, and they were given the
right to impose their own taxes. The correspondent went on
to say that the King and Lord North had agreed to the proposals; a ship bearing their reply was on the point of sailing.

The report came from a source which Forth considered
reliable, but it was completely untrue. It contained several
improbabilities which should have put him on his guard: the
fact that Howe had no power to conclude an agreement with
the insurgents was one of them. But Forth believed it; he took
no steps to check the report. His sanguine temperament made
him credulous; he believed the good news because he wished
to do so.

Lord Stormont could have undeceived him, but Forth had
other plans. He sent the news to Maurepas: 'write to Timeo,
tell him the news, pathetic and spirited'. This letter, written
at 3.00 on Sunday morning, is in the archives of the French
Ministry of Foreign Affairs. It finishes: 'Milord Stormont
knows nothing yet; he will hear by the official courier tomorrow evening or Tuesday morning. My true affection for
you prompts me to send you the news at once, since I know
how important it is for Your Excellency, surrounded as you
are by enemies, to be informed of so great and momentous
an event . . . my greatest wish is to serve you and to convince
you of my true and disinterested friendship. My present action
is the strongest proof that I can offer you, for if my letter were
to be seen I should for ever be branded as a traitor. But I trust
you implicitly, Monseigneur; being entirely devoted to you I
serve you with my whole heart. I do not do so out of interest
as you know well, since this advance news might earn me,
if I wished, 100,000 écus'.[4]

By sending this letter Forth risked his position as Special
Envoy. It is true that he received his correspondent's information in his private capacity, but he was a salaried servant of
the British government, and his first loyalty was to his

Ambassador. No doubt he argued that since peace between England and America would lead to the resumption of good relations between England and France, it could not be said that he was betraying information to his country's enemies. He certainly saw a more promising future for himself in France than in England: his recent interview with the English Ministers, when they sat while he remained standing, probably contributed to this impression. The idea of being the Lieutenant-Governor of a French royal castle pleased him, nor would he be the first Irishman to find a new name and an influential position in foreign service. He relied much on Maurepas's friendship which he believed would be strengthened if he was given this important news ahead of his ministerial colleagues. But the benefits which Forth anticipated would follow only if the news were correct.

In fact Forth's letter greatly alarmed Maurepas. The report that England had come to terms with the Americans was exactly what he dreaded to hear. The Abbé Véry, once his confidant and still well informed, wrote in his *Journal*: 'During the night Sieur Forth sent Maurepas a courier to inform him of the debate in the House of Commons on 17 February on the proposals put forward by Lord North for conciliation with the colonies. With this news he sent a letter announcing that the Americans had already come to terms with the Court of St. James . . . In revealing this he was apparently betraying his country's secrets. He even said that he was risking his life if ever it became known that he had passed on this information. All day M. de Maurepas, dismayed at such a speedy reconciliation, was in the greatest anxiety . . . The King, braver or less perturbed than his Minister, disagreed: "Sieur Forth may be lying in order to embarrass us", he said . . . '.[5]

It would of course have been possible to ask Franklin and the other American Commissioners if Forth's information was true, but in the circumstances their denial would have carried no more weight than the diplomatic denials which Maurepas had been making to Lord Stormont during the past weeks. It was therefore little wonder if Forth found Maurepas somewhat guarded in his conversation, when, after attending a musical *déjeuner dinant* at Fullarton's

Pavilion, he obeyed a summons to Versailles on Sunday afternoon.

If Forth's account of the conversation is complete, he began by reading to Maurepas the letter from his London correspondent. Maurepas made little comment on this; the main topic of discussion was the likelihood of war between France and England. Maurepas did not share Forth's belief that a settlement between England and America would lead to a general peace. He thought it much more likely that England, possibly in conjunction with America, would attack the French West Indian colonies. When Forth said that Maurepas had peace or war in his hands, and could ensure peace by countermanding Admiral de la Motte Piquet's orders to sail with a convoy to North America, Maurepas replied, 'Do not you think things have gone too far? . . . We have great reason to fear Lord Chatham's coming in, and he will make war with all the world'. Nevertheless in order to be certain that no orders which might result in war were issued without his knowledge, Louis XVI had instructed his Ministers to submit every order to Maurepas. 'By this means they can do nothing without me, as you see now by all these papers. The only way to ensure the peace is to disarm. If you will do it, I will begin'.

'You said so before and deceived me and them by breaking your word'.

'Yes, the Spaniards were the occasion of it then, *now* they will not have war, and if you disarm, we will. However, stay here, and I will go in to the King, and I will speak to you if it will do, and if it will, we can settle it tomorrow, and you can go or send over and settle, etc.'.

At this point in the conversation Maurepas's colleagues arrived for a meeting of the King's Council. Maurepas left Forth to talk to Le Cler, and later to attend the Queen's card game. Finally he was again shown in to Maurepas's room. 'Well, what have you decided on?' Forth asked.

'We will wait, will see the event: we will not attack, we will only defend ourselves'.

During the next few days Forth felt considerable satisfaction at what he had done. He imagined that he had furthered his own interest with Maurepas and helped the cause of peace.

He told Lord Stormont 'all' (but surely not *quite* all) and wrote an account of his discussion with Maurepas to Lord North and Robinson.

The reality was quite different. When no confirmation came of a British victory in America Maurepas doubted, probably not for the first time, how far he could rely on Forth. He wrote to the Marquis de Noailles, the French Ambassador in London 'I have no doubt whatsoever of the [English] determination to make war on us in spite of the assurances to the contrary constantly made to me by Mr. Forth, of whom you must no doubt have heard more than once. I listen to him because I must, but reply little or not at all; however I do not suppose that this prevents him from attributing remarks to me. You will know in advance what reliance to place on any such reports'. To which the Ambassador replied that he had indeed heard of Forth and of Maurepas's condescension in receiving him: 'you are, M. le Comte, as much above the reports of such an agent as he is below what he ought to be to deserve the smallest credit in your eyes'.[6]

Maurepas retained a personal liking for Forth but he had no further official use for him. This was a distinction which Forth did not understand. Nor did he understand what harm had been caused by his false report. Although there had been no British victory, the danger of conciliation, which Forth's news underlined, remained. If not on that occasion, then at some other time, England might make peace with her colonies. The French government determined to forestall any such possibility. They decided to make public the treaties with America without waiting for a formal ratification from Congress. On 10 March instructions were sent to Noailles to inform the British government that France had recognized American independence and entered into treaties of friendship and commerce with the United States.

3

Goat the smuggler, well informed as ever, came to Forth at midnight on 9 March to tell him that Noailles was about to announce the treaties with America to the British government.

His information was rather in advance of events. The decision
on Noailles's instructions was taken at a Council meeting on
7 March. The instructions were despatched on 10 March, and
delivered by Noailles to Lord Weymouth on 13 March.

Forth was lying ill in bed with violent rheumatic pains when
Goat told him the news. At first Forth could not believe it.
Although by now he probably understood that the report of
a British victory in America was untrue, sub-consciously he
may still have continued to hope. Any further delusion was
now impossible. None the less it was some time before Goat
finally convinced him. Further confirmation came from Robert
Herries on 14 March. Forth was still in great pain, and under
treatment by Dr. Gem, but with the help of Fullarton, Goat
and Pigion, he now began to put his intelligence network into
running order, dictating to Betsy letters for his agents at the
ports.

On Monday 16 March, Forth left his bed for the first time
for a week, and was with Lord Stormont when a messenger
arrived with dispatches containing his recall to England. Lord
Stormont was understandably much affected. His whole mission
had been spent trying to preserve good relations between
France and England, an object which coincided with his own
inclinations; now the two countries were enemies, and might
soon be at war. To show how bitterly England resented the
step which France had taken, Lord Stormont was ordered to
return to England without taking leave.

Forth was quite as much moved as his Ambassador. His
duties as Special Envoy were over; there could now be no
prospect of congenial employment in France; even the broking
transactions which earned him his living would be affected.

That day one of Le Noir's policemen, Agent Buhot, was
keeping the British Embassy and its personnel under observation. He reported that there was much coming and going. Lord
Stormont had spent the morning with Madame Du Deffand
and Madame d'Invau. He had returned to the Embassy and been
closeted for an hour with Admiral Rodney. When Rodney
left he had said in English that he hoped there was no truth in
the rumours that Noailles had delivered a declaration of war.
Fullarton had also been with Lord Stormont, and had been

shown a passage in a letter four pages long. Jeans had been told that he would be needed after dinner. He and Riddell had been kept busy all afternoon writing in the Ambassador's closet. Forth had spent an hour with Lord Stormont while Betsy waited in a carriage outside. Finally Lord Stormont had ordered all his silver to be packed and told his servants to hand in their liveries; his kitchen would cease to function the following evening.[7]

Lord Stormont's departure did not proceed altogether smoothly. The formidable Countess Forbach, from whom the Embassy was rented, protested that Lord Stormont had not given the notice required under his lease. She proposed to foreclose on his carriages. The French government were embarrassed. They had waited to issue Lord Stormont's passports until they knew how their Ambassador was being treated in London, but once they were satisfied on this point, they wished to preserve diplomatic courtesy. It was a relief when the lawyers of the two parties concluded a satisfactory settlement. At 6.00 in the evening on Saturday 21 March, only five days after he received his recall, Lord Stormont left Paris.[8]

The Ambassador had been forbidden to take formal leave of the French King and his Ministers, but Forth was permitted to see Maurepas once more. He was again to be offered a snuffbox as an expression of Louis XVI's gratitude for the suppression of Morande's Libel. Forth had instructions from Lord Stormont what to do, but Forth was out of charity with Maurepas. He knew that he had made a fool of himself; his disappointment and disillusion took control. The interview followed a most undiplomatic course.

Maurepas began by asking about Noailles from whom he said he had heard nothing. Forth taxed him with perfidy and breach of his word. While the two men were talking, the Prince de Bourbon came to see Maurepas about his duel with the Count d'Artois, and Forth left. Maurepas sent Le Cler after him with the snuffbox. Forth refused it. Maurepas called Forth back when Bourbon had gone, and again pressed him to accept the box. There followed what Forth rightly describes as a curious scene. The dialogue in Forth's Diary is in French in which a certain lack of grammar increases the sense of pent feelings at last finding expression.[9]

'*Forth*: Do you think I am so base as to carry in my pocket
the portrait of a man who has played the treacherous part
which your Master has played. He has dishonoured the name
of King and Frenchman by signing a treaty with rebels and
pirates, and do you imagine that I am the kind of *fier anglais*
who would accept this box from a Minister without a heart
and without a title [Maurepas was never actually given the
title *premier ministre*] who passed his youth in low intrigue,
his [middle age] in exile for his crimes, and is ending his life in
timid betrayals, dishonouring his nation and his king. Take it
(*throws down box violently*). I pity and I pardon the young
King who is your dupe. I despise and punish the old lackey
who dies like a serpent, spitting out poison in its death agonies.'

'Much affected, cries, takes up the Box, picks up three
diamonds. Says, "I am lost for ever if you breathe a word.
I was obliged to do what I did, or resign. In a little while everything will become plain, and you will see that I will still be
your friend".'

'*Forth (enraged): Je me fous de votre amitié, Vieillard.*
But do not believe that you ever deceived me. You tried to do
so, but I was well aware of your knavery. (*Go away furious.*)'

Perhaps Forth did not say quite what he recorded in his
Diary. Certain blanks and erasures in the text suggest this.
It is none the less the description of a painful scene. Forth was
much the younger man; he had received great kindness from
Maurepas; it is sad that they parted on such terms.

From Maurepas Forth went to Vergennes. Here again he
allowed his temper to take control, but in Vergennes' case
there is less reason to regret it.

'Go to Vergennes. Wait for him ten minutes. He comes.
Go into his Cabinet. Pretends not to know me. Upbraid him
with his being shortsighted; *persiflé* him.

'*Forth*: I do not blame you so much as M. de Maurepas.
You have dishonoured your nation in order to win money by
gambling in our funds. Only a gambler's throw could save you'.

'He is furious, desires me to think where I am, and to whom
I am speaking. I say, "I have entered the Cabinet of a lackey,
and I am speaking to a stockjobber".'

'*Vergennes*: You deserve to be arrested'.

'*Forth*: You would not dare. I have your trial and sentence in my pocket. Look! (Here tell of Grand, when and how he played for him, different payments, rescounters, etc.)'.

'Greatly alarmed. Begins to apologise. Break away saying, "Remember that I am alive, that you are in my power, and that if you ever dare to arrest me, I will see that you yourself are arrested".'

When giving instructions for these interviews Lord Stormont certainly never imagined that Forth would end by accusing the French Foreign Minister of speculating in British funds. Forth took a great risk in doing so. But on this occasion he seems to have made sure of his ground; the evidence of payments and settling days sounds convincing, nor is there anything improbable in the accusation. There had been an outbreak of speculation at the time of the Falkland Islands crisis in 1771 when it seemed likely that England would go to war with Spain. More than one public servant was involved, including, it was thought, the French Ambassador in London. Now, in a similar situation, when war seemed likely between England and France, speculation began again. If Vergennes was speculating, Georges Grand was an agent he might well have chosen. Grand was the banker favoured by the American Commissioners; through his bank French subsidies were paid to Sweden where Vergennes once served as Ambassador. Although an accusation of this kind is almost impossible to prove after the event, particularly when the men concerned would have acted through intermediaries, it is true that Vergennes's contemporaries believed that he tripled his fortune during his years in office as a result of successful speculation based on inside information. Forth was also of this opinion, and risked a *Lettre de cachet* in saying so.

Meanwhile Betsy was waiting for Forth at the inn. As he returned there, after unsuccessfully trying to call on Necker and the Minister of War, he met Le Cler coming out.

'Mrs. Forth tells me he had brought the box, and that I had forgotten it. Shows it, praises the diamonds, etc. She says I told her I had rejected it with disdain, and she refuses it'.

4

There was much to be done during Forth's short remaining
time in Paris: purchases to be made, bills to settle, farewells
to be said, and final instructions to issue to his agents. No
wonder that the entries in his Diary read, 'run about all day',
and 'go about for intelligence; employ all'.[10]

The purchases included a supply of commissions. Forth
would continue to buy stock on behalf of clients in France
as long as he could; if communications between France and
England became impossible, transactions could be transferred
to Amsterdam.

One of many farewell gatherings which Forth attended took
place on 30 March at Lady Dunmore's. Admiral Rodney was
there, still desperately anxious about the debts which prevented
him returning to England and active service. He had already
consulted Jeans about his problem because, as he told his
wife, 'he is a good man, and feels the distress I am drove to'.
On this occasion Marshal Biron, who was one of the guests
'took Lady Dunmore, Mr. Forth and Mr. Jeans the Parson
into another room and told them he heard my stay in Paris
was occasioned by the want of a remittance to discharge the
debts I must necessarily have contracted. That his purse was
at my service, and begg'd that I would make use of it, that
whatever sums, even to two thousand pounds might be
necessary he would immediately pay . . . On the Marshal's
return into the room they beckoned me out and made me
acquainted with his generous offer, for which I begged they
would make my acknowledgements, and how highly sensible
I was of his friendship; but as I made no doubt but that I
should soon receive proper remittances, I could not possibly
avail myself of his generosity, but should ever retain it in my
memory. Besides my enemies would take advantage of my
receiving pecuniary favours from Frenchmen of his high rank,
and instill insinuations to my disadvantage. Lady Dunmore
and the two gentlemen were of my opinion . . . '. But some
days later, finding no other way of resolving his difficulties, Rodney accepted the offer of this most chivalrous
adversary.[11]

This encounter was more important for his country than for Forth. Much more significant from his own point of view was his farewell interview with the Duke de Chartres. Forth saw him on 1 April, his last day in Paris. He undertook to carry out several commissions for Chartres in London, and received in return many expressions of friendship which were to count for much in the future.

Forth had his last interview with Goat on 28 March to settle methods of communication if war were declared. On 1 April he saw all his agents in Paris, and paid the 'port people'. His agent, Langlacé, would act as paymaster in his absence.

In the intervals of all his other activities Forth found time to sit once or twice to Judlin for his own portrait as a companion-piece to Betsy's. He collected his debts and paid his bills. He auctioned all but two of his horses, Mousquetaire, for which he refused 126 louis, and Smugler, already sold for 80 louis to Prince Bariatinski. A red chest containing some of his most treasured possessions was already packed and consigned to England in the care of Jeans. In this chest were books, pictures, eau de cologne and tea; with them went Forth's violin and viola, and Betsy's piano, perhaps one of Pleyel's earliest instruments.

By 30 March Forth was ready to ask Vergennes for passports for himself and *his suite*. This phraseology was altogether too ambassadorial for Vergennes. When sending Forth's request to the Lieutenant General of Police, the proper official to deal with such matter, he replaced the word *suite* by 'servants, luggage, horses and carriages'.

On the same day that Forth wrote to Vergennes he wrote to Maurepas to ask for a letter to the Governor General of Calais, and a safe-conduct for the vessel in which he would sail to England. This may have been his first communication with Maurepas since the 'curious scene' at Versailles. The letter contains no direct apology, but Forth expresses a wish to depart at peace with everyone, and he acknowledges Maurepas's many kindnesses in the past. He leaves Maurepas surrounded by *continental* friends, but as soon as he wishes to be among *insular* friends, Forth will hasten to rejoin him. Because he has never flattered or deceived Maurepas, he feels able to subscribe

himself, with the deepest respect, his true and zealous friend.
There is no record of Maurepas's reply, but later he was to
show that he harboured no ill feelings against Forth.[12]

On 2 April Forth received his passports. The wagons loaded
with his heavy baggage included 900 bottles of Sillery wine
which he had undertaken to sell in England on behalf of the
Count de Genlis at 6 livres the bottle. That evening, at 5.00,
a time which allowed for an easy four-hour stage to Chantilly,
Forth and his party set out. Next morning Lady Dunmore and
her party overtook them at Chantilly. She allowed Betsy to be
introduced, and the two parties continued in company to
Calais. While they waited there for a vessel, Forth spent a good
deal of time in conversation with Chartres's friend, the Duke
de Lauzun, who was on his way back from England to join the
French volunteers in America. Forth's vessel sailed at 12.00 on
8 April; at 2.00 a.m. on the 9th he was in London.

1. Nathaniel Parker Forth in middle age. Portrait by an unknown artist.

2.   Forth aged 59. Miniature painted in Paris in 1803 by an unknown artist,
and given to Eliza Petrie at Christmas 1803.

3. Eliza Forth, who on her second marriage became Baronne Rouen des Mallets, *c.*1809. From a portrait by François Pascal Simon, Baron Gérard.

John Petrie, Forth's father-in-law, :puty Lieutenant of Surrey, M.P. for Gat-n. Miniature by Andrew Plimer.

Forth's sons: 5. Capt. Frederick Henry Alexander Forth in the uniform of the 75th Foot, now 1st Battalion the Gordon Highlanders. Gazetted 21st Royal Scots Fusiliers in 1832, he was afterwards Lieutenant Governor in the West Indies, and Acting Colonial Secre-

8. David Murray, 7th Viscount Stormont, later 2nd Earl of Mansfield, in 1780. Engraving by an unknown artist. Lord Stormont was at that date Secretary of State for the Northern Department.

7. William Murray, 1st Earl of Mansfield, Lord Chief Justice. Bust, 1779, by Joseph Nollekens.

9. Louis Philippe Joseph, Duke de Chartres, afterwards Duke d'Orléans (Philippe Egalit
Drawing by Angelica Kauffmann as a study for a portrait painted in Rome in 1783.

0.  Pamela (on the left) at a harp lesson given by the Countess de Genlis to Mademoiselle 'Orléans, daughter of the Duc d'Orléans, in the Chàteau of Saint-Leu. Engraving by Iauzaisse of a picture painted by Giroust in 1787.

Jean Phélypeaux Frederic Comte de Maurepas.

11. Jean Frédéric Phélypeaux, Count de Maurepas. Engraving by Dupin.

*Chapter Seven*

## THE PORTSMEN

### 1

IN LONDON Forth's life, although no longer directly concerned with the great issues of war or peace, was none the less active and lively. As soon as he was installed at Somerset Street, and before the carpets were laid, he set about renewing his connexions in the government and in the City of London.

His first call was at the Treasury. He saw Robinson, and finally, Lord North. Forth was 'spirited and respectful', Lord North 'clear, candid and communicative'. From the Treasury Forth went on to visit the bankers, Robert and Henry Drummond. While he was with them they were joined by Anthony Chamier, one of their chief cronies, and a member of the group known as the Gang. This 'voluntary association, cemented by private friendship and congeniality of disposition', originated in a convivial dining club of 12 members, and continued to bring together an influential group of men with interests in public affairs, commerce and finance. Forth 'roused' Chamier, and all three were 'very merry'. Afterwards Forth dined with Lord Dunmore, and at 8.00 visited Lord Mansfield, who received him affectionately. At 11.00 he returned to Somerset Street where he sat up discussing all the City news with Lord Dunmore and John Amyand until 2.00 in the morning.[1]

The following day, Easter Sunday, passed quietly. Forth spent the time settling accounts with servants and tradesmen. But on Monday the round of visits began again. Forth saw both Secretaries of State: Lord Suffolk praised him, and even Lord Weymouth, usually so stiff, was remarkably civil. In the interval of his official visits, Forth managed to obtain orders from Robinson and his colleague, Brummell (father of the Beau) for some of Count de Genlis's Sillery wine. He was certainly not wasting his time.

79

During these first weeks after Forth's return to England
he saw much of Lord Dunmore and his wife. Perhaps one
reason was that in this household at least Betsy was accepted
as Forth's wife; indeed when Nat was christened, Lady
Dunmore was one of the godmothers. But Forth and Lord
Dunmore had several interests in common: some were financial;
another was music. When Lord Dunmore abandoned the
Governor's House at Williamsburg he left behind a harpsichord,
a pianoforte, several other instruments, and no less than three
organs. In London he was a member of the Noblemen and
Gentlemen's Catch Club which Lord Sandwich had founded
for 21 aristocratic members and a proportion of professional
musicians. The Club met once a week for a dinner at which
each member proposed a toast. Catches, songs and glees alter-
nated with the toasts, and if any singer sang out of time or
tune, he was bound by the rules to drink a glass of whatever
wine was on the table; no tea or coffee, 'or other such heterogeneous beverage' was allowed. Not surprisingly, as the evening
went on, the proceedings became increasingly hilarious; but in
spite of this the Club was said to have greatly improved the
performance of catches, canons and glees, and the prizes offered
had called into being many new compositions. Lord Dunmore
often took Forth with him to the Club, which Forth found
much to his taste. Nor was music confined to the Catch Club.
After an evening at Lord Dunmore's house Forth wrote: 'dine
at Lord Dunmore's with Drummond and Lord Rosse. Sing,
dance, etc., play, till late on'. In this instance perhaps play
may be taken to mean not gaming but music.[2]

When Forth's house in Somerset Street was arranged to
his liking, the carpets laid, and the china and Jasper ware from
Wedgwood delivered, Forth borrowed Lord Dumore's cook, and
gave a dinner for 15. The guests included Lord and Lady
Dunmore and some of their family; Robinson and Brummell
from the Treasury; Count Belgiojoso, Minister of the Court of
Vienna; one of the Drummonds; and John Amyand. The party
was evidently a success: 'very merry; drink, sing, etc., until
2 am'.

Forth had not forgotten his promise to purchase horses
and hounds for the Duke de Chartres. He spent several mornings

at the sales at Tattersall's, Lord Dunmore, Fullarton and Jeans
accompanying him to give their opinion on his choice. When he
had bought both horses and hounds, he was faced with the
difficulty of shipping them across the Channel in wartime,
when communications were limited to six vessels between
Dover and Calais. However Lord North authorised the ship-
ment, and on 10 May eight horses and 20 hounds were sent off
under the care of Forth's groom, Tom, who was given 30 guineas
for his expenses on the journey.

But whatever his other occupations or diversions, Forth's
main concern at this time was his career. He hoped that his
services as Special Envoy would qualify him for another
government post, preferably diplomatic. Such a post would be
hard to obtain. Demand was always high, and the number of
those whom the government wished to oblige outnumbered
a supply now very much contracted by the closing of the
Paris Embassy, the probable closure of the Embassy at Madrid,
and the return of numerous Governors of North American
colonies from posts no longer tenable. At one time there were
three governors, of whom Lord Dunmore was one, attempting
to administer their territories from a cabin aboard one of
H.M. ships. And plainly an ex-ambassador or ex-governor had
no need of a staff.

In his search for government employment Forth was in
competition with his former colleagues of the Paris Embassy;
their claims indeed were considerably stronger than his, since
they had been chosen for their posts by the British government,
while Forth owed his appointment as Special Envoy to
Maurepas's caprice. Lord Stormont of course was out of the
running: he was too able, and his government connexions
too good, to remain unemployed for long. Towards the end of
1778 he was made Justice-General of Scotland, and the following year he succeeded Lord Suffolk as Secretary of State for
the Northern Department. Fullarton's great wealth and East
Indian interests gave him considerable advantages. He obtained
a seat in Parliament (Forth was with him when he discussed
preliminaries with Robinson) and he also proposed, with the
help of friends to fit out four privateers for an expedition to
the Spanish Main. He would be commissioned Lieutenant

Colonel for the purpose, and allowed to raise a regiment, although he was completely without military experience. Not unnaturally the proposal to put 'this embassy clerk, this *commis*' in command of troops roused a great deal of opposition in Parliament and in the Army, but to everyone's astonishment Fullarton made an excellent soldier, and ended by commanding an army in India. Jeans, who did not possess a fortune, and could not bring much influence to bear on those in authority, was eventually given the New College living of Witchingham in Norfolk. He was a near neighbour of Parson Woodforde, who inducted him into his living, and frequently dined with him. Parson Woodforde was somewhat critical of the quality of his dinners, especially when he was offered a roast hare, half raw and half burnt to a cinder. But he enjoyed Jeans's society, and availed himself of the services of Godolphin his fine grey stallion.[3]

Forth, in a position rather similar to that of Jeans, had nevertheless one asset of his own creating. This was his intelligence network. It had already proved useful, and now made it possible for Forth not only to oblige the government by supplying intelligence when this was badly needed, but also provided an opportunity to keep in constant touch with Lord North.

2

Forth's system, originally designed to produce commercial intelligence, was based on informants in the chief north and west coast French ports and in some English ones: Forth called them *the portsmen*. There were 'the miners' who dug out the information, and 'the greyhounds' who carried it. Some informants were wine merchants such as Byrne of Bordeaux, and O'Gorman, a brother-in-law of the Chevalier d'Eon; others were Irish officers in foreign service. Yet others were sea captains such as Goat (or La Chèvre) who operated principally between Dover and Calais, and may have been connected with the banking firm of Minet and Fector, who also ran the cross-Channel packet service. Forth himself acted as the chief distributor of intelligence; he did not conceal this fact from the agents, but he was careful not to reveal who received the information. Dr. Gem and Knight (perhaps a connexion of Betsy) helped Forth to keep in touch with the agents. He usually, but not always, paid them himself. One of the intermediaries employed when communications were cut between England and France was a certain Levasseur from Boulogne, perhaps related to an innkeeper of that port. While the system was used for commercial purposes, funds were probably forthcoming from the financiers who benefitted. But during the War of American Independence, when Forth began to send information to the British government, funds were provided from the Secret Service account of the Treasury. Forth accounted for these to Robinson or Lord North.[4]

There were of course other intelligence systems besides Forth's. Both the Admiralty and the Secretary of State for War collected and received intelligence; William Eden of the Board of Trade and Plantations was the main channel through which flowed reports on Franklin and the other American Commissioners in Paris. There was also the information received at Lloyds Coffee House from the masters of merchant ships, and transmitted by Lloyds to the Admiralty. Forth's aim was to satisfy Lord North that his system could stand comparison with any other.

He proceeded to do this in a series of interviews, some of which took place in Lord North's Treasury room, and some at his country house at Bushey. Lord North showed himself not only accessible, but eager, to hear what Forth had to tell him, in particular if it had any bearing on the movements of the French Mediterranean fleet, which for obvious geographical reasons was always difficult to keep under observation. On 22 April Forth showed Lord North an intercepted letter which had been sent him by Payne, a correspondent at Dover. Two days later the two men had a 'long familiar chat' at Bushey: 'very merry; tell several Parisian bawdy anecdotes; drink tea'. On 26 April Forth hurried out to Bushey again with news about the Toulon fleet: 'Lord North runs out; most cordial reception; tell him of Toulon fleet and every particular; letter from Le Kerbonne when under way: he is greatly affected; long confidential chat; stay there some time; go into parlour; drink tea

with ladies . . . take leave; Lord North follows me; go into his
Cabinet; he is remarkably civil and gracious . . . '.

At this interview Lord North promised his official support
for Forth's system. He agreed that Forth should station portsmen at Le Havre, Cherbourg, St. Malo, Brest, Lorient and
Nantes, leaving it to Forth to arrange prices and terms; funds
would be forthcoming. This was just as well; Forth had already
made arrangements for portsmen in precisely those places
before he left Paris.

Now that Forth had received Lord North's sanction, he
wasted no time in adapting his system to operate from London
instead of Paris. He sent one of his greyhounds to the ports
with 50 guineas, and he forwarded a draft for a further 50
guineas to his financial agent in Paris; the dispatch of horses
and hounds to the Duke de Chartres provided an opportunity
to send this letter (and other relevant correspondence) across
the Channel. Forth's next task was to arrange further links
between the French and English Channel ports. He was satisfied
with communications between Calais, Boulogne and Dover,
but more were needed with 'the Sussex coast. Forth visited
suitable landing-places at Seaford, Newhaven and Saltdean,
and with the help of a trusted agent, Killick by name, and
Muttlebury, who was probably a smuggler, he made arrangements for transmitting news between the coast and London.

For help at the London end of the chain of communication
Forth approached Samuel Swinton. The two men were already
acquainted, and Swinton had been useful to Forth when he was
tracking down Morande. Swinton, an enterprising and adven-
turous character, started life in the Navy, but left it for naval
intelligence and journalism. His newspaper, *Le Courrier de
l'Europe*, much disliked, and in fact banned by the French
government, nevertheless enjoyed a considerable circulation
in France. Swinton had a French mistress, and a family settled
in Boulogne. His varied contacts made it easy for him to collect
intelligence which for many years he had been passing on to the
Admiralty. He also acted as a channel of communication with
other agents, including those working for Madame Wolters at
Rotterdam. He now agreed to perform a similar function for
Forth's agents.

Forth did not leave the collection of intelligence entirely
to his agents. One day he spent a guinea in a fruitless attempt
to discover information about the Brest fleet; another day he
came home tired after a whole day hunting all over the City
of London for 'one La Ferriere supposed to bring over Adams's
letter'. Some news brought by Robert Herries on 2 May
was more to the point: he had heard that the destination of
Admiral D'Estaing's Mediterranean fleet was certainly Delaware
Bay; ships with supplies for America were to join him in the
Toulon roads, whence the fleet would sail to Cadiz; four
Philadelphia captains had left London to join D'Estaing, and
to act as pilots. This was a useful supplement to intelligence
which the government had already received from the Hague that
D'Estaing had sailed on 26 April. But when Forth passed this
news on to Lord North, he found him 'cautious' about
believing it.[5]

This was a difficult time for Lord North. An English fleet
under Admiral Byron was being hastily fitted out at Portsmouth
with Gibraltar as its destination in the hope of intercepting
D'Estaing. Lord North was being sharply criticized in Parliament for delaying Byron's instructions. He could not afford to
make mistakes. Forth apparently succeeded in convincing him,
and through him King George III. The King wrote from Portsmouth where he was spurring on the naval preparations: 'the
person from whom you have got the intelligence of the
destination of the French fleet is in my opinion much the best
of the many that have been employed'. This was high praise
from someone who was usually critical of Forth and once
described his reports as 'extraordinary narrations'.[6]

Every day Forth summarized for Lord North the principal
points in his agents' reports; if he had obtained information
from his contacts in the City, or received letters from correspondents in France (he still heard from time to time from
the Duke de Chartres, Maurepas, and Madame de Genlis among
others), he included this news also. The information was often
very trifling, as Forth admitted, but Lord North seemed to be
glad of it; two or three times a week he sent for Forth to discuss
his summaries. At one such interview on 11 May Lord North
was called away to the House of Commons to reply to a motion

by Barré calling for a state funeral for Lord Chatham. That
bright particular star, whose return to power the French so
much dreaded, was now extinguished for good.

Frequent and friendly intercourse with Lord North encouraged Forth's hopes of another government appointment. Lord
North, at this time, was threatening to resign: Forth could ill
afford to lose so promising a patron. He wrote Lord North a
letter of advice, and with it sent the splendid edition of Tasso's
*Gerusalemme Liberata* which he had himself been given by the
Duke de Gontaut. A few days later Forth returned from visiting
Lord Mansfield at Kenwood to find that Lord North had been
waiting at Somerset Street for his return, and left a message
asking Forth to follow him to the Treasury. 'Go to Lord North;
he is amazingly kind and civil; go over everything relative to the
Toulon fleet, the man from Lezoutte, intelligence, etc., . . .
Irish Bills, change of administration, etc. Speak of Tasso's
*Gerusalemme*, of Lord and Lady Stormont; whole story of Lady
Clermont relative to me. He is in great spirits; make him laugh,
talk funny till quarter past four'.

But amazingly kind and civil as Lord North might be, he was
still First Lord of the Treasury. Forth was disagreeably
reminded of this on 19 June when he was summoned to the
Treasury to account for the sums which he had expended on
intelligence. 'Stay an hour; go over the account; various remarks
make it clear that I have lost. Press him to be explicit and clear.
Settle from 1st June at 12½ guineas per month for each of six
men at ports—75 guineas. Go over every article of the account;
explain fictitious names, contractions and differing services'.
Evidently Lord North jibbed at subsidizing the portsmen at
Le Havre, St. Malo, Cherbourg, Brest, Lorient and Nantes
during the weeks before he gave Forth authority to station
anyone in those towns.

To most men this would not have seemed a propitious
moment to raise the subject of his future; Forth thought
otherwise: 'talk of myself; desire to be on the same footing as
I was while Lord Stormont and Fullarton are so. He says he
will write to me soon, will consider and let me know. N.B.
Upon the whole treats me with his usual affability, though
at first hurt my delicacy'.

Forth was right in thinking that Lord North was still well
disposed. Payment for the portsmen was satisfactorily settled
when Robinson allowed Forth £2,855 for different services,
and provided a salary for the useful 'greyhound' Killick, by
putting him on the payroll of the Imprest service, one of the
Audit departments of the Exchequer. Better still, Lord North
suggested two possible posts for Forth. One was some kind of
unofficial mission to Poland, the other a similar mission to
Brussels. At that moment Poland and Brussels were both
backwaters in either of which Forth would have been far
removed from the centre of events, as Lord North knew very
well. In suggesting these posts for Forth he showed that his
opinion of Forth's diplomatic talent was not very high. Forth
may not have suspected this, but perhaps Lord Mansfield,
whom Forth consulted, made the right inference. On his advice
Forth refused both appointments.

At this time Forth hoped that Lord Suffolk was going to
offer him the position of Under Secretary in the Northern
Department. Such a post would have opened up excellent
prospects; it might in time even have led to a seat in Parliament.
Several future Ministers began in just such a way. On 23 June
Forth saw Lord Suffolk: 'long confidential discourse, explains
all about the Foreign Department'. This seemed promising,
and in later years Forth claimed that he had actually been
offered the post of Under Secretary. But if the offer was made
at this time, there is no mention of it in Forth's Diary. The
question of his career was still unsettled when in July he left
London for the summer.

Earlier that year, at a dinner at Fullarton's house, when 'all
went cheerful', Forth encountered James Boswell. Other guests
were the Earls of Glencairn and Balcarres; John Wilkes; the
pamphleteer Richard Tickell; and Parson Jeans. 'Claret', Boswell
recorded, 'made no impression to hurt me at all'. The conversation touched on Wilkes's speeches; Pope's *Essay on Man*;
Garrick's character; wit and parliamentary eloquence. Tickell
imitated Burke, and Boswell told Tickell that Dr. Johnson
admired his poem *Anticipations*, an imaginary forecast of parliamentary speeches. Seen through Boswell's eyes, Forth was
'an Irish intelligencer, good countenance and bold talker'.[7]

Even on holiday Forth remained in contact with his portsmen. He hired a house on the south coast at Rottingdean whence he could communicate with agents on both sides of the Channel. A new contact was Beaulard, a smuggler from Fécamp. Forth had a 'long chat' with him at Newhaven on 11 July, and agreed to pay him five guineas for information.

At Rottingdean, too, Forth was within easy reach of Brighton. This was not yet the fashionable watering place it was to become, but several of Forth's acquaintances had taken houses there, partly for the sea bathing, and partly to be near Dr. (afterwards Sir Lucas) Pepys, the King's physician. Forth himself had need of Dr. Pepys's services when in mid-July he was seized with a violent fever which lasted for several weeks.

3

In this looking-glass warfare the French too were running a very effective intelligence system. Before leaving England, the French Ambassador explained to Vergennes how it worked. There were correspondents in Portsmouth, Plymouth and Deptford, in the Admiralty itself, and in the War Office. Others had access to Parliamentary papers and to the transactions of the East India Company. None of the agents knew each other, nor were they aware that they were working for the French. The Ambassador proposed to supplement these well-tried informants by an agent who was capable of organizing a secret correspondence with the Continent; the existing agents (unlike Forth's) had no experience of this kind of work. The new agent must have a pretext, 'agriculture, aboriculture, or any other plausible reason', for his stay in England, and it would be useful if he could pass as a German.[8]

The men who fulfilled the Ambassador's requirements were La Motte and Luttersloh. La Motte was a British subject of Alsatian origin; Luttersloh, a Brunswicker, recruited by La Motte, had been employed to raise German auxiliaries for service in America; he then settled at Wickham, near Gosport, where (impeccable cover) he ran a pack of hounds.

La Motte and Luttersloh worked successfully together until the unlucky day in 1781 when La Motte was visiting the

Secretary of State's Office in Cleveland Row, and dropped his portfolio on the stairs, spilling documents which proved to contain detailed lists of the British fleet. Luttersloh turned King's evidence, and La Motte was executed as a traitor. But not before he and his fellow-agent had done a great deal of damage, and supplied much information for use in the Franco–Spanish invasion which threatened England in 1779.

# II. DUKE'S AGENT

## Chapter Eight

# IN SEARCH OF TWO FOUNDLINGS

### 1

A SCHEME FOR invading England was being discussed almost as soon as the treaties of commerce and friendship with the United States were signed at Versailles. Based on others which had been under consideration in the Ministries of Marine and War for many years, the final plan envisaged the defeat of the British Channel fleet by the combined fleets of France and Spain, the capture of the Isle of Wight, and the landing of a powerful expeditionary force at Portsmouth. With the British Navy dispersed, and many seasoned troops in America, there was a very good chance of success. England stood in greater danger than at any time since the Spanish Armada. Nevertheless much more by luck than skill the invasion fleets were scattered and the troops, badly suffering from cholera, never embarked. By the end of September 1779 it was plain that there would be no invasion that year.

While hostile fleets divided England from the Continent, the Duke de Chartres was unable to continue his correspondence with Forth. But when action once more shifted from Europe to North America he approached his English acquaintance once again. By that time the situation of both men had changed.

Chartres had not distinguished himself in the war. Determined to serve in the Navy, the first French Prince of the Blood to do so, he was given command of one of the Brest squadrons, and saw action at the battle of Ushant in July 1779. It was an indecisive battle; the English and French fleets both claimed a victory, but both set up inquiries to determine why they had not done better. On the French side Chartres was blamed for misunderstanding a vital signal; it was also said that his cowardice had kept his ship from closing with the enemy. The fault lay much less with Chartres's conduct than with a system that gave responsible command to a prince who had next to no training as a naval officer, but no such allowance was made; it was more convenient to make Chartres a scapegoat. The idea that he was a coward persisted until the end of his life.

Ushant was a turning point for Chartres. From that time public opinion was against him, led by the King and Queen. As a young married woman Marie Antoinette had taken pleasure in Chartres's company, and shared many of the same amusements, dancing, gambling, horse racing. Now, at last both wife and mother, her preoccupations were different; she began to share the suspicion with which Louis XVI had always regarded the younger branch of the Bourbons and their dynastic interests. Her friendship for Chartres turned to dislike; she did not hide her feelings, and her circle followed her lead. Pamphleteers made the most of the situation; needless to say one of the most spiteful was Morande. In public or private Chartres could do no right. He found the change hard to understand or forgive. Cynicism, which may at first have been protective, became habitual. He withdrew into his own circle, which inevitably became a focus of opposition to the King and Queen, and pursued his own interests and amusements. Many of these lay in England where Forth could help him.

It so happened that at this time Forth also was dissatisfied with his situation. The government still made use of his intelligence network but withheld employment. Lord North did what he could. When government loans were being raised Forth was one of the brokers that he employed. He was also granted a quarterly pension amounting to £600 a year from the King's Secret Service funds. He could count on receiving payment regularly but because it was a royal favour and not a right he must write to ask for each instalment. Forth was delighted that the King had recognized his services to his country, and he welcomed the addition to his income (£600 compared very well with other allowances made from the Secret Service fund). Nevertheless he regarded this as monetary compensation for the loss of his post as Special Envoy; he always referred to it as his 'compensation', not as his pension. Such payments to out-going officials were customary in France where office holders bought their positions, but in England the situation was different. In obtaining a pension for Forth, Lord North was making it plain that although he recognized services in the past he would not be prepared to consider any claim in the future.[1]

Forth continued to hope. In October 1779 when Lord Suffolk died, and Lord Stormont took over as Secretary of State for the Northern Department, Forth wrote in terms which Stormont thought very unsuitable, to ask for an Under Secretaryship: 'I did not think I had a wish to gratify, I find I have. It is a wish dictated by my zeal to serve my country, and the ambition of serving it under your Lordship's orders. I will avoid entering into the manner in which I am capable of making your Abilities and Integrity confirm my being an usefull and faithfull servant to you. My attention and punctuality to my duty, my Attachment to your Interests, will justify your Lordship's choice if you will be so good as to make me Under Secretary of State. I earnestly request it, and conjure you not to refuse me, as it will give me many opportunities of convincing your Lordship of the inalienable affection and gratitude of your servant.'[2]

It was certainly not the kind of letter to convince Stormont that Forth would make a suitable civil servant. In Paris Stormont had found Forth extremely useful. But the qualities that made him a good intelligence agent and Special Envoy were not necessarily those that he would require as Stormont's second-in-command in a government office. There was in any case a most suitable candidate already working in the Department. Forth was therefore told that the post had been filled.

Although he acquiesced, according to Stormont, 'with great seeming good humour, and pretended that from that moment he gave up all thoughts of it', the refusal was a disappointment. When therefore Chartres reopened correspondence he found Forth in a receptive mood. When peace was finally restored between England and France a connexion with a French Prince of the Blood might help to achieve much in a country where Forth believed that he had a future.

In their different spheres Chartres and Forth each sought compensation in another country for disappointments in his own.

2

Chartres's first request was a strange one. 'I suppose, Monsieur', he wrote on Sunday 3 October 1779, 'that when one wishes to withdraw a child from the institution which we call the Foundlings, provided one fulfils certain formalities, one can obtain possession of the child. If this is so, you would greatly oblige me by choosing from among those nourished at the King of England's expense a pretty little girl with dark hair, not more than six years old; she absolutely must not have a long nose, and she must not know one word of French. I should like you so to arrange matters that no one will ever be allowed to reclaim her. My plan is that she should be brought up with my three-year-old daughters, who will learn English by playing with the child. I apologize for putting you to this trouble, but my dealings with you are so pleasant that I cannot help myself. If it is not practicable to obtain a little girl by the means I have suggested, I should be grateful if you would proceed in any way that suggests itself to you. I should like the child to arrive this winter'. A later letter made another stipulation: the child must have a good English pronunciation, and if that meant choosing a slightly older child it would not matter.[3]

The plan which Chartres put forward so lightheartedly was not his own. It derived from his mistress, Etiennette Félicité, Countess de Genlis, who exercised a strong influence on Chartres, and intended to keep it by any means in her power. The education of his children offered remarkable opportunities so that it was with much satisfaction that in September 1779 she obtained the appointments of Gouvernante to his twin daughters. Her views on education, based to a large extent on Rousseau's novels *La nouvelle Héloise* and *Emile* were decided, and often sensible, especially on the subject of learning languages. Chartres's letter to Forth was one of the first signs that she was at work in her new capacity.

Forth did not find his search an easy one. He was helped by the parson Jeans who finally, through his family connexions in Hampshire, found a child who seemed to fulfil all Chartres's requirements. Little Anne or Nancy Syms, aged six, dark eyed, dark haired, lively and pretty, was the illegitimate daughter of Mary Syms, whose father was a merchant in the salt and cod trade operating between Lisbon and Newfoundland where, on the island of Fogo, Nancy had been born. When Jeans heard of Nancy she was living at Christchurch in Hampshire. Mary Syms, now married to a ship's captain, William Brixey, had other children, a situation which probably reconciled her to parting with Nancy in return for a sum of money, unspecified, but probably quite substantial.[4]

There were still no regular communications between France and England, but even in wartime Chartres could obtain permission for a packet to cross the Channel with carpets or horses which he had ordered from England. By 12 February 1780 arrangements had reached a stage where Chartres could write that Saint-Denis, his horse-dealer, would be in London at Easter, and could bring Nancy back with him to Paris. Chartres had his reservations about Forth's choice: 'I cannot conceal some misgivings about the birth of the little girl that you are kindly sending me. I fear that when she has been carefully brought up her relations will want her back, or that I shall have to do something for her family which appears to be a large one. I should have preferred a child who was completely alone in the world.'

Nancy was sent off to France with Saint-Denis in April. 'I am sending you', Forth wrote, 'the finest mare and the prettiest little girl in England'. From her first appearance in a little red cloak and hood, no doubt chosen by Betsy, she charmed everyone. Many years later she described how the Duke de Chartres took her from Saint-Denis, carried her through many long corridors to a room where Madame de Genlis was sitting, and introduced her with the words, 'Here is our little treasure'.

'I don't know whether you are a god or a devil, but one or the other you assuredly must be, to have found the little angel that you have sent us', Chartres wrote to Forth on 17 April: 'I feel that I can never show you sufficient gratitude; you must have put yourself to untold trouble to discover such a delightful creature, so closely fulfilling all my requirements. I hope very much that you may wish for something from this country; I assure you that nothing could give me greater pleasure than the chance to prove to you the extent of my obligation.'

Madame de Genlis was just as appreciative. She took a great fancy to the child, who was adaptable and anxious to please. When she showed a talent for acting Madame de Genlis taught her poses somewhat resembling Lady Hamilton's famous attitudes. Soon Madame de Genlis wanted a closer relationship than that of instructress: she wished to be made the child's godmother, and on the grounds that Christchurch was full of anabaptists, she persuaded a somewhat unwilling Archbishop of Paris to allow the little girl to be rechristened. Nancy Syms now became Anne Caroline Stephanie, but everyone called her Pamela after the heroine of Richardson's novel which Madame de Genlis very much admired.

As time went on Madame de Genlis's affection for Pamela increased. When Chartres asked the painter Myris to make a drawing of his daughters with Madame de Genlis and hers, Pamela was included in the picture. Forth was asked to have the drawing engraved in London: 'in [it] you will also see the portrait of the little girl you sent me: Madame de Genlis loves her as though she were one of her own, and I cannot thank you enough; she really is delightful . . . '.5

Now Madame de Genlis began to worry about the possibility that Pamela's relations might try to reclaim her. She wanted Forth to tell Pamela's mother that her daughter was in Poland or Spain: 'I go in mortal fear that one fine morning this woman will appear and make me a scene that would make my blood run cold'. To prevent such a disaster Madame de Genlis wanted a form of agreement that would bind Pamela's mother. Forth thought the best plan would be to take out Indentures of Apprenticeship: Pamela was indentured to him, and he undertook to maintain, clothe, educate and furnish her with all necessaries at his expense. Then on the grounds that he could not do any of these things as he would like, he transferred Pamela to Madame de Genlis: 'I think myself in duty bound to transfer the care, protection and authority which the contract empowers me with to the Countess de Genlis . . . '.6

Still Madame de Genlis was not satisfied. She wanted to have Pamela naturalized, and she asked Forth for a certificate to prove that Pamela was English by birth. If Lord Mansfield would sign the certificate so much the better: 'all that's needed is a certificate from Lord Mansfield . . . it can take whatever form [he] pleases, so long as it is signed by him . . . the testimony of a man so eminent is an authentic document in any part of the world'. But although Madame de Genlis was determined to have her certificate she was also parsimonious. She would pay the expenses of bringing Pamela's mother to London to swear an affidavit before Lord Mansfield, 'but I hope that they won't amount to much, and that you won't encourage the woman to travel in luxury'.[7]

By this time Forth must have been out of patience with the exigencies of Madame de Genlis. But her influence on Chartres was such that by obliging her he also obliged the Duke. He set to work with his usual energy until at last he was able to send Madame de Genlis her 'cher certificat'.

3

Pamela was such a success that two years after she arrived at the Pavillon de Bellechasse where Madame de Genlis was educating Chartres's children Forth was asked to find another little girl. This child could be either dark or fair, but not red haired, she should be aged between six and seven, and should know no French. She must also have been inoculated against smallpox. 'I do not flatter myself that she will be as charming as Pamela', Chartres wrote to Forth on 26 July 1782, 'but I know that I can rely on your choice. I should like her to be here next March'.[8]

Once again it was not Chartres but Madame de Genlis who had plans for the child. She was to be brought up by her daughter Pulchérie so that she too could have the pleasure of educating a child who would owe everything to her.

By November Forth had found a suitable little girl, and on the 10th Madame de Genlis was making arrangements for her to travel to Paris with Mrs. Henry Swinburne's maid: 'my dear little Pamela is still an occasion for gratitude, and every day I realize more clearly how much I am beholden to you . . . Pamela asks me kindly to tell Mrs. Forth that she loves her with all her heart, and kisses her a thousand times . . .

But the little girl never went to Paris. Her inoculation took badly, and she lost the sight of one eye. Madame de Genlis wrote to say how concerned she was, but her letter shows no genuine awareness of the suffering which her caprice had caused. Pulchérie appears in a more sympathetic light: 'my younger daughter for whom the poor child was intended, is inconsolable over the accident. She considers herself the innocent cause, because if the child had not been coming to her she would not have been inoculated. My daughter's first thought therefore was to let the child come just the same so that she could as she said, look after her, and make her as happy as possible. This proof of humanity in a young girl of 15 naturally afforded me the greatest satisfaction. My daughter then begged me to let her pay a pension of 50 écus out of her pin money to the poor child, and this seemed entirely right. I have the honour, Monsieur, to forward the pension for the first year, and I beg you to pay it at once to the child's mother. May I also beg you to make certain that the child is taken to the best eye surgeon in London, and if it is possible for her sight to be preserved, and the remaining eye cured, I will gladly pay the surgeon's fee'. Madame de Genlis promised to augment the pension which Pulchérie had offered, and to send an additional sun in a few months' time. But she finished: 'I am infinitely touched, Monsieur, by your kindness in undertaking to find another child, but I do beg of you to make certain that she is healthy as well as pretty, so that we shan't have the same trouble next time'.

Hermione Compton, the child eventually chosen by Forth, was an orphan, her father had been an army officer and her mother the daughter of a clergyman. Betsy and Forth looked after her for some time before she was handed over to Madame de Genlis, and they became very fond of her. Fifteen years later Forth was still in touch with her, and always made a note of her birthday in his Diary, a sign of his continuing affection for 'la chère et charmante Hermine'.

In the spring of 1785 Forth and Betsy escorted Hermione, or Hermine, as she was now to be called, to Paris where Madame de Genlis and Pulchérie took charge of her. Her arrival at Bellechasse was the occasion for a great deal of speculation and gossip. Pamela's arrival five years earlier had gone unnoticed; at that time Madame de Genlis was then merely Gouvernante to Chartres's daughters. She was now Gouverneur to his sons. The appointment shocked public opinion, which considered it outrageous that Chartres should entrust a woman with the education of boys who might well one day succeed to the throne.

Everything that happened at Bellechasse was closely watched in the hope that further scandals would emerge. The arrival of Hermine promised well. At the same time people began to take notice of Pamela, and to ask who was the pretty child who appeared so often in the company of Chartres's children.

Most contemporaries believed that Pamela and Hermine were the daughters of Chartres and Madame de Genlis; they supposed that they had been brought up out of sight until an opportunity came to produce them. The school for princes at Bellechasse provided the opportunity. No one wanted to believe the denials of those most concerned, although Chartres told his son Louis Philippe that he had not children by Madame de Genlis, and she for her part swore as solemnly as she could, on one occasion after confession and communion, that Pamela was not her daughter. The story persisted; even one of Madame de Genlis's novels, *Les Mères rivales*, was brought forward to confirm it. In telling the story of a mother who adopts her own illegitimate daughter Madame de Genlis was thought to have been drawing from life, though this is surely to misunderstand the imaginative process by which a real situation is transmuted into a fictional one.

Later generations have for the most part believed the contemporary version of the story of Pamela and Hermine. In Forth's life such gossip matters only because he is involved. It has been supposed that he was Chartres's pimp; that because he was responsible for introducing the children into Chartres's household it was he who had looked after them and kept them out of sight. But the children were born in the early 1770's, some years before Forth was introduced to Chartres, and the entries in Forth's Diary which record the progress of his acquaintance with Chartres also make it clear that he did not take Pamela and Hermine to England with him when the British Embassy left France in 1779. The letters which have been quoted show what part Forth really played in this odd transaction.

The later lives of the two little girls so strangely introduced into a princely household developed quite differently. Pamela, always exceptionally pretty, married Lord Edward Fitzgerald, a younger son of the Duke of Leinster and one of the first of the United Irishmen. After some years of happy married life her husband became deeply involved in the Irish Rebellion of 1798 and was fatally wounded while resisting arrest. Pamela who greatly needed protection and stability was left to make her way in a post-revolutionary world for which Madame de Genlis's education had not prepared her. She remarried briefly and unsuccessfully, and after more than one adventure died under the protection of one of the Dukes de la Force.

Hermine's destiny was happier. She remained with Pulchérie de Genlis when she married, and looked after her children during the Revolution when Pulchérie and her husband were imprisoned. Later she herself married a country gentleman named Collard, who had business connexions with the House of Orleans and owned the château of Villers Hélon near the headquarters of the Orleans estates at Villers Cotterêts. Collard was a friend of General Dumas who, when he died, made Collard one of the guardians of his four-year-old son Alexandre, the future novelist. An illustrated bible belonging to Hermine, perhaps an inheritance from her grandfather the clergyman, was one of the books in which Alexandre learnt to read and to use his imagination. Of Hermine he said that it was impossible to picture anyone possessed of greater charm and distinction.[9]

In his search for foundlings Forth had chosen well.

*Chapter Nine*

## DUTIES OF AN AGENT

1

THE SUPPLY OF two foundlings was the oddest but by no means the only demand which Chartres made in the course of his correspondence with Forth. Sometimes it was information to enable him to settle a bet: precisely what was the armament of the *Rainbow*, a 50-gun naval vessel which had captured the French frigate *Hebe*; or what were the Newmarket rules for accepting a wager—supposing a man bets in front of several others that something is nor is not so, and another man replies Done, is the better committed? Hats, gloves, saddlery, needles were some of the items that Forth procured for Chartres. He also handled transactions with the engravers who reproduced some of Chartres's pictures in mezzotint, producing, as Chartres, a connoisseur, admitted, magnificent results.[1]

In June 1781 Chartres required passports for his head groom to return to France after buying horses in London: 'very foolishly, Monsieur, I forgot to write to ask you to obtain passports for Thomas and Singleton ... if you could at the same time obtain an order for three vessels capable of transporting 30 or 40 horses, I should be infinitely obliged'. In another letter Chartres told Forth that the famous (and conceited) dancer Vestris was coming to London and had asked for a letter of recommendation: 'I thought that I could not do better than recommend him to you, knowing your good taste and your willingness to oblige'.[2]

After almost five years Forth and Chartres again met in Paris. For a brief spell Forth was again acting as Special Envoy.

During the course of the war many peace feelers were put out and as often withdrawn. In July 1780 Forth received an

approach from the Count de Maurepas. Evidently he still
trusted Forth, and had forgiven him his rudeness the last time
that they met. Forth showed Maurepas's letter to Lord North
who referred it to the King with the guarded remark that he
supposed that Maurepas wanted to end the war at least while he
was writing the letter. The King was equally mistrustful; but
he thought it might be useful to send Forth to Paris to hear
what Maurepas had to say, and if he had some weighty reason
to wish for peace. It 'makes me a little more hopeful that Spain
is resolved to end the war . . . One circumstance at least is
agreeable, that America cannot make part of any proposition
Forth might be entrusted to communicate. On the whole I
desire Lord North will see Lord Stormont before any answer is
given to Mr. Forth (whom Lord North knows I always think
a very dubious negotiator) and if that able negotiator does
not see, from his perfect knowledge of Maurepas, that we can
be drawn into any difficulties by Forth's journey I shall not
object to it, but I certainly should to Forth's having any instructions but to hear what the Minister has to say'. Stormont
however thought an approach at that moment would be unwise,
and it was not until two years later that Forth was sent to
Paris. By that time Maurepas was dead, and Forth never had an
opportunity to make peace with his old friend.[3]

By 1782 all the European belligerents, who now included
the Dutch, were ready for peace. But the approaches were
complicated by the different treaties which governed the
relationship between the various allies. The Austrian Emperor
and the Empress of Russia had made a tentative offer of mediation, which at first the English were ready to accept, later they
changed their minds, hoping to separate the French from their
American allies and treat each nation separately. In March
1782 Forth was asked to go unofficially to Paris with
instructions to make it clear to the French foreign minister
Vergennes that England preferred direct negotiations to a
settlement through intermediaries. He was empowered to offer
certain concessions to the French in the hope that they could
be persuaded to negotiate without the Americans.

Forth was happy at the chance to return to the diplomatic
trade and the life that had pleased him so much. It would

probably have horrified, but not perhaps altogether surprised, the King and Lord North to know that although his mission was secret he had written to Chartres to ask if he would allow him to lodge in one of his houses in Paris. Chartres saw, as Forth did not, how unsuitable it would be for a French Prince of the Blood, who was already regarded as an Anglophile, to offer houseroom to an unofficial envoy from England. He replied on 12 February: 'I am extremely sorry that I have not an apartment that I can offer you in any of my houses. I hope that you will stay near the Palais Royal and that I shall see you frequently. You can depend on me not to speak of your arrival. Pray believe how delighted I shall be to see you and to be of use to you in this country . . . '.[4]

Forth arrived in Paris on 8 March and returned to the once familiar corridors of Versailles for an appointment with Vergennes. At their last encounter Forth had accused Vergennes of using his position to speculate in English funds, an accusation which both men must have remembered with embarrassment. Whatever his personal feelings Vergennes did not refuse to receive the English Envoy; he saw Forth on 14 March, and gave him an opportunity to explain the English position. Forth said plainly that his government did not want the services of a mediator, somewhat too plainly according to the Austrian Ambassador's report to his own government; he also offered the concessions that it had been hoped might induce the French to enter into separate peace negotiations. Vergennes refused to consider such a step; he was non-committal on the subject of mediation. But here, although he could not admit it to Forth, his views were similar to those of the English Ministers. It was awkward because one of the proposed mediators was the French Queen's brother.

This fact made Forth's mission of great interest to Marie Antoinette. When she knew that he had been with Vergennes she persuaded Louis XVI to give her a full account of the interview. However when she saw Vergennes she found that he, rightly fearing her Austrian bias, was unwilling to talk about it. As he was about to take leave of her without even mentioning Forth's visit she stopped him with the words, 'Why do you not refer to Forth?'[5]

Forth's reappearance as Special Envoy did not last long. On 20 March, a few days after he saw Vergennes for the second time, Lord North's Ministry fell, bringing down with it most of those on whom Forth relied for advancement.

2

Luckily he now had other prospects. His meetings with Vergennes might not have been very fruitful, but he had seen a good deal of Chartres, and found that he was still prepared to be friendly.

Forth had brought presents for Chartres; one of them, a special kind of warming pan from Betsy, was the admiration and astonishment of everyone who saw it. This was a good beginning but it was even better to know that Chartres was grateful for all that Forth had done for him in England, and proposed to find still more for him to do in future.

The prospect of working for Chartres was exactly what Forth liked; there was no doubt that it would give him considerable standing to act for a man in Chartres's position. Chartres would certainly expect a great deal of him, as the search for Pamela had shown, but Forth liked to be put on his mettle. He recognized this; more than once he compared himself to a flint that shines only when struck by someone else. Chartres on his side was pleased to find someone as active and competent as Forth to carry out his commissions.

Even though the relationship that evolved over the next few years served the interests of both men, it was never entirely a business one, nor was it merely the connexion between client and patron. However widely separated in rank Chartres and Forth might be in eighteenth-century eyes, the link between them came very close to friendship. It was for Chartres to set the tone of the relationship, and it was he who placed it on the remarkably informal footing which his letters, one of them dictated from his bath, gave proof. Forth's response, which he would probably have described as spirited and manly, also struck the right note, and his integrity won Chartres's respect. Some of Chartres's other agents were far less scrupulous.

It would have surprised those who thought of Chartres as insolent and overbearing to read some of his letters to Forth, and to find how much sympathy he showed, particularly when the point at issue was Forth's integrity and independence. Forth always refused to make money out of any of his business transactions for Chartres apart from the half commission to which he was legitimately entitled on any money which he invested for him. Once when Chartres suggested Forth might profit by some transaction, and Forth, as usual, refused, Chartres wrote: 'Before coming to business, Monsieur, I must make my statement of belief. You have given me a great deal of pleasure, you have always endeavoured to do what would please me; I always have been and I always shall be grateful. I have never seen any sign that you were looking after your own interests. Therefore I beg you to believe that I have never suspected you of dealing dishonestly with me, and for that reason I am distressed that you won't profit from one of my business undertakings. I should not regard it as dishonest in the least, and I should be delighted for you to derive some personal advantage in carrying out one of my requests.'[6]

In another very important respect Chartres showed consideration for Forth; this was in his treatment of Betsy. He and all his circle, including Madame de Genlis, always treated her as Forth's wife. Chartres knew the position, having been at Fontainebleau when Marie Antoinette took offence, but he accepted it. He began his renewed association with Forth by ordering Betsy a very handsome present to show his gratitude for all the charming things that she had sent him by Forth. 'As I think that what we make best here is porcelain, I hope that you will accept some pieces which I found attractive because they depict the birds from M. de Buffon's illustrations. The set is not yet complete, but I shall make sure that it is added to as the pieces are finished'. In fact it was some time before Betsy received her china, partly because Chartres suggested a slight improvement in the design which further delayed the already very busy factory at Sèvres. Chartres explained that there was only one workman who specialized in painting birds and he had to work full-time on a set which the Count d'Artois was taking with him as a present to the Spanish Royal family when he went to inspect the troops which were besieging Gibraltar. More than once Chartres

wrote to Forth or Betsy apologizing for the delay: 'I am
ashamed that [Mrs. Forth] still has not received the porcelain,
but workmen in this country are very dilatory'. But after a
year's wait Betsy received a dessert set consisting of 12 fruit
dishes, 2 butter dishes, 2 ice pails, and a punch bowl with
mortar, all decorated with paintings of Buffon's birds on a
speckled ground of *bleu du ciel*.[7]

### 3

While Forth was in Paris Chartres discussed with him one of his
most cherished plans. He wanted a house in London, a
pied-à-terre where he could arrive whenever he liked as easily
as if he were arriving at his house at Monceau. He would live
there as a private individual, the Count de Joinville, the name
which he used when he travelled incognito. He asked Forth to
look for such a house.

At first Forth misunderstood what Chartres wanted. 'I must
have explained myself badly, Monsieur', Chartres wrote on
26 July 1782, 'and led you to suppose that I want to live in a
style quite different from the one I envisage. Among other
things you suppose that I am going to London to live in state.
That is not at all my intention. The house that I wanted you
to look for . . . would rent furnished at 5 or 6,000 livres, and
sell at about 40,000 écus, which is what I should prefer . . .
Obviously I couldn't live on a princely scale in a house of that
size . . . but, to tell you just what I have in mind, once I had a
pied-à-terre, and had lived in it long enough to know the lie
of the land, I might from time to time rent a really large house
where I should live in the style you speak of, and receive his
Serene Highness the Duke de Chartres, and perhaps my
children. For the time being I just want somewhere to live,
but with stabling for 12 horses, and as I explained giving
directly on to a street. I don't mind in the least if it's in an
elegant part of the town . . . Please send me a plan of London.'[8]

By mid-August Forth had found a house of the kind Chartres
wanted at 35 Portland Place at a rent of 350 guineas. Chartres
was pleased and excited: 'here I am with a house in Portland
Place . . . all I need to know is how I am to pay the rent, what

is due in taxes, and to ask you to be so good as to engage a concierge until I have made my own arrangements'. He was a little disappointed that he might have to take over furniture with the house: 'I am strongly of the opinion that furniture, like women, should be chosen to suit one's fancy at the time'. The situation of the house however pleased him greatly: 'all the English here tell me that it is in an entirely new quarter'.[9]

The question of a concierge was settled when Forth suggested that he himself should live in Chartres's house, and run it for him. The arrangement might not have suited Chartres at all, and Forth took a chance in proposing it, but the idea appealed to Chartres so much that he refused to accept the third of the rent which Forth offered: 'apart from the satisfaction it will be to me to do you this small favour, I shall be completely certain that my house will be well kept and maintained. I shall be delighted to use whatever furniture you put in the house until I have bought some of my own choosing'. His gratitude to Forth was wholehearted: 'all my dealings with you increase my indebtedness . . . if in future you find me importunate you have only yourself to blame; why do you carry out my wishes so much to my satisfaction?'[10]

Forth moved into Chartres's house in October 1782 before Chartres had had a chance to see it. The move suited Forth's circumstances very well. He now had two children, Nat, and a girl named Eliza born in 1779. This second child was not strong, and Forth, hoping that she would benefit from country air, took a house outside London for Betsy and the children. There was less need for him to live so constantly in London at a time when the war was ending and his intelligence system was no longer so useful.

One of Forth's duties while living in Chartres's house was the entertainment of his guests. One of these was the Marquis Ducrest, Madame de Genlis's brother, a lively minded man to whom Chartres entrusted many of his financial undertakings. Ducrest knew Forth's competence in money matters, and was glad of the opportunity to consult him. Another guest was Madame de Genlis herself. When she visited England for the first time in 1785 Forth and Betsy looked after her and escorted her on all her visits.

Chartres's house was spacious but not as large as it looked.
there was no more than comfortable room for the owner, two
guests and their servants. This meant that the joint tenancy
sometimes ran into difficulties. Once when Forth asked if Betsy
might remain in the house while Chartres was in residence he
received a very firm refusal: 'I must tell you frankly, Monsieur,
that it would not suit me at all if Madame Forth remained in
the house. The situation is quite different if there is a woman
present, and I must consequently ask you to give me the free
occupation of my house ... I am truly sorry to disturb
[Madame Forth] but since you ask me, I state the position'.
On another occasion Forth moved out of Portland Place for-
getting that he had carried away the keys of the water closets
causing, as Chartres remarked quite good naturedly, considerable inconvenience. Apart from such difficulties the joint
tenancy worked well; in December 1784 Chartres was able to
tell Forth how glad he was to have entrusted him with the care
of his house, and congratulated himself every day for giving
him his confidence.[11]

4

It was close on a year before Chartres was able to see his house.
But in May 1783 when the preliminaries of peace had been
signed, but before a French ambassador had been appointed,
Chartres at last received consent to visit England and discover
whether it fulfilled his expectations. He had betted that he
would cover the distance between Paris and London in 30
hours, not counting stops on the road, so his journey was a
rapid one. He arrived in the evening of 4 May, and found time
to write a note to Forth to tell him how delighted he was with
his house. Soon he was to be seen everywhere. He attended a
debate in Parliament, and said that if he had been an Englishman he would have found great pleasure in attending the House
of Lords. He dined with the Royal Family, went racing, and was
made a members of Brooks's.

English first impressions of Chartres differed considerably.
The King and Queen were reserved; they knew that the French
King and Queen mistrusted him, and they feared his influence

on their volatile son George Prince of Wales, then approaching
his twenty-first birthday, and about to set up his own household at Carlton House. As it happened, the Prince of Wales
began by disliking Chartres; he told his brother Frederick that
Chartres was rather clever but a great beast: 'in short I cannot
bear him'. English society was also rather reserved. Lady
Bessborough was shocked by some very indecent buttons that
Chartres was wearing; members of Weltje's club in St. James's
Street were stiff and formal until one young man clapped him
on the back, saying, 'There's a fine Duke of Chartres'.[12]

Gradually, as he continued to visit London, society became
accustomed to Chartres. In 1784 he was at Epsom for the fifth
Derby in which his horse Cantator was running. His pink and
black colours also became familiar at Newmarket. Soon it
was being said that Chartres was as much at home at Brooks's
as Fitzpatrick or Charles James Fox.

The Prince of Wales revised his impressions of Chartres, and
was often in his company. Chartres, fifteen years older than the
Prince, adopted the role of elder brother, ready to give sympathy and advice when the younger man found himself in a
scrape. When the Prince of Wales secretly married Mrs. Fitzherbert, Chartres offered them hospitality in Paris. But the
great bond between them was a similarity of situation. Both
were at odds with the reigning monarch; each tended to become
a focus of opposition. The Prince of Wales was the luckier: in
England there was a· distinction between the King and his
government so that it was constitutionally possible for the
Prince to oppose his father's Ministers without attacking the
King himself: Chartres could not criticize either without
suspicion.

When the friendship between the Prince and Chartres reached
a point where they agreed to exchange portraits, it was Forth
who made the arrangements with Sir Joshua Reynolds. The
splendidly romanticized full length of Chartres in the uniform
of a Colonel General of Hussars cost 250 guineas; this, Forth
told Chartres, was considered rather high by amateurs of
paintings. Chartres agreed, but he told his bankers to settle
the account. It was also Forth who arranged for the portrait
to be engraved by John Raphael Smith, and took the

finished portrait to Carlton House to present it to the Prince of Wales.[13]

Chartres's preoccupations during his visits to England were not entirely social. He was busy with an ambitious property development for which he needed to raise capital, and he relied on Forth's knowledge of the money market to help him.

Ever since the beginning of 1781 when his father the Duke of Orleans gave him possession of the Palais Royal Chartres was bent on exploiting so promising an asset. In spite of strong opposition he cleared the gardens behind the palace, cut down the famous central avenue of chestnuts under which so many Parisians had strolled and gossiped, and enclosed the site on three sides with houses and shops. The scheme required far more capital than Chartres, deep in debt, could supply. He planned, with Ducrest's assistance, to raise money by setting up a life insurance company, for which he hoped Forth would be able to find him support in England. He also planned to raise a loan in Holland; here again he counted on Forth's help.[14]

Forth soon came to play as important a part in Chartres's business as in his private affairs. Eventually Chartres gave him a power of attorney to act for him in London, and allowed Forth to describe himself as his London agent. Even when Chartres's financial position improved he continued to make investments in London, and to watch the movements of stock on the London Market.

Business and finance had become subjects of real interest to Chartres, and continued to hold his hitherto wandering mind. Forth was able to meet him on this new ground; an acquaintance which began on the race course endured because he shared Chartres's new found enthusiasm.

5

In the autumn of the year in which Chartres paid his first visit to England Forth decided to try his luck in France. Perhaps the death of his little daughter on Good Friday 1783 influenced his decision. He certainly thought that Nat, at the age of eight, was old enough to profit by an education in France. Chartres, repaying Forth's efforts in kind, promised to find the Forths a house.

Betsy and Forth arrived in Paris on Friday 26 September 1783. On Monday, from the Hotel de la Paix in the Rue de Richelieu, Forth, remembering that he no longer enjoyed diplomatic protection, and that Vergennes had once threatened him with prison, wrote a very characteristic letter: 'I feel that it is my duty to inform Your Excellency that I have been in this country since Friday last. The marks of kindness and protection with which you have so signally honoured me allow me to hope that you will continue them so long as I do not abuse your kindness, and provided that you judge me worthy of so great an honour. I have arrived with my wife, some servants, ten horses and three carriages. I plan to stay for some time and perhaps to settle here for some years in order to educate my son, at present my only child. As I am sufficiently wealthy and I only have this one child, I shall spare nothing that might contribute to his happiness. For this project I seek not only Your Excellency's approval but your advice and protection, and before I proceed further or take a house, I beg you to spare me a quarter of an hour so that I can explain my plan and receive your orders as to my conduct . . . No one in this country knows about my plan but in England all my friends and patrons, including the King, are aware of it . . . '[15]

Vergennes's reply is not among Forth's papers; it was probably diplomatically non-committal. Although he was not one of Forth's admirers he could not reasonably object to his residence in Paris, particularly when he enjoyed the protection of so powerful a prince as the Duke de Chartres. Forth certainly continued to live in Paris and even sometimes appeared at Court.

For the next six years Forth and Betsy spent much of their time in a house which Forth had taken in the Rue Neuve des Mathurins near the boulevards and the Chausée d'Antin. It was not altogether a happy time for Betsy. When Forth was Special Envoy her position had been ambiguous and she had lacked company. This was no longer the case. Madame de Genlis and her circle received her, and she could if she wished appear anywhere except in official circles or at Court. Madame de Genlis was kind and even affectionate, at least on paper: she lent Betsy her box at the Theâtre Français, and praised 'le charmant petit Natty'; Pamela gave Nat an elaborate comfit

box. But Betsy was in poor health, and did not go out much.
It is possible that she found Madame de Genlis a little over-
whelming; nor can Betsy have failed to notice that however
amiable her letters they were also ever so slightly patronizing.
Whatever the reasons—a certain Countess de Genetines may
have been partly accountable—it seems that Betsy was happier
in England, perhaps in the house which Forth had taken at
Egham.[16]

Forth on the other hand with his three carriages and ten
horses was in his element, leading an active life in Paris, or
attending the wine harvest at Sillery with Chartres and Madame
de Genlis's husband, the owner of the vineyard. He had timed
his arrival in Paris very well. In November 1785 when Chartres
succeeded his father as Duke of Orleans, Forth found himself
working for one of the most potentially powerful men in
France, the possessor of lands covering perhaps a twentieth
part of French territory, and revenues running into several
million livres.

Orleans, to use his new title, was determined to run his
estates efficiently and profitably. He formed a company to
administer them and presided very regularly over its meetings.
His successful exploitation of the gardens of the Palais Royal
encouraged him. Building on the site was now almost complete;
the gardens newly laid out, and lighted with lamps (which may
have been some which Forth bought for Orleans in England)
were planted with mature trees. Once again they were a
favourite haunt of Parisians. They were even beginning to prove
profitable to Orleans himself. He rightly had little doubt that
he could be equally successful in the development of his estates.
He planned to build canals, and to introduce industries, a
factory for cotton thread spinning, and a plant for the manu-
facture of alkali bleach. Where these plans required capital it
was Forth's task to help raise it.[17]

Forth had little to do with the political side of Orleans's life,
and the activities which placed him among the opponents of
the King and his government. Nevertheless as the time
approached for the Assembly of Notables, and later the meeting
of the States General, he sometimes met at the Palais Royal a
clever ex-artillery officer who was Secretary of Orleans's

Council; this was Choderlos de Laclos, author of *Les Liaisons dangereuses*. It was Laclos's responsibility to co-ordinate the preparation of Petitions of Grievances from the various parts of the Orleans estates for submission to the States General. These *Cahiers* were being drawn up all over France but those from the Orleans estates were very carefully prepared in answer to a standardised form of inquiry sent out by Orleans's Council.

But it was with the men who handled Orleans's business and financial enterprises that Forth had most to do. He came to know some of them very well, in particular Maître Denis André Rouen, one of the notaries in charge of Orleans's legal affairs. A wealthy man himself, Rouen was the head of a prosperous notarial practice in the Rue Neuve des Petits Champs. His predecessors in the practice had a long experience of high finance, one of them having acted as notary to John Law.

Forth also had many dealings with Rouen's relation Claude Odile Baroud, with whose very pretty sister, Madame de Genetines, Forth also became acquainted. Baroud was deep in the multifarious schemes and speculations so characteristic of the last years of the *ancien régime*. He was a native of Lyons where he practised as a notary until, needing a wider field of operations, he came to Paris and settled in the house next door to Rouen. His main concern was speculation in shares, those of the revived East India Company and the Discount Bank among them. He was also involved in marine assurance and the foundation of a company to supply Paris with water, but above all he specialised in the many forms of investment in life annuities which were then the rage.[18]

This was the period when the Thirty Young Ladies of Geneva flourished. They were not the heroines of a limerick, but thirty young girls carefully chosen by Genevan doctors from families known to be healthy and long-lived. Investors bought a group of annuities, not for the duration of their own lives, but for the duration of the lives of the thirty young ladies of Geneva. Every year the girls were medically examined, and certificates were issued to confirm that they were alive and well so that the annuitants could continue to receive their yearly payments. There was more than one group of young ladies of Geneva, but the original band lived to justify the actuarial calculations of its

inventors, most of the thirty surviving to a very ripe old age.
Although these annuities had been intended for private individuals, it was not long before banks began to deal in them as if
they were another form of investment. Many fantastic and
highly speculative variations were devised to enable investors
to postpone making a down payment as long as possible and
benefit as soon as practicable. Baroud was an adept at doing
this; some of his schemes, however, were so complicated that
the permutations were almost impossible to follow, and were
still being unravelled many years later.[19]

Forth did not invest in annuities on the lives of the thirty
young ladies of Geneva. When he bought annuities they were
for the lives of Betsy and himself. But the speculative climate
was favourable for men who like Rouen and Forth derived their
incomes from commissions on the preparations of documents
or the sale of stocks or shares. A good income could be made
from such transactions, especially if a man was in the know.
Forth was very well placed in this respect because many of the
commercial developments in France not only derived from
schemes canvassed before the war, but echoed similar ones on
the other side of the Channel.

One such was the struggle for control of the East Indian
trade. In England Forth's close friend David Scott was at the
head of a group working to end the English Company's shipping
monopoly. In France another group of financiers and shipowners, with some of whom Forth was also closely connected,
were working on broadly similar lines. In 1786 they made a
successful bid for control of the newly revived French East
India Company.

It was by no means their first attempt. Ever since the British
gains in India in the middle of the century the French Company
had been in difficulties. But if its trading position was weak
the Company was nevertheless a financial prize, with its share
capital secured on the tobacco farm, and several profitable subsidiary operations such as the trade in piastres from Spain.
Before the War of American Independence a group with
Necker at its head, and his bank behind it, successfully fought
off two take-overs from the group with which Forth had links.
The leader of this group was Isaac Panchaud, an ingenious

but unlucky financier of Anglo–Swiss origins. He was backed by
Sir Robert Herries and the various Herries banks in Spain and
the Netherlands, together with certain other Low Country
banking houses. Necker's group represented finance and banking and the maintenance of the Company's monopoly; while
Panchaud's supporters represented trade and shipping interests
and the extension of trading privileges to the so-called inter-
lopers. Forth's main connexion with this group was through Sir
Robert Herries and the Foleys whose bank was also involved.
But Panchaud and his associate, Thomas Sutton, Count Clonard,
were business acquaintances of long standing. Walter Boyd
and John Kerr, junior partners in the Herries Antwerp bank,
concerned in the final successful take-over, were also known to
Forth. With his friends now established in influential situations
Forth was in an excellent position to take advantage of the
traffic in shares that followed.[20]

Annuities and commercial undertakings were only some
of the schemes that attracted speculators in these pre-
revolutionary years. Urban property development also offered
opportunities which Orleans was by no means the only land-
owner to exploit it. The King's brothers, the Counts of Provence
and Artois, planned to develop respectively the gardens
surrounding the Luxembourg Palace and the nursery gardens
in the Roule area of the Faubourg St. Honoré. The Duke de
Choiseul had already begun to build on his wife's property
near the Rue de Richelieu, while Hosten, known as 'the
American', but in fact a Bordeaux merchant with trading
interests in Martinique, had plans to build on ground in the
St. Lazare quarter. Some of the plans for these developments
reflected others to be found on the English side of the Channel.

It is perhaps unlikely that Forth had anything to do with
the fact that the architect Ledoux's plans for Hosten's site very
much resembled Henry Holland's plans for the Hans Town
development of the Sloane estate in Chelsea. It is just possible
that because Forth recommended the Adam brothers to the
Count d'Artois one of the first plans for the Faubourg St.
Honoré development was named *lès Adelphes* in close parallel
to the Adelphi Development in London. It is far more likely
that Artois's architect Bélanger borrowed directly from the

Adams. Nevertheless such resemblances illustrate the cross-
fertilization between France and England in the 1780's, in
which Forth was unquestionably one of the carriers.[21]

For five or six years Forth disappeared into this jungle of
schemers and speculators; no diary and almost no correspondence survive to chart his path. It is certain that he prospered on
both sides of the Channel. By May 1789 when the States General
met, and the familiar France of the *ancien régime* was about to
disappear for good, he possessed a richly furnished apartment in
Paris, 332 Rue St. Honoré, on the corner of the Place Vendôme.
In London he was a Justice of the Peace for the County of
Middlesex; he had a house at Egham and another at 8 Manchester Square. He had many influential friends, and was
firmly and pleasantly established in the world; he had lived, to
quote his own words, in the strictest familiarity with the first
men of his age and acquired a steady settled opulence.

# III. PRINCE'S CREDITOR

## Chapter Ten

## RAISING THE WIND

### 1

EACH STAGE IN Forth's life developed logically from the preceding one: his failure to secure a permanent government post caused him to concentrate on his City interests: these in turn led to his employment as the Duke of Orleans's agent; this position, and his own increasing wealth, now brought him to the notice of the Prince of Wales.

George, Prince of Wales, who was not yet the Prince Regent, was a young man of great charm and little sense. Handsome and active, he found the Court of his father, George III, lacking in entertainment; the round of conscientious work and mild amusements in the company of a small circle of trusted members of the Household had little to offer a lively young man. He made it plain that when he succeeded to the throne there would be great changes. In politics he favoured the Opposition, whose leader, Charles James Fox, was his friend. He enjoyed pretty women, horses and cards, his taste in pictures was discerning, and he liked ostentation and display. He was determined to transform his comparatively modest residence, Carlton House, into something more nearly resembling the palace of a royal prince in other European capitals. This, and indeed all his amusements, cost an enormous sum of money. Before the Prince was 21, he was deep in debt. At his coming of age George III allowed him £50,000 from his own Civil List; together with £12,000 from the Duchy of Cornwall, which with its revenues traditionally belonged to the Prince of Wales, gave the Prince an income of £62,000; Parliament agreed to settle his debts. The King was prepared to double his son's allowance when he married, but the Prince was secretly married to Mrs.

Fitzherbert, and though the marriage was strictly illegal, the Prince regarded himself bound by it (for the time being) and could not take this way out of his difficulties.

The King considered that he was treating his son generously. He himself as Prince of Wales had managed on much less. He did not take into account the difference between his son's temperament and his own, or allow for the fact that while he did not become Prince of Wales until his father's death, the Prince was born in the purple; he had never known a time when he was not the heir to the throne, or lived among people who did not, when in his presence, put on smooth and smiling faces. Nor did the King provide enough serious alternatives to the Prince's expensive amusements to occupy him during the years which must pass before he succeeded to the throne; George III was only 24 years older than his son, and this period might well be a long one. But in 1788 the King fell ill. If he lived it seemed likely that he would no longer be fit to rule, thereby completely changing the Prince's position.

Financially this was as desperate as ever: the previous year Parliament had once again provided a large sum to pay off his declared debts, it could not prevent him from incurring others. If he were made Regent, however limited his powers, he could have faced his creditors, and his difficulties would have been at an end. It happened otherwise; in February 1789 George III recovered, and the Prince was driven back to the old expedients of raising money how and where he could.

His needs brought him into a strange company of lenders and go-betweens. One of the oddest was his Comptroller and Clerk of the Kitchen, Louis Weltje, 'a German of no ordinary bodily dimensions ... [who], though he had resided some years in England ... spoke no language except a barbarous Anglo-Westphalian jargon ... '.[1] It may not be true that he had once kept a ginger-bread stall in Leicester Fields, but it is certain that he had made a large fortune while in the Prince's service; he not only lent the Prince money, he also acted in cases in which his master was unwilling to appear as principal. In August 1789 Weltje suggested that the Prince should ask the Duke of Orleans for a loan of £200,000; Thomas Hammersley, banker both to the Prince and to

Orleans, would suggest the best intermediary. Hammersley suggested Forth.

On 18 August, according to an account of the transactions written by Forth some years later, Hammersley came to see Forth in Manchester Square. Forth told him that Orleans himself could not lend so large a sum, but his 'consequence and great property', would make it easy to raise an even larger loan. On 5 September Forth was at his house in Egham when he received an express summoning him to Carlton House. There the Prince explained the embarrassed state of his affairs, and told him that those of his brother, the Duke of York, were almost as bad; he would like Forth to persuade Orleans to lend the two princes £250,000 on the security of the Duchy of Cornwall. Hammersley, who was also present, said he did not think the Prince could find anyone with more inclination or better abilities to serve him than Forth. 'I know Mr. Forth very well', said the Prince, 'I know him to be a very worthy honest man in whom I have the greatest confidence. I have a very long correspondence with [the King] in my possession, which he little imagines how it came into my possession. All his letters are carefully tied up in a parcel by themselves, just as they were given to me during [the King's] late unfortunate malady'.

No doubt it was highly flattering to Forth not only to be consulted by the heir to the throne, but also to hear that the Prince knew so much about his work as Special Envoy; the letters tied up in a parcel by themselves were the reports which he had sent to North from Paris twelve years ago. He might have been shocked to know that the Prince ought never to have seen them. During George III's illness his Ministers did not give the Prince possession of his keys, nor did they allow him access to his father's papers. His remark to Forth shows that he managed to circumvent their arrangements.

At the Egham Ball on 8 September the Prince drew Forth into a private room, and told him that his brother, the Duke of Clarence, also wanted to borrow money, he would like to share in the loan, the total of which should now be raised to £300,000; Hammersley was unable to suggest precisely what form the loan should take. 'Forth', said the Prince, 'you can make out a plan better than anyone. Prepare one with your usual clearness and method, and come to me next Sunday morning to Carlton House with Hammersley'.

Forth explained his plan to the Prince and Hammersley on 13 September. He proposed that the Prince and his two brothers should give their joint bonds to the Duke of Orleans for £300,000, paying 5 per cent half-yearly from the revenues of the Duchy of Cornwall. This interest would not be payable until after the death of George III; therefore to cover the risk that the King might oulive his sons, Forth proposed that the Princes should execute further bonds for £36,000 (12 per cent on £300,000). Hammersley was to be appointed Receiver General of the Duchy, and receive a profit of 5 per cent on the receipts. Forth did not include a reward for himself in his proposal; his recompense was to be left entirely to the generosity of the Princes.

The Prince was delighted with Forth's plan, and encouraged him to leave for Paris as soon as he could. He and his brothers were concerned with their financial necessity, they did not take into account the situation in France. A Revolution was taking place there, and it was thoughtless, to say the least, to send an emissary to Paris with bonds signed by English princes at a time when it was generally believed that 'les guinés de Pitt' were being used to raise mobs and undermine the government. To an Englishman there was a clear distinction between the revenue of the Monarch and of the State; there was no such distinction in France; it could not be supposed that in a time of crisis any Frenchman would distinguish between the practices of the two countries. The Princes placed their country, and indeed their emissary, in an embarrassing position by their single-minded pursuit of their own ends.

If these considerations occurred to Forth, they did not deter him. As he journeyed through France he had plenty of opportunity to observe the effects of the Revolution. Its effect on property was what immediately concerned him, and here it was plain that anyone with valuables of any kind was anxious to move them out of the country as soon as possible. In one convent near Lille, on the border between France and the Austrian Netherlands, Forth saw more than £350,000 in sterling and gold packed into casks ready to be moved at once.

Forth left London on 26 September, arrived in Paris on 30 September, and on 1 October went to the Palais Royal. He arrived there just as the Duke of Orleans's affairs were moving to a climax. Ever since the Estates General met in May the Palais Royal had been a centre of revolutionary activity. Mirabeau, Talleyrand, Sieyès, Barère, Lauzun, were all intimates of the Duke; Choderlos de Laclos was in command of a permanent headquarters of pamphleteers and journalists, producing a stream of manifestoes and reports; every evening popular orators harangued crowds in the Palais Royal gardens. In all probability the leaders of the crowds received funds as well as instructions on when and where to stir up public feeling. The object of these activities was the establishment of a constitutional monarchy, but not under Louis XVI, who would be set aside, perhaps deposed. It is not clear what was supposed to happen next: there were probably as many plans as plotters. Orleans certainly had a place in the scheme, as Regent, as Lieutenant General, or possibly as king. Whether he was prepared to go all lengths to achieve any of these objects; whether so essentially frivolous a man could ever have carried out the duties of a constitutional monarch; whether indeed his supporters intended that he should, are unresolved questions. For the time being, Orleans was the Constitutionalists' candidate. But their first step was to bring Louis XVI from Versailles to Paris.

An opportunity occurred in October at the very time Forth arrived in Paris. Bread was scarce and dear, the Parisians, especially the women, were in ferment, ready for action. On 5 October, a wet, misty day, a violent crowd, which included many viragos from Les Halles, marched on Versailles. In the evening they attacked the Palace, murdered two of the Gardes du Corps, and reached the Queen's Apartments, from which Marie Antoinette barely escaped in time. The arrival of Lafayette with the National Guard prevented worse disorder, but the crowd insisted on the return of the Royal Family to Paris the following day.

Public opinion blamed the Duke of Orleans for everything. Witnesses testified to seeing him marching with the crowd

on 5 October; some said he was disguised as a woman, others
that he was inside the Palace, pointing out the way to the
Queen's Apartment. The Court was convinced of his guilt.
It is likely that his money helped to rent this particular
revolutionary crowd, and it is true that on the morning of
6 October he drove out to Versailles, where he was acclaimed
in the Place d'Armes just when Louis XVI appeared on the
balcony above the Cour de Marbre to announce that he and his
family were willing to remove to Paris. But he himself told
the Enquiry which investigated these events that on 5 October
he was in Paris all day; in the morning he was with his men of
business, he dined at Monceau, and slept at the Palais Royal.[2]
Forth was one of these men of business, and the matter which
they were discussing was the Princes' loan. Forth also says,
'the ever to be lamented night of the 5 and 6 October with all
its horrors, the use which the Duke of Orleans attempted to
make of the Princes' bonds, the bold manner in which Mr.
Forth defeated his atrocious purposes, shall here be passed over
. . . the transactions of the 2, 4, 5 and 6 shall never again be
mentioned by him . . . '. This tantalizing statement seems to
suggest that if Forth had not prevented him, Orleans would
have used the Princes' bonds to show that the English Royal
Family were stirring up rebellion by sending money into
France. But it would be unwise to rely too much on an
innuendo made a decade later, when Forth's feelings towards
Orleans had changed. The business talks are facts. The rest
is conjecture.

As a result of his discussions with Forth Orleans agreed to
guarantee the Princes' loan. Forth next consulted Orleans's
notary Brichard, and his uncle Rouen on the best ways of
raising the sum required. The two men assured him that con-
sternation in Paris was so general that he might raise a million
in sterling, gold, diamonds or pictures, provided the borrower
took the valuables out of France. They also suggested some
alteration in the form of the bonds; Forth would return to
England to adjust this, but would be back in Paris before the
end of October.

While Forth was sounding the money market, Orleans was
being made to feel the effect of the march on Versailles. One

result was an almost complete break with the Royal Family; there was also a change in his relations with the Constitution-alists; his presence in France was now embarrassing to them, so Lafayette planned to have Orleans sent to London on a pseudo-diplomatic mission. Ostensibly he was to sound British opinion on events in France and the Low Countries and to dis-cover what part English gold had played in the happenings of 5 and 6 October. Discussions between Lafayette and Orleans about this mission were taking place at the same time as those between Orleans and Forth about the loan for the Princes. It is the measure of Orleans's serious interest in money that even when his future was at stake, he found time to consider such problems. It was his influence which enabled Forth to procure passports, and on 9 October he had the gates of Paris opened for him.

On 16 October Forth was in London reporting to the Prince of Wales and the Duke of York: 'nothing could exceed the joy of the two princes except their protestations of friendship to Mr. Forth, and their promises of what they would do for him and his family'.

## 2

Up to this time Forth could congratulate himself on his luck. He was using his energy and ability in the way he liked most on an undertaking which, if it succeeded, would gain him recognition at a very high level indeed. It was a great thing to be known as a confidant of the Prince of Wales, to hear himself described as his best friend, and to be summoned to urgent discussions at Carlton House. Forth's friends and acquaintances began to treat him as a man known to have influence in the right quarters, someone who might obtain favours from the Prince.[3] It would have been odd if Forth did not find this gratifying. It was too good to last; affairs took a different turn with the arrival of the Duke of Orleans on his mission to England.

The Prince was delighted when he heard Orleans was coming to London where he could put pressure on him. Just so did the young men at the Drones' behave when they heard that Oofy

Prosser was entering the Club. News that Orleans had been stopped at Boulogne caused the Prince to send Forth post haste to meet him there, and to deliver a letter which, though Forth does not say so, must have stressed the Prince's desperate need for cash; among other outgoings was a loan of £4,000 to Georgiana, Duchess of Devonshire, whose needs were perennial, and her means of raising money practically exhausted; he was also being hard pressed by Gray, one of his jewellers.

Forth, with his chaise and post horses, left early on the morning of 21 October, but he had not travelled two stages when he met Bengald, Orleans's courier, who rode ahead to make sure that all would be ready on his master's arrival. An hour later Forth met Orleans himself in his coach 'with a Monsieur Laclos'. Orleans transferred to Forth's faster moving vehicle, sending a courier ahead to ask the Prince of Wales to meet him at his house in Chapel Street. The two princes asked Forth to take part in their discussions, and later in the afternoon, when the Duke of Queensberry and Colonel St. Leger arrived to take Orleans to dinner at Queensberry House, the Prince insisted on having his 'best friend, Forth' with him.

It was now time for Forth to continue his negotiations in Paris. He left London on 23 October for the convent near Lille, where on his previous journey, he had seen casks full of gold and valuables. Brichard, Orleans's notary, met him there. The state of unrest and uncertainty was such that the convent authorities were very willing to agree to a loan of £50,000, provided the casks containing that amount were shipped to London immediately.

When he arrived in Paris on 28 October he entered a hornet's nest. A virulent pamphlet, No. 124 of *Les Actes des Apôtres*, had appeared while he was in England, alleging that he had been sent to France by Pitt and the Prince of Wales with 15 million livres to finance the events of 5 and 6 October. Brissot's paper, *l'Union*, had also published an article about Forth, calling him a thorough-going royalist, nursed in the lap of despotism, the most dangerous man to be found on the soil of France, and the first to be got rid of. These two articles roused feeling against Forth to such a pitch that there was a mob outside his lodgings, and his friends warned him that if he did not leave Paris at once

he would very likely be torn limb from limb. Forth ignored
their advice. He went to the Palais Royal gardens, and, using a
table for a rostrum, stood up and asked for attention. 'He then
told the people his name, and who he was. After some hisses
and applause he gained their silent attention. He then read part
of the pamphlet which related to him, and refuted the groundless charge . . . '. He next called on Brissot, whom he supposed
to be the author of the libel, and anyone else who was prepared to support the accusation. 'He then told the people that
he lived opposite to where he stood, pointing to his apartments
in the Palais Royal Hôtel, and that he should again present himself next day at 12 o'clock to answer any questions . . . [he
was] loudly applauded and walked home gently amidst the cries
of Vivent les Anglais'.

Next day at precisely 12 he returned to the gardens. Once
again he climbed on a table. He was surrounded by a crowd
'mostly of the respectable class; a great many of the National
Guards attended'. He asked twice 'in a loud tone of voice,
"Has any person pretence for saying that the calumny in the
pamphlet is in any shape founded?" No answer. Upon this,
an Aide-de-camp of General Lafayette, the Viscount de St.
Germains, came forward and asked . . . "Pray, Sir, where is
the Duke of Orleans?" . . . "Sir, I dined with him in London,
at the Duke of Queensberry's, in company with the Prince of
Wales, the Duke of York, and others, on Wednesday the 21st
. . . ". The Aide-de-camp then said, "Mr. Forth, the people and
National Guard are perfectly satisfied with your conduct, and
are convinced that the accusation is false and groundless". The
people dispersed, and Mr. Forth retired to his lodging where
certainly none of his friends expected to find him alive . . . '.

It was brave indeed to face such a crowd in Paris in those
times, Forth says that he did it because he felt it was a duty
which he owed the Prince of Wales and Mr. Pitt. But it is
questionable whether in the long run he achieved much. The
French continued to suspect that Forth was the bearer of
English funds, and they had grounds for their beliefs, even if
they misunderstood the object of the transaction.

After a fortnight of discussions with prospective lenders,
notaries and lawyers, Forth successfully completed this stage of

his mission. On 17 November he was back in London and in a position to tell Hammersley that he had brought £50,000 in cash and bills as a first instalment of the Princes' loan; when the bonds were signed he was sure he could raise a further £250,000.

During Forth's absence the Prince of Wales had continued to press the Duke of Orleans for a loan. He believed that Orleans had an investment in East India stock which could easily and profitably be sold to provide funds. Orleans indeed possessed £15,000 of stock, but it was invested to produce an annuity for Forth. He therefore most correctly refused to sell out unless Forth agreed. The Prince of Wales and the Duke of York now put pressure on Forth to give up his claim on the stock, and to take one of their bonds in exchange. It was not a good bargain, a highly marketable security in exchange for a promise by the Princes to pay the Duke of Orleans after the King's death. However, the Princes declared themselves 'bound by every tie of justice to secure Mr. Forth's annuity', and at length, against his friends' advice, Forth agreed to the sale, which produced £25,000. But when Forth asked Orleans for the bond in order to deposit it in his bank, the Duke said that he had forgotten to put it in his pocket. This was only the beginning of Forth's difficulties over the bond which he calls Bond A.

The next incident had some of the ingredients of comedy, but it was not comic for Forth. On 14 December the Prince of Wales sent for Forth to come immediately to Carlton House. He had been told by Lord Loughborough that it was treasonable to mention the King's death in a document, and this was precisely how the bonds were worded. Loughborough was a sound lawyer, who had been Attorney General in North's Ministry and was now Chief Justice of the Common Pleas; if he said anyone concerned in negotiating the bonds was rendering himself liable to transportation, his opinion was to be respected. The Prince was in a great state of agitation when Forth obeyed his summons to Carlton House; he kept going into his bedroom, and every time he returned, he appeared more uneasy. He, and the Duke of York, who was also present, insisted that Forth must give up any further attempt to negotiate

the bonds; he was first to recover Bond A from the Duke of
Orleans, and then return to France for Bond B, which had
already been sent to Brussels in accordance with the arrangement with the convent near Lille. 'The Prince of Wales and the
Duke of York both said some of the following strong words,
"My dear Forth . . . our honour, our reputation depend on your
bringing us the bonds and papers. We would do anything for
you, you have often said you would sacrifice your life for our
family, why not give us who love you, who will always love
you, some proof of all your protestations. Do this for us, and
whilst you live you may command us." Mr. Forth was so
affected that he could scarce speak'.

He went from Carlton House to Chapel Street. At Carlton
House all had been agitation; Orleans retained his accustomed
cynical composure. He was very sorry for the Princes' difficulties, but he could not return Bond A, he had sent it to Paris.
Forth, too stunned to reply, returned immediately to Carlton
House. The Prince, in a rage, declared that the whole story was
a gross falsehood. He said Forth must obtained an order from
Orleans to his agent in Paris authorizing him to hand over the
bond. 'Here some very warm language and some menaces
passed'.

Forth returned to Chapel Street to ask Orleans for an order
to his agent. This would be useless, the Duke said, his own
distresses were such that when he sent Bond A to Paris he
ordered it to be negotiated. If Forth was really so anxious to
recover it he could give him his own note of hand promising to
pay £25,000 in monthly instalments; in that case Orleans would
order his agent to deliver Bond A. Forth had thus not only
been manoeuvred into a position where he had parted with the
stock producing his annuity, he was being asked to lend Orleans
considerably more than its face value. In this wretched dilemma
Forth put his obligations to the Princes first. He gave Orleans
his note of hand, and returned to his own house.

Ten years later when he looked back on these events Forth
commented, 'It might here be asked with great propriety if
Mr. Forth was a fool or a madman, or what could be the motive
of giving up the counter-security of £25,000 in India stock
for a sheet of parchment, or why bind himself to pay £25,000

to get back this same sheet of parchment. Mr. Forth would answer, this memoir is a simple narrative of occurrences, and a plain state of facts'.

His troubles were far from being at an end. 'About 6.00 in the evening, 14 December, Mr. Forth, ill, fatigued, vexed and dispirited, set out for Lille and Paris—dreadful weather, racking pains, and a dark night were his only companions'. The night was so black, and the road so slippery that on a steep chalk hill near Rochester his chaise entangled with a waggon, and was overturned. Forth's jaw was broken, and he received head wounds. He was taken to an inn at Rochester, where his wound was dressed, and at 2.00 next morning before it was light he set off for Dover. He arrived in a high fever, and was forced to spend two days in bed at the *Ship* inn, but he sent his valet ahead to Brussels to make arrangements to recover bond B. On 18 December, with his head bandaged, Forth reached Calais; there he saw a surgeon who thought him too ill for the journey to Paris, so he sent a messenger to Brichard, the notary, summoning him to bring Bond A to St-Omer. He also wrote to tell the Princes his misadventures, ending, "You shall see me arrive with the bonds, or you shall never see me. You told me, Sir, with a taunt that I had often said I would sacrifice my life for your family. You shall see, Sir, even in that instance I will not break my word". The Prince of Wales wrote in answer a most gracious letter, as tender, as consoling as possible.'

Forth, with Souville, the surgeon, and an English male nurse, arrived at the Hotel de Poste at St-Omer on 23 December. Brichard's chief clerk was already there, bringing with him, to Forth's great relief, Bond A. In the evening a Flemish monk came from Brussels with Bond B. The whole of the following day, Christmas Eve, was spent in discussions, sometimes acrimonious, with the bondholders. One bondholder became violent, and wounded Forth with a clasp knife. But at last Forth persuaded them to hand over the bonds. 'The agents, monks and notaries left St-Omer in the evening, some for Paris, some for Brussels . . . '. On Christmas Day Forth returned to Calais. He remained there too ill to go further, while letters reporting his success were dispatched to the princes and their

banker. On 31 December he was in London, and on New
Year's Day 1790 he saw the Princes at York House, where the
bonds were examined and burnt. The Princes were friendly
and grateful, they also agreed to recompense Forth for the
loan which he had been forced to make to Orleans. It seemed
as if everything would end happily: unluckily there was no end
to the Princes' indebtedness.

3

The Prince of Wales called on Forth's help once more in July
1790. Forth was abroad at the time; he was constantly on the
move that year, partly on his own affairs, partly on those of
the Duke of Orleans. He journeyed to England as fast as he
could, and on 29 July met the Duke of York at Reigate. York
at this period of his life was learning to be a competent soldier,
but his private affairs were as disordered as his brother's.
When Forth was in Holland he had encountered one of York's
agents, Colonel Frederick; he came, like Weltje, from West-
phalia, and he finished his career by committing suicide in
Westminster Abbey. Frederick was also engaged in raising
money for the Princes, offering better terms than Forth had
been empowered to offer.

York proceeded to explain his own and his brothers' circumstances, which were quite as bad as they were in the previous
autumn. Forth says that York cursed Lord Loughborough for
preventing the former abortive loan, 'and accused Mr. Sheridan
of having frightened the Prince of Wales on purpose to have
him more in his power'. The Princes, Wales, York and Clarence,
still needed £300,000, and hoped that Orleans would be
willing to back this loan as he had done before. Once again
money would be raised by means of bonds, on which the names
of Orleans and Forth, this time acting as one of the principals,
would appear as guarantors of the loan; interest would be paid
half yearly, and the principal repaid when any one of the three
princes became possessed of revenues worth £200,000 a year.
Interest on the bonds guaranteed by Forth was to be derived
from the revenues of the Duchy of Cornwall, and his claim
was given priority.

Forth set to work at once. By 7 September he had 'examined
several places where money was deposited in Flanders, the
Netherlands, and Paris', and worked out a plan of operations.
In October he took the bonds to be negotiated. While he was
doing this he heard from the Duke of York, perhaps with some
satisfaction, that Colonel Frederick had been feathering his
own nest by making deals on his own account; York therefore
asked Forth to do his best to recover Frederick's bonds, and
withdraw them from circulation.

Negotiations were well advanced, and the bonds already
in the hands of prospective lenders, when the Princes sent for
Forth to tell him that a committee headed by the Duke of
Portland 'and nine of the first men in point of rank and fortune
in England' had offered to raise a loan large enough to pay off
all their debts. But Portland and his Committee insisted, first,
that the Princes should cancel all other arrangements which
they might have made to raise loans; next, that the revenues
of the Duchy of Cornwall should be assigned for the payment
of interest on their loan, and that these payments should take
priority over any other claims, which would of course include
Forth's. He would also have to recover the bonds which he had
already placed in the lenders' hands. He was naturally unwilling to forgo his advantage, nor did he wish to go back on
the arrangements with the bondholders, some of whom had
already been disappointed when the previous loan fell through.

The Princes wanted to have their cake and eat it. They
wanted to take advantage of the Portland Committee's offer,
and therefore urged Forth to yield his claim to priority; they
also told him they did not wish to go back on the arrangements
with the bondholders. The Portland Committee's loan was
intended to place the Princes' affairs on an open and business-
like footing, but the Princes, like other large debtors, shrank
from making a full disclosure of their liabilities. The extent of
the loan was limited by the revenues of the Duchy of Cornwall:
their needs were greater than that. They said that they would
continue to pay interest punctually to the bondholders, if only
Forth would yield his claim.

In spite of pressure from the Princes and their legal advisers,
Forth held out for some time. They renewed their efforts at a

meeting which took place on Sunday, 28 November, at the banking house of Ransom, Morland and Hammersley in Pall Mall. The Duke of York was present and took Forth into an adjoining room. Forth reports their conversation:

'What is the reason that you will not give up the priority?'

'Because, Sir, I cannot get the bonds from the holders without a great sacrifice, as they have been already disappointed; perhaps, also, the agents have put them into other hands.'

'If you will promise Mr. Baldwin[York's chief legal adviser] to give up the priority, and get back the bonds, there is nothing that the Prince of Wales and I will refuse to do for you.'

'Self interest, Sir, has never influenced my conduct.'

'Well, give up the priority, and get back the bonds, and you may depend upon being recompensed for all your losses and trouble when the bonds are brought back. Besides, I really assured the Prince of Wales and others, that at our meeting yesterday you had positively promised me to give up the priority, and get back the bonds.'

'Then, Sir, you shall never appear to have asserted an untruth, if I can prevent it. I owe all I have to your Royal Father's personal protection, and I cannot make a better use of it than by relieving my Master's favourite son. Let us now return to the next room, and I will declare my assent.'

'The Duke of York then pressed Mr. Forth's hand, and said "this shall never be forgotten". After some very kind expressions he then preceded Mr. Forth into the next room, where the latter made his declaration . . . '.

Forth had now given up his claim, the Princes on their side had decided after all to recall the bonds. An express messenger was sent to Paris and Flanders for this purpose, returning with the bonds about two weeks later. But he was obliged to advance £825 before the bondholders would consent to hand them over.

On 17 December Forth was summoned to the Princes: 'all the bonds were counted and examined and Mr. Forth proposed to burn them as the others had been, but the Duke of York said "No, no, we may want them" . . . Then they thanked [Forth] in the kindest manner for all the trouble, fatigue, expenses and vexation he had had, declaring that when the day should come, that they could acknowledge all the obligations they felt themselves under, then he should find them sincere and grateful. As soon the the Duke of York was gone, the Prince of Wales said, "here, my good friend, here are three bonds of £5,000 each for you; this, my dear Forth, I owe you, and is the only recompense that I can *now* make you for all you have done for me, as also for the sums you have paid, and as some small compensation for the loss of the counter-security which the Duke of Orleans cheated you out of; but be assured a day will come when I shall liberally and honorably reward all your friendly services to me" '. Forth was to wait a long time before that day came.

## Chapter Eleven

# WATERSHED

### 1

FOR THE PRESENT he could afford to wait. His own fortune, modest in comparison with some of those possessed by many of his aristocratic or merchant contemporaries, was nevertheless sufficient to keep him in considerable comfort. Meticulously, and mainly in French, the language which came to him most naturally when dealing with money matters, Forth drew up a balance sheet shewing his income and expenditure in the early 1790s.[1]

His running account at his bankers was over £26,000, but this sum included funds which he was handling on behalf of others. He estimated his own total annual revenue at £6,650. His main sources of income were an annuity of £2,000 from the Duke of Orleans; his pension of £600 on the Secret Service fund; £40,000 in East India stock, producing annually £2,150; ten renters' shares in Drury Lane Theatre, producing £600. He also owned three houses: at Manchester Square, the contents of which were valued at £4,000; at Egham; and an 11-roomed house in Paris, Rue St. Honoré. This, 'richement meublée', and provided with linen and china, was let in 1792 to M. Gojard, Receiver General of Paris, for £450 a year.

Out of his annual income Forth reckoned to set aside £1,950 for reinvestment, which, as a result of arbitrage transactions on rates of exchange, discounts, commissions from bankers and others, and other unspecified incidentals, produced, according to his calculations, never less than £1,050.

Forth estimated the total running cost of the Manchester Square house at £2,200. Apart from Forth and his family the household consisted of a Dame de Compagnie or companion

137

for Betsy, six men, and six maidservants. Betsy's successive companions, Miss Vaughan, Miss Brown and Mademoiselle Heyner, were paid £50 a year. The highest paid of the men-servants was the valet at £36 15s. a year; the others were paid £18 18s. or £15 15s. and, unlike the valet, who did not wear livery, they were provided with stone coloured liveries worth £13 10s. There were two coachmen on board wages, receiving liveries worth £16 16s.; they were also supplied with a box coat every other year. Forth evidently set a good deal of store by the smart appearance of his servants, and the liveries are described in great detail. The highest paid of the women servants was the housekeeper at £21, the lowest the nursery-maid at £8 8s. A tax of £1 15s. was payable on each manservant, and 10s. on each maidservant.

One year's food and drink for the household, both family and servants, totalled about £450. Forth budgeted for an expenditure of roughly £1 a day. He allowed an extra £50 for dining out, and £54 for food consumed when travelling. A year's supply of drink cost about £82. This included £20 for beer and starkey at 14s. the barrel, and £62 for wine of various kinds. Port cost 1s. 8d. a dozen bottles; sherry, 1s. 9d.; madeira, 3s. 6d.; claret, 1s. 5d.; burgundy, 6s. 0d.; champagne, 7s. 0d.; graves 3s. 0d.; and hock, 5s. 0d. A Portuguese table wine which appears in Forth's list as Lisbon (abbreviated as 'lis') was possibly a Colares; it cost 1s. 9d. the dozen. 'Lis' and port were the items most often re-ordered, 130 and 128 dozen bottles a year respectively.

Heating was another considerable item of expenditure. The eight coal fires, including the kitchen range, burned 3¾ bushels of coal a day in the cold months of the year. Stacked in the cellar near the kitchen, the knife-hole, the area and the mews, 73½ chaldrons of coal were consumed in one year; coal, together with wood for kindling and other purposes cost £48. Forth carefully noted the dates when each store was emptied; he was not going to allow his household to run short of fuel. Candles of wax and tallow for lighting cost about £5 annually.

Other household expenses were insurances, the upkeep and replacement of furniture, and personal and household laundry. Forth's accounts do not show the amount of his insurance premium, but the total value insured was £8,000. Forth estimated that insurances, maintenance and taxes cost him £80 a year. There is no annual figure to show the expenditure on laundry, but bills for seven months in 1790 totalled £16 16s. 7d.

The expenses of the house in Paris were slightly higher than those of the London house, £2,500 yearly. They are not set out in detail, but an account for the month of April 1972 shows outgoings of 12 livres for servants' wages; 14 livres for job horses, carriages and coachmen; 6 livres for an arrangement with a restaurateur to provide food and drink; 2 livres for heating; and 1 livre each for laundry and barber. The total expenditure that month was 60 livres, or about £2 10s. in English money. The comparable expense in Manchester Square was £1 11s.

To a man who travelled as much and as often as Forth, his horses and carriages were essential pieces of equipment. He stabled his saddle horses with a livery stables keeper named Welch, from whom he jobbed carriage horses at whatever rate was current. Forth paid Welch £135 11s. in 1790 for these services and the wages of a coachman, apparently in addition to the two mentioned earlier. Two carriages, a town one and a chaise, were both housed in the Manchester Square mews. They cost Forth £17 a year in tax, and £26 for repairs to vehicles and harness, and the replacement of saddles, bridles and whips. The coachmen received 1s. a day extra on the road, and two guineas a year in addition to their liveries to keep themselves in boots and breeches.

Since he might have to leave at any moment on one of his journeys, Forth kept a list in readiness setting out all the items which he found it convenient to take with him. One such list 'for a week's jaunt at any time' is pasted into his copy of *Paterson's Road Book* for 1799.[2] Clothing included 1 hat; 1 greatcoat (surtout or cloak), 2 coats; 2 pairs kersey, and 1 pair black silk breeches; 3 white, 2 flannel and 2 jean waistcoats; 6 shirts; 2 chemisettes; 6 striped fichus; 4 muslin and 4 embroidered cravats; 20 white lawn or silk handkerchiefs, some of which were bordered; several kinds of stockings, white silk, or black and white ribbed wool; 2 flannel and 4 cotton nightcaps; 2 pairs of shoes, 1 pair of slippers and 1 pair of boots. Among the miscellaneous items were a bootjack; shoe and knee buckles; 2 wigs; powder box; shaving tackle; tooth-box, sponge, nailbrush, soap and perfume bottle. Forth also took cocoa, cocoa pot and strainer; a teapot; sugar; wine and brandy; a housewife for his mending; a watch; spectacles; pistols; a therm-ometer; maps and writing materials; an umbrella and a cane.

The choice of articles envisages a great variety of needs and occasions, but most of the items would probably have figured in many travellers' lists at that date. More surprising and personal to Forth were a Bible, a pedometer, a measuring tape, and his violin. When he was absent for more than a week he took a viola as well.

2

It was no coincidence that so precise a statement of Forth's financial position and household affairs should have survived for the early 1790s. In many respects these years were a water-shed in his life.

Hitherto his health had been excellent, allowing him to meet any demands which his energy might put on it; he had been in-jured, as any hard rider always may be, but he recovered. Now he began to suffer from a violent pain, which had already afflicted him: it was eventually diagnosed as the stone. He was to suffer from it at intervals for the rest of his life. This was already giving him pain when he set out in December 1789 on the journey during which his chaise was overturned and his jaw broken. The fracture was badly set, and continued to trouble him. A painful abscess was treated by John Hunter, the surgeon, a year later, but without completely curing him. The two conditions, not at first noticeable, gradually undermined Forth's strength.

A more immediately visible break in his life was his separa-tion from Betsy. Forth was 46, she was 31, and they had been together for 14 years. The 'dear Betsy' of the earlier diaries has become 'Mama', the mother of his children. She was still very much part of his life, his children were dear to him: why did they part? There is nothing in Forth's papers to explain this, but the reason was almost certainly the Countess de Genetines.

Françoise de Genetines was the sister of Claude Odile
Baroud, the notary whom Forth already knew as one of the
most ingenious of those who invented and underpinned the
speculations in annuities. Their father, Louis Joseph Baroud du
Soleil, was one of the rich and restricted oligarchy which kept
such a tight hand on the government of Lyons. He was also a
distinguished member of the Parlement of Lyons, and a firm
defender of its dignities. In May 1788 during the Assembly of
Notables, when the King published an edict from a *lit de
justice* overriding the powers of the provincial parlements,
Baroud refused to obey, and was imprisoned very uncomfort-
ably on an island off the Mediterranean coast. In his private
capacity he was a charming, cultivated man, a member of the
Academy of Lyons, and a translator of Sterne and Gay. Coming
from a rich and cultured family it was not difficult for the two
older daughters to make good marriages among the *noblesse
de robe*, but Françoise surpassed them by marrying into one of
the great families of the Lyonnais, Charpin de Feugerolles.
Her husband, descended from a younger branch of this family,
was François Régis de Charpin, Count de Genetines, a captain
in the Bourbon Regiment of Dragoons. Evidently beauty was
an important element in Françoise's dowry.[3]

She was married in July 1784. Nothing has survived to say
how or when she met Forth. It was probably in Paris, perhaps
through her brother. She became Forth's mistress; again, it
is not possible to say when. At the beginning of the Revolution she came to England with her little daughter Mimi, and
settled in London.

Betsy could perhaps have ignored the new relationship;
she was the woman in possession, with the advantages of that
situation, but she had a hot temper. When she knew from
many small, cumulative signs that she had a serious rival,
younger, fresher, and perhaps more sophisticated than she was,
she decided to leave Forth.

It was not so simple to sever a bond which had been a
marriage in fact if not in law. Betsy must be provided for;
there were also the children, Nat, aged 13, at Dr. Thomson's
school at Egham, under the general supervision of Parson Jeans,
and Eliza, usually called Betty, who was only two. Forth

treated Betsy generously: he paid her £600 a year; with the income on the annuity of 12,000 livres, which he had bought for her in Paris, this provided a reasonable income for herself and Eliza. He continued to pay for Nat's schooling, and, until a formal Deed of Separation was drawn up in 1793, he also paid the wages of Betsy's companion.[4]

The final parting took place at Spa on 12 November 1790. For the time being Betsy remained abroad, and Forth returned to Manchester Square.

### 3

It was also during the early 1790s that Forth's relations with Orleans began to change. The connexion which had been such an asset gradually became a liability.

The process began during Orleans's diplomatic appointment in London. The mission lasted nine months, and it brought him no credit. During the whole of his stay he was watched with suspicion by the official French Ambassador, who employed the blackmailer of Marie Antoinette, Théveneau de Morande, to spy on all the comings and goings at Chapel Street, where Orleans had taken a house for himself and his mistress, Madame de Buffon. Morande, still living on his ill-gotten annuities, and contriving to make himself useful, sent in detailed reports on everything, including the movements of his former acquaintance, Forth. Among other things Morande reported that Choderlos de Laclos used Forth as a channel of communication with his political friends in Paris. Since these were Orleanist supporters, some of whom were living in the Palais Royal, Forth could not easily refuse. But it harmed his reputation to be associated with this faction at a time when feeling against Orleans ran high on both sides of the Channel.[5]

In London the government was embarrassed at the existence of two French diplomatic missions; the King and London society generally were not anxious to receive the man believed to have been responsible for the march on Versailles. It is said that when Orleans visited Ranelagh people drew back as his party walked through the gardens: Georgiana, Duchess of Devonshire, warned the Prince of Wales to be on his guard

against him.[6] The Prince however was linked to Orleans by
his financial needs, and a similar link bound Orleans to Forth.

Orleans was speaking no more than the truth when he told
Forth during the negotiations over the Prince's bonds that he
was in financial distress. Indeed the later history of Bond A
shows to what expedients he resorted. In order to recover this
document Forth had bound himself by his note of hand to pay
Orleans £25,000. This he did in monthly instalments throughout 1790, and obtained the Duke's receipts. But three years
later a most respectable London banking house applied to Forth
for payment of £25,000, and he discovered that Orleans had
been borrowing on the note of hand. 'This wretch', says Forth,
'had assured Mr. Forth that he had burnt the note at Paris as
it was cancelled by his legal receipts'.[7]

There were good reasons, apart from lavish spending, why
Orleans should find himself short of money at this time. In
abolishing feudal privileges, the French National Assembly
necessarily reduced the income of all feudal landowners, not
least the Duke of Orleans with his vast estates. His former
Chancellor estimated that in spite of substantial compensation
he had lost at least a million and a half livres. Nor was this the
full extent of his losses. He must make the most of his other
resources, among them his collection of pictures and
objets d'art.[8]

He asked Forth to find purchasers for his pictures. Forth
approached the auctioneer James Christie who in September
1790 made an offer of 100,000 guineas for the contents of the
Palais Royal Gallery. The Prince of Wales and the Duke of
York were both interested in acquiring some of this famous
collection. When Forth was raising money for them in July
1790 he planned to use the princes' bonds to pay for the
pictures. But when the princes accepted the loan offered by
the Portland Committee the scheme fell through. Two years
later the French banker Laborde de Méréville succeeded in
bringing the French and Italian pictures from the Orleans collection to England, and soon afterwards the Dutch and Flemish
paintings were bought by an English collector Thomas Moore
Slade, with the backing of Ransom Morland and Hammersley's
bank. Slade only just managed to outwit Orleans's creditors,

who, with a group of French artists, were determined to keep
the paintings in France. Thus it was owing to Slade's ingenuity
that in 1792 English buyers were given the incredible good
fortune to acquire the Raphaels, Titians and Correggios, the
Rembrandts, Rubens, Claudes and Poussins with which Cardinal
Richelieu and the Regent Orleans had endowed the gallery of
the Palais Royal.[9]

A note in Forth's accounts may relate to these transactions.
A page headed 'dimanche 29 avril 1792' records gains and losses
during a gambling session at Raincy. The players were Orleans,
Lauzun (who had inherited his uncle's title, and was now
Duke de Biron), Sillery, the husband of Madame de Genlis,
and Louis, Prince d'Aremberg. The presence among the players
of the banker Walckiers and Forth suggest that the gambling
took place in the intervals of business discussions. the games
were crabs (played with dice) and billiards. The score cannot
have been at all easy to keep when some of the party were
wagering assignats, others golden louis, and Sillery, bottles of
his own wine. In the afternoon the men were joined by Madame
de Buffon and Grace Dalrymple Elliott. This ravishing demi-
mondaine, Scottish by birth, had been the mistress of the
Prince of Wales and of the Duke of Orleans; at this time she
was apparently being kept by Biron. At the afternoon session
the whole party played billiards, and the stakes became even
more heterogeneous: rings, jewelled buttons, golden buckles; a
snuff box; a carriage; a miniature of Mrs. Elliott; and a deer. By
nine o'clock in the evening Forth was 1,667 louis or 40,000
livres to the good.

Perhaps it was at this gambling session that Walckiers
won from Orleans all the Italian and French paintings in the
gallery of the Palais Royal. There is a story that he did so,
and, whether it was a gambling debt, or, as seems likely, a
ruse to prevent Orleans's creditors obtaining possession of
the paintings, this may well have been the occasion when
the transaction took place. Pictures were certainly among
the stakes; Forth himself won a Rape of the Sabines by Salviati.
The session began again the next day at Monceau, so that
there were plenty of opportunities for spectacular gains or
losses.[10]

At about this date Forth himself acquired some Dutch pictures, but whether they came from the Palais Royal or from one of the other private cabinets then being dispersed is now almost impossible to say.

Among Orleans's other disposable assets was the urban property surrounding the gardens of the Palais Royal. The lease or sale of this property, including the newly completed theatre, brought in a considerable sum, but Orleans needed larger resources than those derived from sales of pictures or premises. While he was in London he embarked on a series of loans which he continued to negotiate when he returned to France in July 1790. The banking houses mainly concerned were Boyd, Ker and Company and Greffulhe, and the firms with which they were closely associated, Laborde and Walckiers. Forth's numerous journeys to France, Germany and the Low Countries during the early 1790s show that once again he was acting as intermediary in at least some of these transactions. It is also likely, but hard to prove, that Orleans entrusted Forth with some of the money raised by these loans to speculate on foreign exchanges, where considerable profits were being made as currencies rose or fell with the unsettled state of European affairs.[11]

By this date Orleans was known by the name to which posterity has become accustomed, Philippe Egalité. He acquired this description, which he himself thought ridiculous, when he was standing for election to the Convention, and asked the Procureur of the Commune of Paris to find him a suitable surname. Thereafter it was decreed that he and his family should bear the name Egalité; the Palais Royal became the Maison Egalité, and the gardens, *les Jardins de la Révolution*. For a short time, between the return from the attempted flight of the Royal Family and the invasion of France by foreign armies, Orleans was popular, and his prospects of becoming at least Lieutenant General of France seemed promising. But as the Revolution gathered momentum Orleans, although he aligned himself more and more with the Jacobins, gradually lost his influence, and this complex, vulnerable and by now very frightened man became little more than a cipher. His financial affairs were still a major preoccupation, and Forth continued to help him. But when Austrian and Prussian troops invaded France such international dealings appeared treasonable. Some believed that Orleans was taking money out of France, others that Forth and he were using English gold to foment counter-revolution. Sénar, the *secrétaire rédacteur* of the Committee of General Security, compiling a dossier from the papers of one of Orleans's supposed accomplices, was convinced that English letters referring to the transfers of millions of livres must mean that Orleans was being financed by Pitt.[12] Neither Orleans nor Forth had foreseen this. Both men grew up in the milder climate of earlier eighteenth century opinion when a man could pursue his private affairs in spite of wars. Now, at the end of the century, the climate was becoming colder; the interests of a private individual were becoming identified with those of his country, and he was blamed for trading with his country's enemies.

But while the frontiers between France and England were still open Forth became involved in a business of a different kind.

## Chapter Twelve

# THE DU BARRY AFFAIR

1

IT WAS SOME TIME since Forth, shortly before he left Paris for the last time as Special Envoy, met Madame Du Barry and had a 'long affecting chat'. But he was now to spend two years closely involved in her affairs. He could not guess that his efforts to help her would one day endanger her life.

When Forth was in Paris in 1790 on the princes' business the notary Rouen, who was also Madame Du Barry's notary, had given him a list of her jewels in the hope that he might find purchasers for them in England. Her income was very much reduced as a result of the French Revolution; she hoped that her jewels would supply an alternative source, but so many jewels were being sold by others in a similar position that Forth found no one willing to buy at the price that Madame Du Barry was asking. Nevertheless it was because of the enquiries that he had made on her behalf that on 10 February 1791 James Christie the auctioneer brought him two visitors, a Jewish diamond merchant named Lyon De Symons, and his solicitor Edward Allen.

They had a very odd story to tell. The previous day a man had called at De Symons's house in Prescot Street, Goodmans Fields, with some spectacular diamonds for sale. He said that he was a French nobleman, and it struck De Symons that he was remarkably ignorant of the value of the jewels that he was trying to sell. De Symons was not at all the man to be concerned in shady dealings. He was rich and highly respectable, enjoying an assured position in the City of London, and married to one of the influential Goldsmid family. He was suspicious of the pretended nobleman, in particular because it seemed to him that some of the jewels resembled some described in a list of valuables recently stolen from Madame Du Barry's country house outside Paris. De Symons was cautious. He bought some of the jewels, and to keep negotiations open asked to be shown others the following day; meanwhile he consulted his solicitor. Together the two men decided to enquire if Madame Du Barry had an agent in England who would take on himself the responsibility of what might prove to be a very awkward business. They knew Forth had been trying to sell some of Madame Du Barry's jewels, and hoping that he was her agent, they asked James Christie to introduce them.[1]

At first Forth was reserved. He knew nothing of the theft, although it had caused a considerable sensation, and he sent round to the French Embassy for confirmation. He also produced the inventory which Rouen had given him. As De Symons examined it he became more than ever convinced that the jewels which he had been offered had belonged to Madame Du Barry. But he was not at all anxious to become too far involved. Allen, his solicitor, agreed: he did not want his client to make himself responsible for the arrest of thieves who could not, as he knew, be prosecuted in England for a crime committed in another country. If they were jailed they might bring an action for false imprisonment against their accuser.

As Forth watched what he later described as the timid and cautious conduct of De Symons and Allen, he became more and more irritated. He saw that the jewels would never be recovered unless someone took decisive action. He decided to take a hand. He suggested that while De Symons returned to keep his appointment with the suspicious nobleman and his equally suspicious companions, he and Allen should go to Bow Street for two constables to assist Forth, as a Justice of the Peace, to take the thieves.

Unfortunately De Symons's house was in the City of London where the magistrates of Bow Street had no jurisdiction; Forth found that he would have to rely on the help of his coachman and his footman. He explained what he wanted them to do, and

took the unwilling Allen with him in his carriage to Prescot
Street. There he asked a hackney coachman to hold his horses
while he posted his own coachman and footman on either side
of De Symons's front door to prevent anyone coming out. De
Symons's wife heard him give these orders, and begged him not
to cause an alarm in the neighbourhood or make any arrests
in the house. De Symons and Allen supported her. Forth took
no notice of these new signs of 'timidity'. He locked the front
door, pocketed the key, and asked De Symons to take him to
see the 'nobleman', who was now changing his story and assert-
ing that he was a jeweller named Levet.

Forth found Levet in De Symons back parlour sitting in front
of a table covered with paper packets containing jewels. One of
Levet's companions (they were all, like Levet, Jewish) was in
the front parlour, and another in the kitchen with De Symons's
servants. Forth introduced himself to Levet as a friend of De
Symons, who always consulted him about any large purchase
of jewels because he was too cautious and timid to act on his
own account. This was too much for De Symons. 'Now, Mr.
Forth', he said, 'I will leave you. I will have nothing more to do
in the affair'.

As he talked to Levet Forth became so convinced that the
jewels on the table were Madame Du Barry's that he asked
outright if this were not so. Levet, in Forth's words, remained
in some degree cool and collected. He said he knew nothing of
any theft; he had bought the jewels a month ago from a man
named Harris for £3,000. The present price was £4,000, and if
Forth was not prepared to pay so much Levet would sell
elsewhere, on the Exchange or in Holland. Forth replied,
'These diamonds have been stolen from Madame Du Barry's
house in France. I am Milor Forth. I was Secretary to the
Ambassador, and now belong to the Secretary of State, and
have orders to arrest you, and take away the diamonds . . .
by the law of England you must be hanged, and the King of
England cannot save you from being hanged'.

'O, God', exclaimed Levet, 'are you Milor Forth? Do not
ruin me: I will own everything to you'.[2]

At this point Forth called in De Symons and Allen, who
were considerably relieved to hear what Levet said, 'You may

seal up all the diamonds and pearls, and I will bring you to the
man who sold them to me'. They would find him in Grace-
church Street at the *Cross Keys* inn.

When Forth, De Symons and Allen arrived at the *Cross Keys*
Levet took them to a room leading off the first floor gallery,
whereat a table laid for five, three more Jewish men were seated
smoking pipes. Levet indicated Forth, and said, 'This gentleman
has bought the diamonds, and now wants some large ones'. One
of the men took a handful of sealed packets out of his breeches
pockets. While Forth and De Symons examined the packets
Allen sent for some constables, who soon arrived accompanied
by one of the City Marshals.

Levet and his friends were arrested and brought before the
Lord Mayor. Here again De Symons and Allen held back. It
was on an Affidavit sworn by Forth that four of the thieves
were consigned to the special Jewish ward of the Poultry
Street Compter. The fifth thief, an English Jew named Harris,
was the man whom Levet had named as the seller of the jewels.
Because he seemed prepared to turn King's evidence he was
separated from the others, and sent to the Compter in Wood
Street.

The jewels, in a parcel sealed with the seals of Forth, De
Symons and Allen, were deposited in Ransom, Morland and
Hammersley's bank. By a form of triple receipt the Bank
undertook not to release the packet without the written con-
sents of all three signatories.

## 2

Forth's next step was to write a triumphant letter to Madame
Du Barry to tell her that her jewels had been found, and
suggesting that she should come over to London to identify
and reclaim them. On 17 February, only a week after the
arrest of the thieves, Forth crossed to Boulogne to meet her
and escort her back to England.

At the age of 43 Madame Du Barry was rather more plump
and high-coloured than when Forth saw her last, but she was
none the less a beautiful and desirable woman, good natured,
generous and endowed with the serenity of a woman who has
always been able to attract and charm.

Forth made himself extremely useful to Madame Du Barry. He found rooms at Greniers Hotel for her and her party, which included her jeweller; he acted as her interpreter; he accompanied her to the Bank to inspect the stolen jewels; to the lawyers to discuss how best to proceed. He even advised her on the purchase of carriage horses. An unfriendly observer later remarked that Madame Du Barry seemed wholly guided by Forth. She was so grateful for the success of Forth's efforts that she gave him a gold snuffbox with her picture on one side; on the other, in letters of gold on a blue enamel background, was a quotation from the letter Forth had written announcing the discovery of the jewels. She nicknamed him Fortuné because he brought her luck.[3]

At first all went well. Madame Du Barry's jeweller, who had often reset her jewels, was able to testify that he recognized them by certain unmistakable marks. The Lord Mayor decided that there was a case to answer and committed the thieves to Newgate; Madame Du Barry was bound over to prosecute them. Harris, the English thief, volunteered a statement in which he described how the theft had been planned and carried out.

When the preliminary proceedings in London were over, Madame Du Barry, still accompanied by Forth, returned to Paris to follow up the accusations which Harris had made against the thieves' accomplices. Here they were not so successful. The man in whose Jewish eating-house the theft was supposed to have been planned was able to prove that he was out of France on the crucial date. The scar on his head by which Harris said that he could be recognized was not visible, even though Forth, unwisely over-zealous, pulled off his wig to look. It began to seem as if Harris's statement was not to be trusted.[4]

A far worse check occurred in London when the judge at the Old Bailey ruled that the thieves could not be tried in England for a felony committed outside the country. All the thieves, except Harris, were released, and to make matters worse Madame Du Barry was forced to pay for their upkeep in jail. Although this was the usual practice at that time it added to an already lengthening bill for legal expenses.

Forth, on Madame Du Barry's behalf, now set about reclaiming her jewels, the only course that remained open. He arranged a meeting with De Symons at his solicitor's chambers to ask both men to sign the receipts which would authorize the bank to hand over the jewels. But Allen refused outright. He told Forth that De Symons not only intended to claim a reward of £2,000 which Madame Du Barry had offered when the jewels were stolen, but wished her to sign an agreement to indemnify him against any losses that he might suffer if the thieves sued him. This was only too likely. With the support of a rich and litigious money-lender, known to his contemporaries as Jew King, the gang was preparing to bring at least two legal actions against De Symons.

It was now that the latent antagonism between Forth and De Symons and Allen showed openly. Forth tried to convince De Symons that if Madame Du Barry was allowed to take possession of her jewels she would not let De Symons lose by it. De Symons and Allen held firm. Forth had understood that De Symons did not intend to claim a reward. De Symons denied this. Forth remarked crossly, 'well, well, your word is as good as mine, then you did not say so . . . but if there is any reward due you are not entitled to the whole of it; I am entitled to a share, Mr. Allen is entitled to a share'. To which Allen replied that in his opinion De Symons had earned the whole reward, but if Forth was intending to put in a claim, so would he.

The two sides had taken up positions on the merits of which only a court of law could decide. Madame Du Barry was very angry with Forth when she heard how unsuccessful he had been, and understood that the day when she could return to France with her jewels was postponed once again. But her anger did not last long. Soon she was consulting her lawyers on the next step. On their advice she brought an action against De Symons and the thieves in the Court of King's Bench for unlawfully converting the jewels to their own use. De Symons meanwhile initiated a suit against Madame Du Barry in the Court of Chancery to claim his reward. The affair which had promised so well in February, by April seemed to be developing into a series of lawsuits.

At this time Forth too had his disappointments. In March his friend and patron Lord Mansfield died. Ever afterwards Forth kept the last day on which he saw Mansfield as an anniversary, noting in his Diary, '*Dies acerbus semper honoratus*'. In April he attended a dinner given for Madame Du Barry by the Duke of Queensberry at his villa on the river at Richmond. Afterwards the Prince of Wales, who had been one of the guests, stopped Forth just as he was preparing to leave in company with Mr. St. Leger. 'No, Forth', said the Prince, 'you shall go to town in the Duke of Queensberry's coach with Madame Du Barry, the Duke and me, as I wish to speak to you about business'. The coach set down the Prince and Forth at Carlton House, and the Prince entered into a long account of his distressed situation. He said: 'My dear Forth, I am afraid I shall not be able to pay the interests of the bonds regularly, but you may depend on having it as I am able to pay it'.[5]

3

Now that it seemed as if she would need to spend some time in London Madame Du Barry asked Forth to find her a furnished house in which she could live more comfortably and entertain when she wished. He found her one in Margaret Street, not far from 35 Portland Place where he and the Duke of Orleans once lived. 'See Du Barry; fix her in her house', Forth wrote in his Diary on 28 May. Madame de Genetines helped Madame Du Barry to settle in, interpreted for her, engaged servants, and paid household bills.

The whole summer of 1791 was taken up with legal business. But when Madame Du Barry returned to her house at Louveciennes in August, although it has been established by law that the jewels were hers, Lyon De Symons's claim to a reward had still to be settled.

Once again Forth accompanied Madame Du Barry. The French police had been following up the thieves' accomplices who were now to be brought before a Tribunal at Versailles where Forth's testimony was needed. As soon as he had done what was required he hurried back to England to keep Madame Du Barry in touch with the slow progress of her case through the English courts. It was not for another year that in October 1792 he wrote to tell her that her presence was required in London.

In the interval the stately processes of English law had been overtaken by the quickening pace of the French Revolution. Suspicion of the monarchy, and the fear of foreign invasion caused panic; the King and Queen were imprisoned; many of Madame Du Barry's friends were guillotined; her lover, the Duke de Brissac with whom she had lived happily for many years, was massacred. She was still suffering from grief and shock when she arrived at the house which Forth rented for her, this time on the corner of Bruton Street and Berkeley Square.

The French laws about emigration were now very strict. Madame Du Barry took care to obtain the right documents to prove that she was travelling on business, and that her absence would be only temporary. Without knowing it she left behind her a formidable enemy who was only waiting for a chance to attack her.

George Grieve, small, mis-shapen and immensely strong, was an Englishman, the son of an Alnwick attorney. Educated at Eton, and later for a time a clerk in Thellusson's London bank, he now described himself as a prime anarchist, and sub-vertor of despotism in two hemispheres. He had canvassed for Wilkes, befriended Marat when he lived in England, supported the cause of American independence, and claimed acquaintance with Washington and Franklin. In 1791 he settled at Louve-ciennes where he founded a revolutionary club. Madame Du Barry provided a room in her house for its meetings. There, under her own roof, Grieve set about the destruction of this 'Bacchante crowned with ivy and roses', this Messalina 'born of the people and enriched with the people's spoils'.

If Grieve's democratic convictions were genuine his feelings about Madame Du Barry were ambiguous. She was detestable to him as the former mistress of a king, but also because she was a courtesan. His attacks on her, so personal and so venomous, show the kind of pathological hatred of prostitutes that produces a Jack the Ripper. He had other motives for destroying Madame Du Barry. She symbolized everything that he hated; but he also coveted her possessions.[6]

Unluckily Madame Du Barry's friendship with Forth made her particularly vulnerable to his attacks. When Grieve was in Paris at the time of the American War of Independence he was aware of the activities of 'the vigilant Mr. Forth', whom he believed to be an English spy. It seemed obvious to him now that since Madame Du Barry was so closely associated with Forth she must also be working for Pitt and the enemies of the French Revolution. He maintained that the jewel theft was not genuine; it was a plot hatched by Forth to justify Madame Du Barry's journeys to England, and to provide opportunities for her to communicate with the supporters of counter-revolution on both sides of the Channel.

At first Grieve's attempts to arouse feeling against Madame Du Barry did not have much effect. She was very well liked in her village where she had done many kindnesses. But her absence in the autumn and winter of 1792, when everyone connected with the *ancien régime* was under suspicion, played into his hands. He denounced Madame Du Barry as an émigrée, and persuaded the local officials to seal up her house as a preliminary to confiscating her possessions.

Madame Du Barry heard this news in London in February 1793. At long last, two years after the thieves were first arrested, the Court of Chancery decided what reward was due to Lyon de Symons; the moment when she could reclaim her jewels seemed to be in sight. The news from Louveciennes was so serious that she could not wait. Hurriedly, with Forth's help, Madame Du Barry settled her affairs in England. Together they made lists of all the payments to be made to her legal advisers and those who had helped her.

Forth himself was not forgotten. In Madame Du Barry's eyes it was he, not Lyon de Symons, who had earned the £2,000 reward. She did not want to give De Symons any opportunity to object, so, perhaps at Forth's suggestion, she arranged that the reward should appear as a loan. She was in any case borrowing nearly £2,000 from Forth to settle her accounts; a further £2,000 was added, representing the reward. The jewels, still deposited in Ransom, Morland and Hammersley's bank, were to stand as security for payment.

Her financial arrangements complete, Madame Du Barry left London for the last time. For the rest of the year she struggled to justify herself against Grieve's accusations. At last, in November 1793, Grieve triumphed, and Madame Du Barry was brought before the Revolutionary Tribunal.

Grieve drew up the case against her. On each article in the long list of accusations he made copious notes for the benefit of the Public Prosecutor. Some of the accusations referred to the time when Madame Du Barry was the mistress of Louis XV; others referred to more recent events, and made much of the *ci-devant* aristocrats whom she had frequented during her visits to London. There were many references to her association with Forth; the skill with which she had avoided being classified as an émigrée was worthy, it was said, of that adept in the Machiavellian arts.

Madame Du Barry was defended by Chauveau-Lagarde, who only a few weeks earlier had defended Marie-Antoinette. He could not save her. The Tribunal pronounced her guilty, and she was guillotined on 8 December 1793. All Forth's efforts had not succeeded in restoring her jewels to Madame Du Barry, but they certainly contributed to her death.

## Chapter Thirteen

## REAPING A WHIRLWIND

### 1

THE EVENTS in France which led to the death of Madame Du Barry deprived Forth of the major part of his livelihood. When France declared war on England in February 1793 the two countries were cut off from each other, and it was impossible for Forth to act as Orleans's agent any longer.

In some ways this saved Forth from embarrassment. Orleans utterly disgraced himself in the eyes of almost everyone by voting for the death of Louis XVI. His close friends, Biron and Madame de Genlis, and his son, Louis-Philippe, the future King of the French, urged him either to vote against the death sentence, or not to attend the trial; Robespierre himself expected that he would do this; but Orleans insisted on attending and voting. The death sentence was approved by one vote. Feeling against Orleans in England was then so strong that it would have been hard for Forth to continue to work for him and keep his self-respect.

He evidently felt that the British government might mistrust his French associations. In a long, rhetorical letter which he wrote to the Prime Minister, Pitt, in May 1794, Forth said that he knew that people had grossly misrepresented him, and he would like a chance to refute the accusations: 'if such is the fatality of future events that the ruins of my country shall crush me, at least they shall bury me with them with a pure conscience and a loyal heart'. In order to prove his loyalty Forth had already informed Pitt that two men were being sent to England by the Committee of Public Safety to assassinate the King and Pitt; he now enquired if anything further had been heard of them.[1]

Forth afterwards claimed that his information saved George III and Pitt. In fact his was not the only, or the most effective, warning. It was true that two men, Colla and Godoni, were sent off in March 1794 with instructions to kill the King and his Prime Minister: they were to travel to England through Liége and Ostend. But the government had been aware of a plot since October of the previous year, and with the active co-operation of the Imperial Minister in the Netherlands, the men were caught. They were already being detained when Forth wrote to Pitt. He can therefore claim only a very limited share of credit for this lucky escape.[2]

The same is probably true of another rescue which Forth believed was his work. 'It was I', he wrote, 'who prevented the Duke of York from being surprised and carried off by the enemy near Valenciennes in 1794, and from his being now perhaps a prisoner in France'. It is a fact that in 1794, while in command of the army in the Low Countries, York was very nearly captured by the advancing French troops. But accounts of the incident, including one by a staff officer who was present, do not mention Forth. If he played a part, it was only a small one.

Forth's main preoccupations after the declaration of war with France were financial. He had not only lost the income which he derived from the management of Orleans's English interests, he no longer received the income payable from Orleans's revenues on his own and Betsy's annuities. In November 1793 Orleans was guillotined. All his property was confiscated and administered by the French government. Forth's own apartment in the Rue St. Honoré was also confiscated. He now fully felt the loss of the East India stock which had been sold to oblige the Princes.

At this time Forth's responsibilities, and his expenses, were increased by the birth of a son. The boy, Richard Rettfort, was the fruit of his liaison with Madame de Genetines, whose household at 183, Oxford Street Forth was already supporting. When Madame de Genetines's husband returned from campaigning with the émigré armies, Forth's equivocal position involved him in further outlay; he not only had to pay Madame's bills, but the debts incurred by Monsieur. The Count

de Genetines proposed to settle, as many other émigrés were
doing, at Hamburg, and to set up in business there. Forth introduced him to a merchant, William Wennington, of Gray's Inn,
from whom Genetines ordered over £600 of merchandise.
These goods were not paid for when Genetines left for Hamburg.
After a long, and increasingly acrimonious correspondence
with Wennington, Forth finally agreed to settle the account.[3]

In order to meet expenses and make good his losses, Forth
set about making fresh business connexions. One such interest
perhaps was Henry Holland's development of Sir Hans Sloane's
estate in Chelsea; it is certain that in 1798 Betsy became the
first resident of one of the houses on the site, 20 Hans Place.
In all probability, as in other such schemes, he acted as broker
between the architect and the men who could provide the
development capital.

During these difficult years Forth claimed repayment of the
money which he had lent to Madame Du Barry, part of which
represented his reward of £2,000. The Marquis de Boisséson,
the husband of Madame Du Barry's favourite young relation,
was in England on leave from Condé's army. Forth encouraged
him to take out Letters of Administration for Madame Du
Barry's property in England, in other words the jewels, which
were still lying in the bank. The result was not as simple as
Forth hoped. As soon as there was a prospect of laying hands
on this property Madame Du Barry's relations, connexions and
creditors came forward in large numbers with claims far exceed-
ing the value of the jewels. More legal proceedings inevitably
followed. The jewels were sold by order of the Court of
Chancery, and fetched about £13,400 at auction at Christie's
on 19 February 1795. The creditors' demands totalled over
£24,000. The next four years were spent in adjusting the
claim. Forth was paid in full because his agreement with
Madame Du Barry specifically gave him a prior claim; Lyon De
Symons at last obtained a reward of £700; but all the other
creditors received only a proportion of their demands.[4]

His financial situation, and perhaps also his long association
with the Duke of Orleans, meant that to some of his old
acquaintances, in whose houses he had once been welcome,
Forth was now a somewhat embarrassing guest. After the 1st

Earl of Mansfield, Forth's protector, died, Lord Stormont
succeeded him. Stormont's son, years later, described a scene
that occurred not long after the 1st Earl's death.

Forth, who 'narrated agreeably and fluently', came to dinner
one evening, as he often did, 'on the pretence he brought some
news, or some French officer requested my father's interference.
It was like a scene in a play, as father did not pretend to be
glad to see him, my mother evidently did not pretend to be
glad to see him, my father was evidently displeased. He took
no notice, sat down to dinner undaunted, talked incessantly,
told so many amusing stories that it was impossible not to
laugh. One day he took my father out of the room, as I afterwards found, borrowed £1,500 for a commission for his son of
which he never paid principal or interest, and his son sold the
commission'.[5]

Forth owed so much to his link with the Mansfield family
that it is sad to watch so fruitful a relationship cooling to
resentment and distaste.

It was galling to Forth, usually so conscientious in settling
accounts, to be himself a debtor. But his income continued
to diminish until, according to his calculations, it was only
£140 a year. In the winter of 1799 he had an overdraft of
£2,000. He decided that the time had come to press the Prince
of Wales and the Duke of York for payment of the money
which he had lent them.

2

The Princes' circumstances had changed a good deal in the last
ten years. The Prince of Wales married in 1795, mainly in
order to obtain the payment of debts and an increased income.
He chose a wife whom he could neither like nor respect, and
when she gave birth to a princess he separated from her.
Gradually he drifted back to Mrs. Fitzherbert. He had grown
older without becoming noticeably more mature. The Duke of
York, abler than his brother, and lucky enough to have work
which interested him, was in 1799 Commander in Chief of the
Army. Both brothers were still in debt, but they were much
more skilful in keeping creditors at arms' length.

Just when Forth was making ready to approach the Princes, he fell seriously ill. He described his illness as six months of rheumatic headaches, which he believed were the result of his broken head and fractured jaw. Sir Walter Farquhar, one of the Royal physicians, gave him more hemlock than he had ever before prescribed for a patient. Whatever the illness may have been, it caused Forth a great deal of pain, which frayed his nerves, irritated his temper, and sharpened all his dealings with the Princes; many of his letters to them were written from his sickbed.

Forth had two claims against the Princes: in the first place he wanted reimbursement of £825, his expenses when recovering their bonds; next, he required compensation for the sale of the East India stock which produced his annuity. The Prince of Wales had given him three bonds of £5,000 each towards this, but little interest had been paid, and of the principal there was no sign. In assessing his claims Forth took into account not only the specific sums, but the amount of income these would have produced during the last ten years; he accordingly expected the Princes to pay simple, if not compound, interest. The Princes did not regard their obligations in this way; their financial position made it impossible that they should.

It seemed to Forth that as the Prince of Wales's affairs were known to be embarrassed, his chances of recovering his money would be better if he approached the Duke of York: besides it was he, who in 1790 had promised Forth that he should be recompensed for all his losses. Accordingly in November 1799 Forth wrote to the Duke to remind him of his promises. At the same time he sent him some very old Tokay, and some Merregoutte Sillery wine, described in those days as champagne, and very often drunk as a substitute. The Duke of York, unwilling to commit himself, wrote politely, after some delay, to decline the gift. He did not allude to the other part of the letter.[6]

In January 1800 Forth heard from an all too candid friend that the Prince of Wales had said in front of a large company, 'O damn him, don't mind that fellow Forth!'

This was too much. Determined to prove that he was not a fellow, Forth sent an indignant letter setting out his own and

his families' services to the Royal Family during four generations: 'he whom the Prince of Wales and the Duke of York have
repeatedly called their best and sincerest friend, whom in all
their letters they address My dear Forth, and to whom they
subscribe themselves Ever and most affectionately yours, ought
to demonstrate that the epithet is misapplied . . . Even private
individuals like me, by faithfully serving their Prince do not
diminish the lustre of their dignity . . . and although, conscious
of the vast distance that nature has placed between us, and
acknowledging the immense superiority that Your Royal
Highness possesses over me in every respect, I may yet with all
humility say, This world 'tis true Was made for Caesar, but for
for Titus too'. The Prince did not reply.[7]

Another letter to the Duke of York brought a reply from
William Adam, his legal adviser, asking to see the bonds. This
letter offended Forth, partly because he thought himself
entitled to deal directly with the Duke, and partly because it
did not address him with proper respect: Adam had not written
out his name in full, or followed it by the three etceteras which
good manners required. Forth's protests were ignored.

In his irritation Forth began to think that his only remedy
against the Duke of York was a legal action. He consulted Sir
Francis Buller, Justice of the Common Pleas, and on his advice,
drew up a Memoir of everything that had happened in connexion with the loans. He called this Memoir *A Plain State of
Facts*. If it gained the publicity of a Court of Law it would
undoubtedly be very embarrassing for the Princes. Forth did
not say in so many words that payment of the original bonds
was contingent on the death of the King, since this might have
resulted in a charge of High Treason against the Princes and
himself, nor did he mention that the guarantor of the loan was
the regicide Duke of Orleans. But it would be sufficiently
awkward to disclose that in 1790 the Princes were proposing
to borrow money from any source except the Portland Committee. Nor was Forth's aim solely to embarrass the Princes;
he hoped in making the affair public, he would have public
sympathy on his side.[8]

At this point, fortunately as it turned out, Forth was brought
into contact with Lord Moira. Lieutenant General the Earl of

Moira, to give him his full title, was an intimate of the Prince of Wales, a member of the Opposition, and a soldier both energetic and successful. He was also one of the few able and honest men in the service of the Prince of Wales. He was helping the young Duke of Orleans, Louis-Philippe, to disentangle his father's business affairs in England. Forth was asked to explain these to him. At the meeting Forth found it necessary to mention the loans of 1789 and 1790 and the loss of his East India stock. He showed Moira his Memoir. Moira was therefore in a position to mediate between the Prince of Wales and Forth at the very moment when a disinterested adviser was needed most.

In the negotiations that followed it is plain that Moira sympathized with Forth, and thought that the Princes had treated him shabbily, though of course he did not say so. But he also realized that Forth would damage his own interests if he threatened a law suit. He agreed to meet Forth and Lord Kinnaird, who was now one of Forth's bankers, at Forth's house on Sunday 20 April 1800. The two men spent three hours looking at Forth's papers, particularly the three bonds which the Prince of Wales had given him. Afterwards they reported their findings to the Prince of Wales, who asked them to see Forth again a few days later, on 29 April.

Meanwhile the Duke of York and his advisers decided to make a separate investigation. Their investigator was the banker, Thomas Hammersley, who had first involved Forth in the Princes' financial affairs and now had a banking house of his own. He was obliged to ask Forth to remind him what had happened. His letter enraged Forth. He suspected that Hammersley was making himself useful to the Duke of York in the hope of being offered a baronetcy, and commented, 'it is curious to remark that this interloper, who was held as omniscient in the business, and was the Princes' compass to guide them among the shoals of forgetfulness (as to having given the bonds) and the rocks of uncertainty (how far their letters might contradict their assertions) was obliged to apply to me for the first letters of the alphabet of this hypothetical creed . . . to this Baronet of the future I answered in a simple conscientious manner'.

It would have been wiser if Forth had allowed matters to take their course until he saw Moira and Kinnaird again. But he heard that the Duke of York was urging the Prince of Wales to delay the investigation, and he wrote to Moira begging to be allowed to see both the Princes so that he might justify himself to them. He ended his letter with a paragraph which could only be interpreted as a threat: 'I shall impatiently wait for orders till Sunday next, May 4. *After* that day I shall entertain no further hopes, and I here inform your Lordship that *after* that day I shall no longer be able to do what I now can. With all my natural frankness, I will tell you my intentions. Viz: First I shall begin by justifying my character, my situation in life, and ancientry, and when the world knows who I am, and why I am forced to apply to the laws of my country, they will compassionately participate in my sufferings. Then, but not till then, I shall commence a suit against the person whom eminent counsel shall point out, and abide the decisions of an English jury and, if necessary, an English Chancellor.'[9]

Moira answered immediately. He advised Forth to meet Kinnaird as planned, and added, 'I cannot, retaining any view of amicable termination, shew that letter either to the Prince of Wales or Duke of York, for I am confident that they would insist on taking legal steps accordingly. As I am sincerely desirous that such extremities should be avoided, I will, with your permission, suppress any mention of that letter, and the business shall go on in the track I was pursuing'.[10]

At 12.00 on Tuesday 29 April Moira and Kinnaird once again came to Manchester Square to examine Forth's papers. At last they told Forth that the Prince of Wales would like to complete the whole business before 10 May. They discussed various alternatives, until Kinnaird said, 'Give me a pen and ink, and I will reduce them to writing'. Forth and Moira stood by while he did so. Forth says that at this point their only difference of opinion concerned the amount of the first down payment. Moira thought this should be £3,000, while Forth said that since he owed his bankers £2,000, he would be content with this for the present. Kinnaird, said, 'Egad, as I am to find the money, Lord Moira, you must consult me, nor must you distress yourself neither by your gallantry'.[11]

It was finally agreed that Forth should receive a down payment of not less than £2,000; the agreement also provided that in the presence of Moira and Kinnaird Forth should burn all the papers, except the three bonds. In order to invalidate any spurious papers which might appear later, he would afterwards sign a declaration to say he had done so. In return, interest on the bonds would be paid regularly, and the arrears would be repaid in regular instalments.

Forth asked Moira if he was authorised by the Prince of Wales to make these proposals. Moira answered, 'I have full power from the Prince to act as I please. I will not pledge myself to say that the Prince will punctually fulfil the terms, but I pledge my word of honour that I will be responsible for paying the money'.

The meeting had lasted two hours. As soon as it was over Forth went to ask his lawyer to draw up an agreement embodying the terms suggested by Kinnaird. The next day he attended at the Public Office at Marlborough Street, and swore an affidavit that when Moira and Kinnard fulfilled their side of the agreement, he would burn all the papers in their presence. He then fetched the agreement from his lawyers, put all the Princes' letters and other papers in a box, and put the box in his strong-room.

Friday 2 May, had been appointed for the meeting when the agreement was to be signed, the papers burnt, and the first instalment of the arrears paid. At 11.00 Forth was ready. There was no sign of Kinnaird or Moira. At 12.00 Forth sent a servant with a note to Kinnaird. Kinnaird was not at home. Forth sent again an hour later, with the same result. He also sent a note to Moira, but he had gone to Carlton House. Forth waited until 6.00, when a note arrived from Kinnaird: 'Half past five—just come home to dinner. *Tranquillisez-vous, je vous prie.* I this day received a letter from the noble Lord, dated last night, but delivered to me at 11.00 this day, as I was going out to fulfil an engagement which has detained me until a quarter of an hour ago. I am therein desired to make an appointment with you to receive us any morning you please. If Tuesday morning at 11.00 exact should suit you, I will write and fix that hour.'

3

It was the Duke of York who had caused the delay. The previous day he had been with the Prince of Wales, and told him that as he himself had not been present when the bonds were given to Forth, he was not a party to the transaction, and did not consider himself under any obligation to pay interest. The Duke went even further; he managed to persuade the Prince that he had not given Forth the bonds at all. The Duke was ready, and indeed anxious to refer the matter to his law officers: if a law suit did not decide in his favour, it would undoubtedly delay a settlement, perhaps for years.

All this was very bitter for Forth. He had never expected the Princes to deny their part in the transactions. By doing so they implied that he was lying, and that his claim was a fraudulent one. He was now not only reclaiming his money, he was defending his honour.

Happily he had the support of Moira and Kinnaird. For the third time they examined his papers; 'They authenticated that I had £15,000 Indian stock standing in my name in the years 1787, 1788 and 1789, worth £25,000 at 170, the then price; likewise that my banker's book proved that for four years prior and subsequent to the year 1789 my running account was above £26,000 a year. They contrasted the dates of the sale of my Indian stock, the time of the annuities purchased for me of £2,100 per year; the time of the money being given to the Prince of Wales by draft on my bankers.' They were completely satisfied with what they found. Moira said that on the Prince of Wales's instructions, he would let the Duke of York know their conclusions, and arrange a meeting between Forth and the Duke. But he also said that he was opposed to any kind of legal action, and he had told the Prince of Wales that if legal men were to take up the affair, he would from that moment wash his hand of it.

A meeting was eventually arranged for 13 May at Ransom and Morland's bank. At 11.00 the evening before, Kinnaird visited Forth, and sat talking for two hours at his bedside. He particularly warned him not to let his feelings run away with him, whatever might be said next day. Forth gave his word of honour that he would restrain himself. It was as well that he did so; the meeting proved a severe test of his temper.

At 9.00 in the morning Forth was at the banking house at 57 Pall Mall, where, in a long, chilly room on the first floor, the meeting was to take place. Moira arrived soon after Forth, bringing with him Charles Bicknell, the Prince of Wales's legal adviser. The Duke of York, with his legal adviser William Adam, was also there, and so was old Mr. Morland, the senior partner of the bank. Kinnaird was late, and although Forth asked if they could wait until he came, the proceedings began without him.[11]

Forth began by saying that he understood the Duke of York wished to know just what bonds were in Forth's possession. The Duke nodded assent. Forth continued that he supposed it unnecessary to relate the history of the bonds.

'Yes, yes', exclaimed the Duke and Adam together, 'they are precisely the bonds which we wish to have accounted for.'

'Then', said Forth, 'your Royal Highness must find them or their ashes at York House, as they were burnt there before you and the Prince of Wales by Mr. Hammersley on 1 January 1790; but I will shew those bonds which the Prince of Wales gave me.' He then produced the three bonds, with the princes' signatures and seals. They made a considerable sensation. Forth says that there was a visible change of countenance and tone of voice; the lawyers affected a mild deportment and more civility, while the Duke of York twisted and turned about, and bit his nails. Forth demanded, 'Am I now a forger?'

A general cry answered, 'No one said it, no one ever supposed it'.

Forth replied, 'I know by whom it was said.' There was a short silence. Then the Duke of York said, 'These are certainly my signatures and my seals. The bonds are perfectly right—I own that I had totally forgot them.'

But when Forth went on to explain how and when the Prince of Wales had given him the bonds, the Duke of York and Adam still maintained that the Duke knew nothing of his brother's gift, and that Forth had never applied to him for interest. Forth asked if he might mention the conversation in which York had pressed him to give up all claim to repayment from the revenues of the Duchy of Cornwall. Permission was given, and Forth read out the relevant part of his Memoir.

The Duke of York merely said, 'It may be so, but I don't recollect it.' The other men were more impressed. Adam and Bicknell asked what sums Forth had disbursed in order to recover the bonds. Forth produced bankers' and notaries' signed receipts, regularly stamped, specifying that money totalling £825 had been received on account of the Prince of Wales and the Duke of York. Morland, the banker, was able to authenticate the signatures. At that Bicknell said that the sum must be reimbursed immediately. The Duke of York said, 'O yes, undoubtedly.'

In order to prove that he had already applied to the Duke for payment of interest Forth produced copies of his letters. 'Well', said the Duke, 'what does that prove? Where are any answers from me?' Forth read out the answers.

His Royal Highness, Forth's narrative continues, took the answer to my letter of 22nd April out of my hand, looked at it, and said, 'I did not write that, it is not my writing'. Everyone looked at me. I exclaimed, with some emotion, 'What, another suspicion of forgery!' Lord Kinnaird whispered to me, and I, thank God, said nothing disrespectful. I then handed over his answer to my letter of 5 December. The Duke of York said, 'that letter is not written by me.' 'By whom then, Sir, is it written?' He answered, 'By my secretary, Captain Taylor.' I exclaimed, 'Good God! and by whom then it is signed?' He answered, 'O, I believe the signature is my writing.' I lost patience, bounced up from the table, collected my papers, and I am told that, agitated, and in a moment of grateful recollection of the King's admirable uprightness, I shook my head and said, 'Your father would not have spoken or acted thus.' What were the looks or gestures of the by-standers I do not know. I went to the bottom of a long room to lock up my papers, and was so overcome by sorrow that I remained there some minutes to recover myself.

When Forth returned to the table he heard William Adam finishing a legal argument to prove a distinction between acknowledging and not denying a charge. Forth remarked that he did not think that Lord Chief Justice Kenyon and a special jury would be easily persuaded that because a man replied to only part of a letter it proved ignorance of the rest. He began to read

out a letter written to him by the Prince of Wales, but Moira
and Kinnaird checked him. Kinnaird said, 'Mr. Forth, I have it
in command from the Prince of Wales to desire that you will
not read or mention before this meeting any letters or conversation that may have passed between his Royal Highness and you.
I trust to your word of honour given to me last night.'

Forth then mentioned that the Princes' bonds had been a
misfortune to others besides himself; that Brichard, one of the
richest and most respectable notaries in Paris had been guillotined because bonds bearing the princes' names were found in
his office. He was charged with attempting to raise money on
them for the purpose of placing the Duke of York on the
throne of France. At this the Duke and Adam burst out
laughing.

Still trying to bring the Duke of York to acknowledge some
responsibility, Forth remarked that in October 1790, on the
Prince of Wales's instructions, the bonds were sent to the Duke
of Orleans in Paris to purchase his collection of pictures, which
could afterwards be sold to raise more money.

The Duke said impatiently, 'There's where I waited for
you. Now I am sure that I treated with the Duke of Orleans in
England, for I remember perfectly well dining with him at the
Duke of Queensberry's, and likewise at Newmarket.'

'I am morally certain of what I have advanced', Forth
answered, 'I know that the Duke of Orleans was at Paris.'

The Duke of York replied angrily, 'I don't believe it.'

'I know to whom I am speaking, I shall not want respect for
the King's son. But I will not say another word.'

The Duke said more gently, 'Why not? I may be mistaken;
men may differ in dates and in opinions without meaning to
give offence.' Forth bowed, and from his papers proved the Duke
of Orleans's movements from the time when he arrived in
London on Wednesday 21 October 1789, until his departure
on Friday 9 July 1790, from Brighton; he was able to show that
Orleans never left France again.

The meeting broke up into groups. Forth, still weak from
his illness, and feeling the strain of his exertions, sat by the
fire. He heard the Duke telling everyone that as the bonds were
given without his knowledge, he would accept no liability for

payment, but before he left he said to Forth, 'Mr. Forth, I am
not displeased with your conduct, you had a right to demand
payment of the interest due on these bonds. All I pretend to
say is, and I have always said it, that as the Prince of Wales
gave you the bonds when I was not present, and without my
consent, I do not think that I am bound to pay any part of the
interest due on them. But you have answered the chief purpose
of our meeting, which was for me to see the bonds, to recognize
my signature on them, and to bring to my recollection several
circumstances which I had forgotten.'

Three days later Moira and Kinnaird came to tell Forth that
the Princes were ready to repay his £825. But for the reasons
which he had already given, the Duke of York would pay none
of the money represented by the bonds, nor any interest on
them and the Prince of Wales had commanded them to say
that if the bonds were legal instruments, they must be paid,
but he himself did not recollect giving Forth the bonds to hold
as his property.

## 4

From this moment Forth's main purpose was to clear his
reputation. He was still determined to recover his money, but
his strongest efforts were in defence of his good name. His
first hope was that the Prince of Wales would make a private
acknowledgement that he had misjudged Forth; if he would
not. Forth wanted his named cleared as publicly as possible, if
necessary on a Court of Law. This was natural, but Forth was
still a sick man, and some of his proceedings were decidedly
ill-advised.

On hearing what line the Princes proposed to take Forth's
first action was perhaps unwise, but it was also generous. He
said that since the Prince of Wales did not remember giving
him the bonds, he felt he could not honourably retain them;
he said, 'I had declared everywhere, and told my great friend,
Lord Mansfield, that the Prince had given me the bonds as a
present . . . I never would attempt to force a donor, either by
law or menaces, to perform what he regretted he had promised
. . . I know that this is neither according to the rules of law,

commerce or worldly prudence, but it is according to the principles of an independent man, and the sentiments of a gallant
gentleman who says, May hemp bind those that honour can't.'

Moira and Kinnaird both told Forth that he would be imprudent to give up such a material piece of evidence for his claim
on the Princes, but Forth was resolved. Accordingly, he wrote
Bicknell a letter summarising everything that had happened,
and explaining why he felt obliged to give up the bonds. He
later read this letter out to Bicknell in the presence of Moira
and Kinnaird, and asked them to ensure that both Princes read
it. He then handed over the Bonds. In return Forth expected
Bicknell to satisfy himself from his papers that he really had
parted with his East India stock to help the princes.

When Forth had thus thrown himself on the generosity of the
Prince of Wales, he waited for some sign of recognition. When
he thought he had waited long enough, he began to talk about
terrible means of revenge which he could use if he wished. He
himself believed that his letters were respectful, resigned and
conciliating; the Princes' advisers could hardly fail to regard
them as threats. At last, in a letter to Moira written on 14 June,
Forth said that if a settlement was postponed any longer, he
would, before the end of the following week, furnish materials
for an action at Common Law against the Duke of York, and
he would also file Bills of Discovery to force the Prince of Wales
and the Duke to answer interrogatories. He proposed to bring
a further action against Moira.

Fortunately Moira was more patient than Forth. He replied
stiffly, but kindly, trying to show Forth how his proceedings
appeared to an impartial observer. He concluded, 'It is incumbent on me to say that [any intimation of proceedings at law]
must be regarded by me with perfect indifference, and I can
assure you that both the Prince of Wales and the Duke of York
are equally incapable of being influenced by any insinuation of
suits intended against them'. On a later occasion Moira assured
Forth that if he had not allowed for irritation caused by
suspense and ill-health, he would have shown Forth's letters to
the Prince; the result would certainly have been a refusal to
admit Forth's claim, since repayment could not be made in
response to threats.[12]

Moira's remonstrances produced a more temperate atmosphere. Forth wrote an apology to the Prince: 'I dare not implore forgiveness of the Prince for my intemperate letters written after six months rheumatic headaches in a sickroom; all I dare request is that his Royal Highness will forget the passionate heat of my head, and recollect only the warmth of my heart when employed in his service. A broken head and a fractured jaw often remind me of my successful zeal for his wishes, and I hope he will not add a broken heart to them by want of pity.'[13]

By July 1800 it looked as if the Prince of Wales and his brother were about to compensate Forth for his expenses, and pay him an annuity of £740 a year. The business hung fire during the summer, when everyone, including Forth, was out of town. In November Forth heard that the Prince of Wales had accepted his apology, but there was no sign of the annuity. Forth was told that the payments due to the Prince from the Treasury were also in arrears. At last on Thursday, 9 December, Colonel McMahon, the Prince of Wales's secretary, told Forth that Mr. Bicknell would wait upon him on Thursday. 'Reader', comments Forth, 'you now expect, as I did, to see bank notes, drafts of annuities with stamps, ribbons and seals . . . Why then, gentle reader, you will be as much disappointed as I was, for as Swift says, Instead of a rapturous lover, A formal apology came.'

Here Forth does not do justice to the Princes. On their behalf Bicknell offered £1,000 as reimbursement of Forth's expenses, together with an annuity of £200 a year for life. But Forth thought this insufficient. He was prepared to accept the annuity, but he wanted interest on his expenses, and a loan of £500 a year until he was able to recover the money due to him from the Duke of Orleans's estate. The Princes' financial circumstances made such a settlement impossible, and everything was once more in the melting pot.

Again Forth considered going to law. Mr. Justice Buller died in June 1800, so Forth took advice from an unnamed friend, possibly Mr. Justice Cruikshank of the Court of Common Pleas in Ireland. With his encouragement Forth directed his solicitor to bring an action against the Duke of York in the

King's Bench, and to file Bills of Discovery in the Chancery Court to compel the Princes to answer interrogatories on oath.

These cases never came to Court. It is questionable whether Forth intended that they should: their outcome was doubtful; delay, and the high cost of legal proceedings were certain. Forth placed his real hope on something different. He had always planned to make an appeal to public opinion before resorting to law. He would do so by circulating a pamphlet telling the full story of his dealings with the princes. Perhaps he had in mind the highly diverting pamphlets with which, in the 1770s, Beaumarchais had influenced opinion in Paris and confounded his opponents at law. Part of Forth's pamphlet was already written, the Memoir which summarized the loan transactions of 1789 and 1790. During 1801 Forth added to this Memoir most of the correspondence which had passed since, and filled in the gaps with a commentary composed by himself. He called the finished product his *Dikaeology* or *Plea in Defence*.

It was a highly explosive document. If it had been published it might have harmed the reputations of the Princes, low though these already were, but it would almost certainly have rendered Forth liable to a prosecution for criminal libel, the penalties for which were a severe fine or imprisonment.

Towards the end of 1801 there were more discussions on Forth's case between Moira, Kinnaird and William Baldwin, a Member of Parliament, formerly the secretary of the Portland Committee. In the course of the discussions Moira asked Forth to draw up a clear and complete statement of everything that had passed so far. Forth decided to use his *Plea in Defence*. Four copies were needed. But the pamphlet was almost as long as a book, copying it would be a laborious undertaking, and it would be dangerous to entrust it to any ordinary copyist. Forth thought it would be safer to have it printed by hand in his own house. The printers were French émigré priests who, according to Forth, scarce knew ten words of English. He read his notes to their compositor, without connecting the text, and corrected the proofs in his own room. He then gave two copies to Moira, and one to Baldwin, keeping the last copy for himself.[14]

Moira was horrified when he read the document, and was determined to keep it private. He realized the implications much better than Forth did. It was of course his duty to protect the Princes' reputations as far as he could, but he was also anxious to save Forth from prosecution. Even in causing the document to be printed it might be held that he had already published it. Nor was Moira entirely reassured when Forth explained that the priests were by the nature of their calling accustomed to keep secrets, and that these particular priests were about to return to France.

In spite of everything that could be said against it, the *Plea in Defence* nevertheless enabled Moira to bring about a settlement. By convincing Forth of the risks which he faced if he made the documents public, Moira persuaded him to settle privately. He also urged Forth to accept what it was in the Princes' power to offer. Moira then showed the *Plea* to the Prince of Wales, and easily convinced him that publication was undesirable. The Prince, who had been the object of many libellous attacks, was quite prepared to pay to suppress this one. The Duke of York agreed.

At long last, on 19 December 1801, Forth received from Bicknell a payment of £1,240, part payable by the Prince of Wales, and part by the Duke of York. When Forth protested that this was less than his due, Bicknell told him that he was lucky to receive even so much; several creditors of long standing had been put off on his account.

The following year, when he was ill and in great pain, Forth again pressed the Princes' advisers to pay more. His efforts were unavailing; he succeeded only in exasperating Moira, and making the Prince so angry that Forth not only felt bound to write a humble letter of apology, but promised to burn all his copies of the *Plea*. He did so on 3 April 1802, finally acknowledging that he had no real hope of repayment. He had been misled by his too simple trust in the Prince of Wales and his brother. He expected from them the plain dealing which, until the Prince of Wales intervened, he had received from the Duke of Orleans. It must be admitted that as business associates the English Princes compared very unfavourably with the regicide Duke.

# IV.  ELIZA'S  HUSBAND

*Chapter Fourteen*

## THE REVENANT

### 1

WHILE FORTH was still struggling to recover his money from the princes he made the choice which shaped the last years of his life. He determined to return to Paris to reclaim the funds which were due to him from the Duke of Orleans's estate. There was a truce between England and France, and communication between the two countries was now possible.

Even while the war continued Forth began to make his plans. He told the Prince of Wales in November 1800 that he was only waiting to hear if the Prince would give him an annuity before deciding whether, as he put it, to vegetate in his own house in London, or else be obliged to let it, and die of a broken heart on friendless, foreign soil.

Financial considerations and his dispute with the princes were doubtless Forth's main reasons for contemplating a return to Paris, but there was another motive. In November 1800 Madame de Genetines went back to France: 'the constant companion of all my distresses and sickness for ten years', wrote Forth to the Prince of Wales, 'was last week oblig'd to return to her cursed country which murdered her friends, and robb'd her. I could not support the prospect of her starving here.'[1] If Madame de Genetines, Mimi, and the now seven-year-old Richard Rettfort were in Paris, Forth's situation would not be quite so friendless as he painted it.

Throughout 1801 Forth continued to make plans, until the signature of the Preliminaries of Peace in October made it possible to put them into effect. His first approach was to the newly appointed French Plenipotentiary in London.

It was probably at this time that Forth's friend, David
Scott, who had recently resigned the Chairmanship of the
East India Company, proposed that Forth should travel to Paris
with him, and share expenses. In Paris Forth would make
common cause with a client of Scott's Bombay Agency house.
This man, John Petrie who, like Forth, had claims against the
French government, was to play an important part in Forth's
life.

But any idea of leaving England was laid aside when, in
December 1801, Forth fell ill. Much of the time he was in such
pain that his doctors again prescribed large quantities of hemlock. This was Betsy's opportunity; now that her rival was in
France, she came back to nurse Forth. Almost every day she
drove over from Hans Place to Manchester Square. Betty
sometimes came with her, and when her father was well enough,
she solaced him by playing Mozart. Less soothing were his visits
from Nat, who was now planning to take Holy Orders. Married
at 17, and already the father of a young family, Nat was always
in debt. Forth usually ended by settling his demands, but they
were a constant annoyance to a man who took pride in paying
his own debts promptly.

It was five months before Forth was well enough to leave
the house, but in the intervals when he was free of pain, he
continued to prepare for his return to Paris. Gradually he dealt
with his outstanding affairs in England, one of which was the
unsatisfactory conclusion of his dealings with the princes.
There were also letters to be written to his men of business in
England and France, passports to be obtained, an inventory to
be made of the Manchester Square house and its contents,
servants to be dismissed. By the time the Peace of Amiens was
proclaimed on 29 April 1802 most of Forth's arrangements
were complete.

Some of these related to Betsy's comfort. For her bodily
ease he ordered a new carriage at Exalls, and to set her mind at
rest, he arranged a solemn form of reconciliation. On 29 April
in Forth's bedroom, Layard, the Dean of Bristol, administered
Holy Communion to Forth and Betsy in the presence of two
witnesses. The banker, Thomas Hammersley, who was one
of them, did not know that the couple had never been married,

and he regarded the service as the renewal of marriage vows
between a husband and wife after many years of estrangement.
No doubt this was Forth's intention. It is to be hoped that
Betsy derived strength from the ceremony to support her in
the long separation which was soon to take place.

On 11 May Forth left the house for the first time in 20
weeks. During the next ten days he made his final preparations,
and at 9.30 on Sunday 23 May, he left London on what was to
be the last of his continental expeditions. It was quite unlike
his former rapid journeys. He was still far from fit, and he was
accompanied by Macartan, his doctor. At Boulogne he was
taken very ill, and was forced to rest there for 24 hours.
Travelling slowly, he arrived at Paris at 5.30 on 30 May. The
Genetines family were there to welcome him.

2

Paris appeared very different from the city Forth had known.
The buildings seemed shabby and neglected, the streets had
different names, and the people who walked in them wore such
extraordinary clothes that it looked as if they were in fancy
dress. Such costumes were the outward signs of a changed and
disoriented society. It was not surprising that there was little
laughter to be heard. There was hardly anyone whose material
circumstances had not been entirely altered, or who, at a deeper
level, had not suffered loss, anxiety, fear and disillusion. As one
returned émigré said: 'there has been a complete break between
the generation which reached man's estate in 1789 and those
who grew up since that date. For the first time since the world
began, there has been a break in continuity between those who
died and those who survived . . . I feel as if I appear as a ghost
from a different age . . . There is nothing in common between
us, neither ideas, nor memories, nor interests; there is no
common approach to men or facts.'[2]

The English visitors, who were numerous, found that society
in Paris was divided into three main groups: there were the men
who governed France, with Bonaparte, the First Consul,
steadily out-distancing the rest; there was the old nobility,
many of them in very reduced circumstances, and others

feigning poverty because it was fashionable; and there were the
new rich, the bankers, financiers and contractors, who had
made fortunes in the wake of the Revolutionary armies. Most
of the English visitors frequented this group mainly out of
curiosity, but it was with these that Forth's business lay, and
among them that he renewed several friendships.

One of these old friends was the notary, Rouen. He was now
Mayor of the 2nd Arrondissement of Paris, an influential,
prosperous man, the owner of valuable urban property, and the
possessor of an agreeable country house at Taverny in the
forest of St. Leu. Another former friend and colleague, Baroud,
the brother of Madame de Genetines, had survived imprisonment during the Revolution to prosper in its aftermath. During
the war with England, when cotton imports were interrupted,
Baroud, always an opportunist, took advantage of the situation
to develop several industrial companies which exploited new
methods of spinning and carding cotton. Yet another acquaintance was the banker, Perregaux, the Paris agent of Forth's
London bank. An English guide book of the day remarked that
Perregaux 'treats the English who have letters of credit on his
house with the most polite and liberal attention, and the
pleasure of a short residence is much increased by his civil-
ities'.[3] He could well afford to offer generous hospitality; he
was more flourishing than he had ever been as a result of
many profitable contacts with the new régime. He lived grandly
in the Rue de Mont Blanc in a house that had once belonged to
Necker, and had married his daughter to General Marmont,
afterwards Marshal and Duke de Raguse.

All his friends received Forth affectionately. They eased him
through the formalities required for a residence in Paris, and
pointed out the right officials to approach. When, only a week
after his arrival, he had an attack of the stone, and suffered
36 hours of severe pain, he was able to write in his Diary:
'visits and kindness from everyone'. Trochereau, his man of
business for many years, sent him wine.

Forth's main concern was to obtain regular payments on his
annuities, together with repayment of arrears, and the reimbursement of the money which he had lent to the Duke of
Orleans. As a pledge of his indebtedness, Orleans, before he left

England in 1790, had given Forth an extremely valuable diamond. Forth brought this with him to Paris to show that he had claims on the Orleans estate. The young Duke was an exile in England, and his property was in the hands of the administrators of the Biens Nationaux. Forth, as a foreigner with claims on the administrators, must approach the office of Liquidation Général, bringing a sheaf of documents to substantiate his claim. He must produce the official contract for the purchase of his annuities; furnish birth certificates and powers of attorney; and certificates to show that the annuitants, Betsy, Nat and himself were all living. Only after all those documents had not only been lodged but accepted could Forth hope to receive anything. Even then he would be paid only a proportion of his annual payments; the remainder would be paid in French Treasury bonds of little negotiable value. As to the arrears, it seemed likely that repayment might be withheld for a long time.[4]

The requirements were not unreasonable, but they provided plenty of opportunities for bureaucratic delay. It was lucky for Forth that he did not depend entirely on his annuities to meet the expenses of living in Paris. He could still draw on his London bank, and evidently did so to some purpose. Not long after his arrival he rented an apartment and hired servants. Most English visitors found rent, wages and food dear in Paris —fuel in particular at £1 6s. a load of wood was exceptionally expensive. But Forth lived comfortably; he entertained his friends in his apartment, and, as usual, paid his servants' wages on the first day of the week.

Gradually Forth picked up the threads of his former life in Paris. Besides Rouen and his circle, other acquaintances reappeared. Madame Du Barry's relations came forward to discover what had become of her stolen jewels, but Forth could give them little comfort. He had hardly more satisfactory news for Madame de Genlis and her family.

For many years Forth had acted as English agent for M. de Genlis's Sillery wine. It was sold by Forth's wine merchants, Messrs. Christopher and Messrs. Dupuis, and the proceeds were sent by Forth to M. de Genlis. But early in the Revolution Genlis borrowed 12,000 livres of Forth, and arranged for him to repay himself out of the sales of the Sillery. To complicate matters still further, Genlis gave his mistress, who was about to leave France, permission to sell a certain quantity of Sillery for her own benefit in London. 'My wife', he said, 'makes herself agreeable to you at present, but as soon as I am dead, she will show you the door.' Now Genlis was dead, and his wife and family extremely hard up. They hoped that Forth would have money to pay over to them. Instead, to their great disappointment, he produced accounts to prove that Genlis had died considerably in his debt.[5]

A happier reunion was with Hermione Compton, now Madame Collard. During the Revolution she had been invaluable to Pulchérie de Genlis, who had adopted her; she had looked after Pulchérie's children when their mother was imprisoned, and shown her devotion in many ways.

Sometimes Forth amused himself by revisiting the places which he had known in earlier days. One of these was the Palais Royal, where the Tribune now held its sittings; but very few people called it the *Palais du Tribunat,* any more than they called the surrounding gardens the *Jardins Egalité.* One summer day Forth climbed the dusty road to Monceau. In 1802 the now extremely urban Rue de Courcelles was a country road with a drainage runnel down the middle; it climbed steeply between walls, over which acacias leaned, filling the runnel with white petals. The Pavilion, where Orleans once held his liveliest parties, was empty; the park was a public garden, with a restaurant in the lodge at the gates. Beyond the boundary wall of the park was the *Cimetière des Errancis* in which many victims of the guillotine were buried, including, some said, Orleans himself.[6]

As the summer went on, and Paris became very hot, Rouen invited Forth to his country house at Taverny: often Baroud; and the Genetines were also of the party. Billiards was one of the great amusements on these occasions; it was one of the popular sports of the time, and one at which Forth excelled.

Gradually Forth drifted back into his liaison with Madame de Genetines. His Diary entries are cryptic, but the pattern is unmistakable: 'dine Gs'; 'chat at Gs'; 'see Gs home'; and on 5 July, when Forth also recorded the transit of Mars: 'Gs renova'. It was probably inevitable.

3

But while Forth was renewing these old ties, he was also developing a quite new, and increasingly absorbing, set of relationships. They originated in a business connexion with John Petrie.

Petrie was an East India merchant, a nabob, to use the contemporary expression. Eighteenth-century men had a clear conception of this exotic species; in fact it was rarer than they supposed, but Petrie was undoubtedly a genuine specimen. In particular he showed a vein of ruthlessness which was an essential characteristic of a nabob. He began his career in India as a soldier in the service of the East India Company. In 1766, with other officers, he was cashiered by Clive for mutiny. A stricter limitation on allowances was the cause of this, and since a right to make a fortune was one of Pertie's fundamental convictions, it was hardly surprising that, on his return to England, he should have written in defence of his views, and in criticism of Clive. Later he succeeded in making a fortune on the west coast of India in territories over which the Company's power was weak. He also had interests in Madras, where his brother, William, was a member of Council. In the 1790s the Petrie brothers sided with the men who were working to break the East India Company's shipping monopoly; this formed a link with David Scott, whose influence in the Company was directed to that purpose.

A very rich man, Petrie returned to England to enjoy his fortune. A seat in Parliament was the next step in his career, and he, or rather his brother, set out to acquire a suitable pocket borough. Gatton, near Reigate in Surrey, was his choice, a borough represented by two members. The ownership, at election-time, of a particular plot of land in Gatton Park conferred on two voters the right of electing these two members. William Petrie bought Gatton Park and its fine mansion for £110,000 in 1794, and settled it in trust on his brother and his heirs. It looked as if John Petrie could look forward to many years of representing Gatton in Parliament: in fact he sat for a few years in the Parliament of 1796.[7]

Petrie's business concerns were not exclusively East Indian. He also owned mortgages on property in the West Indian island of Tobago. West Indian mortgages carried a higher rate of interest than it was legal to charge in England, and for that reason were considered a profitable investment. But in the peace treaties which ended the American War of Independence Tobago became a French possession, and Petrie found himself a French citizen in respect of his property there. This made it possible for him to represent Tobago in the States General in 1789, as well as in the Constituent Assembly, and to become perhaps the only Englishman to have sat in a French and in an English parliament. When France declared war on England in 1793 Petrie left France, and was entirely cut off from Tobago: when the war ended he returned to Paris to lay a claim against the French government.

This was the man to whom David Scott introduced Forth on 31 May, the day after Forth's arrival in Paris. The two men found each other congenial; the fact that both were viola players was undoubtedly a link. Here as so often a musical thread underlay Forth's relationships. It was also obvious that Forth and Petrie could be very useful to each other. Petrie's term of office in the States General and the Constituent Assembly had made him acquainted with many of the men now in office. Forth, on his side, knew men who had been connected with the administration of the Duke of Orleans's estates, and were now in government posts, for instance Henri Shée, Count d'Alton, once Orleans's Secrétaire des Commandements, and Denis Joseph Delaunay, Orleans's former Receiver General.

Scott, Forth and Petrie agreed to do nothing 'without the clearest mutual communication'. They would work openly with the British Ambassador and the administration in France. But they were prepared, as Forth phrased it, 'to push privately if necessary', and to risk not more than £100 or £150 in presents or douceurs. Such pressure might be exerted on Delaunay, Josephine Bonaparte, and one of her Tascher de la Pagerie relations.[8] It may be said in parentheses that this scale was altogether too modest at a time when, with Talleyrand, the Minister of Foreign Affairs, as an outstanding example, those in official positions felt justified in using them in order to make immense fortunes.

Forth visited Shée soon after his first meeting with Petrie, and on several other occasions. He was also received by Defermont, a member of the Conseil d'Etat with responsibility for the liquidation of the National Debt. Forth found Defermont most amiable, but he temporized: not for nothing had he been nicknamed *Fermons la caisse*. Forth's and Petrie's business could not be hurried. As one Frenchman remarked bitterly after a later Revolution: 'on rasera les palais, on n'abolira jamais les antichambres'.

Through Petrie, Forth met a number of his friends and associates with East Indian interests. Many of them had been involved in the attempts to break the monopoly of the French East India Company, and were now trying to recover the funds which had been sequestrated in 1793. William Bolts, one of the East India Company's most unsatisfactory servants, was one of the speculators concerned; others were the bankers, Walter Boyd and Robert Kerr.

Another of Petrie's friends was Sir Elijah Impey, who had been Chief Justice in Bengal when Warren Hastings was Governor General: like Hastings he had been threatened with impeachment; unlike Hastings he was never brought to trial. While in India he used his salary as a basis for speculation, and because of East India Company prohibitions on taking currency out of India, he remitted his gains to England through other countries, of which France was one. His funds were blocked during the Revolution and he had come to Paris with his his wife and family in an attempt to recover his investment. When he was Chief Justice he had once awarded a very large sum to Georges Grand, the banker, in damages for his wife's adultery. Now he found the former Madame Grand presiding over a house in Neuilly as the mistress, and later, the wife of Talleyrand, while her ex-husband was very much concerned with the financial business which Impey had come to Paris to settle.[9]

Placed in similar circumstances, Forth, Petrie and Impey inevitably saw much of each other. But Forth's relations with Petrie took on a different character when Petrie's wife and daughters came to Paris in August 1802. Successful in so many ways, Petrie had no son to inherit his fortune. Two little Johns, born of different mothers, died in infancy, and were buried in the family vault at Lewisham. Seven daughters survived, Peggy, Nancy, Eliza, Harriet, born of the first marriage, Emily, Charlotte and Jenny of the second: their ages ranged from 22 to seven.

The coming of this family party made a great difference to Forth. He enjoyed the feminine society of the elegant, accomplished elder girls and their stepmother, Petrie's second wife; he was happy with the younger children. Very soon he had made a note of everyone's birthday, including those of Mr. and Mrs. Petrie, so that these fête days could be fittingly celebrated when they came round. With the Petries he visited the sights of Paris, the statues and pictures in the Louvre, the illuminations when Bonaparte was chosen Consul for life. He took the Petries to eat ices at Tivoli or Frascati. In the autumn, when the colder weather came, he entertained them in his own apartment or visited them in theirs. After one party for the Petries, at which the Rouens and the Genetines were also present, Forth's Diary entry reads: 'Laugh till 10'.

In October Forth took a large apartment off the Place Vendôme at 2 Rue Neuve des Capucines. He installed a piano and a billiard table, and prepared to entertain. The Petries were his first guests. On 28 November, the day on which the lamps were lighted for the first time, Forth gave a dinner for 13 people, and 26 came in later to play billiards. To celebrate the Feast of Kings on Twelfth Night 1803 there was a supper for 30 with punch and billiards.

Now there were plenty of sympathisers to care for Forth during his recurrent attacks of stone. But above all there were friends to make music and to laugh with. Nor was the friendship one-sided; to the Petries Forth was the friend of the family, the welcome and expected guest. In the early months of 1803 they moved into an apartment in the Montmartre quarter, 7 Rue Blanche. Almost every day Forth dined or spent the evening there. At last it seemed natural to take rooms in the same house.

Outside the world of No. 7, where Forth was renewing his youth *à l'ombre des jeunes filles en fleurs*, relations between France and England were becoming tense. They were broken off entirely in May 1803.

## Chapter Fifteen

# HUSBAND AND WIFE

## 1

THE ENGLISH, who had so light-heartedly visited the sights of Paris and gossiped in the salons, were now unwelcome guests. On May 12 the British Ambassador left Paris. On 21 May, on the grounds that all Englishmen over 16 and under 60 were potential militiamen, Napoleon decreed that they should be held as prisoners of war. He was resolved, it was said, that on the evening of the day on which the Decree came into force not an Englishman should be found in the most obscure theatre or the worst restaurant in Paris. The final enactment was not quite so severe but, as a preliminary, all Englishmen of military age were ordered to report to some specified centre—for those in Paris it was Fontainebleau—there to declare themselves prisoners of war. If they were willing to do this they were allowed to remain at large on parole; those who did not were to be detained in one of the French fortress towns.

It was a breach of international law to treat civilians as if they were serving soldiers or sailors. The British government refused to consider the arrests valid, but this was no help to the people concerned, many of whom found themselves in very uncomfortable conditions in Verdun and elsewhere.

Forth was not one of them. He did not report to Fontainebleau with his fellow-countrymen, nor at this time does his Diary mention any visit to a Mayor or Prefect. He was ill when the Decree was published, and perhaps this made it possible to delay action. No doubt someone vouched for him; possibly it was Rouen as Mayor of the District in which Forth was living, possibly it was Perregaux the banker. At all events Forth's life continued in a tranquil round of business discussions and social visits as if relations between England and France were still normal.

Petrie was another exception. His status as ex-Representative for the Island of Tobago in the Constituent Assembly now served him well. Tobago was in French hands at the end of the war. In the peace negotiations there was a proposal to restore it to England as compensation for English expenditure on French prisoners of war. But this led to such a complicated series of calculations that the position was still uncertain when diplomatic relations were broken off. Since Tobago had not been handed over to England Petrie was able to claim that he was a French citizen, exempt from the provisions of the Decree, and able, with his family, to come and go freely in Paris and elsewhere.

Petrie's friend, Sir Elijah Impey, was in a more difficult position. Like Forth and Petrie he still had unfinished business in Paris. He did not want to leave until his case had been heard in the French Court of Appeal. But he could not exert quite the influence that Forth or Petrie could. Eventually however with the help of his own friends—one would like to think that these included Madame Grand—he was allowed to remain in Paris on parole.

Although for the present Forth and his friends escaped the most uncomfortable effects of Napoleon's Decree, war had now been declared, and they were in an enemy country. Their immediate friends and associates entertained them, the Rouens, Trochereau, the Genetines, the Barouds, and even Perregaux, increasingly rich and influential, but in other drawing-rooms where Englishmen had been welcome they were now treated coldly. It is with a certain air of defiance that on 4 June, King George III's birthday, Forth recorded, 'King's Health, merry'.

2

The change in the international situation coincided with an emotional crisis in Forth's life. When he first made the acquaintance of John Petrie's family he made no distinction between the three older girls. But gradually his feelings crystal-

lized around Eliza, Petrie's third daughter. She was 18, very
pretty, with beautiful eyes, and the promise of greater beauty
to come. Probably Forth intended no more than a flirtation.
He thought of himself as a married man, and was so regarded
by the Petries. Then in March 1803 Betsy was known to be
very ill. The regular correspondence between her and Forth
ceased on 21 March. Letters came from Forth's daughter Betty,
and from the doctor. If Betsy were to die, Forth would be free.
He allowed his feelings for Eliza full play. 'Disclosure', he wrote
on 24 April; and next day, 'confession, conversation'. On 5 May
he wrote, 'dénouement . . . ill with grief . . . happy issue with
four girls'.

These entries, interspersed between notes of people seen and
other engagements, can be interpreted in more than one way.
But the most likely explanation is that Petrie, believing Forth
to be married, thought that the flirtation was going too far, and
objected. Forth explained his situation, and was allowed to continue seeing Eliza.

This was the position at the time war was declared. The
international situation worked in Forth's favour. In the narro-
ing circle of English people in Paris Forth and the Petries were
necessarily drawn closer together, sharing as they did the
problems of a group of foreigners in a potentially hostile
country. Throughout the summer and autumn of 1803 Forth's
courtship continued. On 5 July, Eliza's nineteenth birthday,
Forth gave her a necklace. By Christmas, when he gave her his
portrait, he was her accepted suitor.

Looked at from any angle it was a surprising match. The
bridegroom was 59. He had one family in London and another
in Paris, and he was in poor health. The bride was 19. No doubt
she liked Forth well enough; he knew how to make himself
agreeable, and was generous with presents and entertainment;
it was flattering to be courted, and to find a husband sooner
than her older sisters. She may even have felt a degree of calf
love. But when a young girl pictures her ideal husband he is not
likely to be a man as old as Forth must have seemed to Eliza.
Moreover she would have to assume responsibility for Forth's
ten-year-old illegitimate son, Richard Rettfort. For Eliza it
must have been mainly a *mariage de raison*.

This is also how it must have appeared to John Petrie. If he had not been cut off in Paris, and restricted in his choice of son-in-law, he might not have chosen Forth. But he could not leave France, he had three daughters of marriage-able age; he was a merchant and an opportunist; he took the best offer open at the time. A man of the eighteenth century, he would not be unduly troubled by Forth's illegitimate families; such things were to be expected. He knew that Forth was kind, and he could be reasonably sure that Eliza would be treated well. He also knew that Forth had money, and what was much more to the point, funds available in Paris. He was also aware of the state of Forth's health, and the increasing frequency of his illnesses. It must have occurred to him that his daughter's marriage might not last long, and that she would then find herself a well-endowed widow.

If Petrie's mind worked in this direction Forth's certainly did not. He was as yet more inconvenienced than worried by his ailments. The fact that he sat for his portrait shows a degree of self-satisfaction. It was apparently without misgivings that he began to make preparations for his marriage. Settlements must be made, and his relations with Madame de Genetines and Betsy must be regularized.

Madame de Genetines did not hide her distress, but she was in no position to forbid the banns. There was in any case no question of a complete break. Relations would be more formal, but she was the mother of Forth's son, and would continue to meet Forth in his own house as well as in the society of the Rouens, and of her brother, Baroud.

The question of Betsy and her children was much more delicate. Forth could not announce his forthcoming marriage without also explaining that Betsy and he had never been legally married. Nat and Betty had no idea of this; it would come as a cruel shock to learn that they were illegitimate. Betsy was too ill to be told anything, but on 26 March Forth wrote to Mr. Morland, his London banker, enclosing a letter for Nat. This no doubt contained Forth's explanation, though what he said there is now no means of knowing. It must have been an appallingly difficult letter to write, and it evidently failed to convince, since, years later, Nat continued to maintain that his parents' marriage was legal.

Forth was leaving Nat and Betty in a very unpleasant situation, but he did what he could to look after their financial interests when the time came to draw up the marriage settlements. By doing so he complicated the discussions about this almost always contentious subject. Sir Elijah Impey was called in to give Forth and Petrie the benefit of his expert legal advice, and to hold the balance between them. The final agreement showed that he tipped the scales very much in Petrie's favour.

By a settlement, signed 24 April, Forth put aside a sum of £10,000 for Eliza. Invested in English funds, it would provide an income during Forth's lifetime; on his death Eliza would keep a life interest in the sum, and when she died her children by Forth would inherit the capital. If she had no children by Forth, the capital would revert to Forth's other children or their descendants. This was the best that Forth could do for Nat, Betty and Richard Rettfort. In return he made himself responsible for all the household expenses which he and Eliza might incur, even if, so the agreement insisted, he had not sufficient funds available. He would pay for 'lodgings, fire and candles, provisions, education of children, wages of servants, and all other expenses, as well in sickness as in health, even the maintenance of the said intended future wife, *whether his revenue be sufficient or not*'. In his eagerness to marry Eliza, Forth allowed Petrie to drive a hard bargain, one which Forth might well come to regret.[1]

Petrie made no contribution whatsoever to his daughter's maintenance. This seems strange from a man who had in the past been extremely rich on his own account, and stood to inherit Gatton Park, and probably a considerable fortune, from his brother. But for the time being he was hard pressed, and only too pleased to have found a prosperous son-in-law to take one of his daughters off his hands on terms so favourable to himself.

Forth's finances were by now in reasonably good shape. By the beginning of 1804 his persistent lobbying and almost daily business discussions were at last producing results. He could count on an income of at least 9,800 francs a year.

Perregaux's bank also allowed him certain advances against the eventual repayments of his debts in Paris, but he had to deposit with Perregaux the diamond which the Duke of Orleans had left with him as a pledge.

His satisfactory financial position encouraged Forth to fix a wedding day, 26 April 1804. He had not quite finished with legal complications. The marriage was taking place in a foreign country, and must be valid under both French and English law; Forth and Eliza would be required to go through a ceremony in the Mairie: Forth called this *mariage à la française*. His Diary shows how busy he was: 10 April 'family meeting; chat about marriage; long conversation and arrangement'; 13 April 'walk about affairs'; 16 April 'communicate to Sir E. Impey'; 22 April 'Sir E. Impey with Bond; Mr. Smith fixes a day; Contract signed'. On 25 April the civil ceremony was performed in the presence of Rouen, Impey, Perregaux and all the Petrie family. And finally on 26 April, in the English chapel, surprisingly still available for use by the diminished English community, Forth and Eliza were married by the Reverend Doctor Nathaniel Smith, in the presence of the same witnesses who attended the civil ceremony.

3

Forth began his married life with Eliza in the apartment at 7 Rue Blanche where he had lived as a bachelor. He altered his rooms, rearranged his bed, repaired the stove, and removed the billiard table, but there was otherwise little alteration in the framework of his life. Eliza's family still lived in the same house, and the same constant intercourse between the two families continued.

Unhappily Forth began his married life in poor health. Only two days after his wedding he was ailing, and two days later in pain. On 11 May he was ill again: 'keep my room, dine there with dear Eliza'. It was an opening in a minor key, which, had Forth been thinking in musical terms, he would have known must influence all future developments.

His illness did not last long; very soon Eliza and he were busy with marriage visits and sociability. On 22 May Forth wrote: '5 marriage visits, 18 at dinner, 15 to Shows'. The Shows formed part of the celebrations for the proclamation of Napoleon as Emperor. Much of May and June was taken up with festivities. Those, who, like Rouen and Perregaux, were closely connected with the men in power, entertained lavishly. Forth and Eliza attended some of the entertainments, notably a great dinner and assembly at Rouen's on 6 June.

At the end of June Sir Elijah Impey and his family received permission to leave France. Their destination was England but they travelled through Rotterdam because in theory communication between France and England was forbidden. This did not prevent the passage of travellers and news between the two countries, thanks to various recognized fictions. A ship that left London for Rotterdam had papers made out as if it had left Emden, and 'Great Emden' was the name by which London was referred to by the port authorities.[2] Such circumlocutions made it possible for Forth to give Sir Elijah Impey letters to his bankers with instructions to invest the £10,000 which he had undertaken to settle on Eliza. Impey left Paris on 29 June, reached Rotterdam on 11 July, and arrived in London on the 21st. He handed Forth's instructions to his bankers on the 25th. It was a roundabout way of doing business, but it worked, and incidentally showed how hard it was to maintain an effective blockade of England.

It was very soon clear to Forth that his old quarters were unsuitable for a married man. After two months search he found what he wanted not far from the Rue Blanche, on the corner of the Rue St. Georges and the Rue de la Victoire. Number 13 Rue St. Georges was a small neo-classical *hôtel particulier* with courtyard and garden. It had been built in 1788, partly as a property speculation, by the architect, Bélanger, for his mistress, Mademoiselle Dervieux, once a dancer at the Opera. Fifty years later it was to belong to Alphonse de Rothschild, head of the Banque de France, and is now engulfed by the head offices of the magazine, *L'Illustration*. On the opposite side of the street was a much larger property development which had been put in hand by the Bordeaux merchant Hosten. Only a few of the houses which Le Doux designed for Hosten had been completed before the Revolution, and the rest of the site was still fields. The open spaces, and air, fresher and cleaner than in the older, low-lying parts of Paris, were the attractions of the Montmartre quarter. Nor was Forth alone in feeling them. Very near the Forths was the magnificent house where Prince Murat lived with his wife, Napoleon's sister, Caroline, and in the Rue de la Victoire, the street in which Napoleon and Josephine began their married life, lived Madame Récamier with her banker husband.

Eliza and Forth moved house on 5 August in hot, sultry weather. Eliza was affected by the heat, and Forth had a sick headache. But it was not long before they were out choosing decorations and furniture, and hiring a piano for Eliza. They celebrated Petrie's birthday on 7 August by a family party at Frascati's, and Forth's sixtieth birthday on 9 August by a party for Eliza's step-sisters and their governess.

Everything seemed to promise well. Nevertheless the impression remains that Forth and Eliza were not altogether happy at 13 Rue St. Georges. They were now on their own, away from the large, merry family party to which both had become accustomed, and it was not easy for a couple so widely separated in age at once to find common ground from which to evolve their own family circle. They could however create their own circle of friends.

At first some of these naturally came from families already known to Forth, but they included the younger generation, nearer to Eliza's age: Rouen's sons, in particular Rouen des Mallets, a protégé of Fouché's, and later a Prefect; Perregaux's son and his daughter, Madame de Marmont.

There were also the Pérignons. This family owned a house in the Rue St. Augustin and another at Auteuil, then a small village in open country. Like other country houses in the neighbourhood, the Hôtel Pérignon stood in its own large grounds. M. Pierre Pérignon, a lawyer and a Senator, was created a Baron by Napoleon. He had a brother in Rouen's notarial practice, and several daughters, some of them near Eliza's age. Forth found the company at Pérignon's 'very pleasant', perhaps because it reminded him of the society which he had known before the Revolution. Like most foreigners who had seen France in those days, Forth no doubt found society under the Consulate and early Empire very stiff, formal and lacking in conversation. But Pérignon's food was not always equal to the company: 'dine at Pérignon's', Forth wrote, 'cold and hungry'; and on another occasion Eliza returned from the Pérignons' with indigestion. Such misadventures did not discourage the Forths from frequent visits to the Rue St. Augustin or Auteuil; indeed they went so often that eventually Pérignon appears in the Diary rather unsuitably abbreviated as 'Prig'.

Sometimes at the Pérignons' the Forths met a witty and amusing elderly man with exquisite manners. He would arrive with his wife in a carriage bearing the arms of the Senate in which he held an administrative post. His name was Jean François Baudelaire. Like Pérignon he came from the Champagne; both had studied for the priesthood at the Collège Sainte Barbe, and remained friends ever since. When his first wife died Baudelaire married Pérignon's ward, Caroline Archimbaut Dufays: their illustrious son was Charles Baudelaire, the poet. But when the Forths met him, Baudelaire's first wife was still living. Before the Revolution he had tutored the sons of the Duke de Praslin, a Minister of Louis XV, and learned much about French politics in an era which had also been Forth's. This common interest, together with the fact that Baudelaire and his wife were both billiard players, led to a regular exchange of hospitality between the two families.

The Baudelaires were little more than acquaintances; a much stronger link attached the Forths to Robert Boyd and his wife, Harriet. Boyd, a Bordeaux merchant with an interest in the wine trade, had known Forth since the days of the Portsmen. He and his wife now lived not far from the Forths, who could rely on them as sympathetic and steady friends.

Such a friendship was valuable in the early days of a marriage which inevitably developed points of friction. One such was Eliza's dislike of housekeeping. Forth had always kept a strict eye on his household: his servants were paid, and accounts balanced every Sunday. From time to time he made a tour of his house to see that everything was in working order. He recorded in his Diary when servants were engaged or left; when firewood was ordered; what stocks there were of oil or tea, powder or pomade, and how long the stocks lasted. He liked stoves to heat efficiently; he disliked smoky chimneys, a fault of which English visitors to Paris were apt to complain. The enjoyment of a smoothly-running household, which paid its way, was very much part of his character. Even if it had not been, the provision in the Marriage Settlement which made him responsible for maintaining the household, whatever the state of his income, gave him every reason to remain in control. It did not leave much for Eliza to do except to give out linen and stores, and to keep accounts of what she spent. Her failure to do these things caused some of the scenes which occurred from time to time.

In plotting the course of this marriage it is a handicap to have only Forth's Diary to draw on. One cannot do more than guess the strains on Eliza, married to a man forty years older than herself and set in his ways. Another cause of friction was certainly Madame de Genetines. She was still a frequent visitor, and Eliza could hardly help resenting this. One 'scene with Eliza' occurred after a day on which Forth had had 'a long chat with Gs'. During another visit to the Forths Madame de Genetines was taken ill, and obliged to stay with them for the night. One suspects that she was curious about the Forths' ménage; staying with them gave her an opportunity to study it. It is unlikely that Eliza relished looking after her.

But it would be wrong to visualize Forth's first year of marriage entirely in terms of stress and strain. He was in love with his bride, and enjoyed taking her to the Opera or the theatres; the Vaudeville in the Rue de Chartres; the Montansier, known for its charming comedies; or the Feydeau with its brilliant company of players. He was pleased and proud when she was admired at assemblies or balls. On the anniversary of their wedding he gave her 150 francs and two valuable gilt-work boxes.

Some of Eliza's and Forth's happiest times were still those which they spent with the Petries, who had moved out of Paris to settle at Ennery, near Pontoise. There they rented a big house—it may have been the Château de Busagny—with a garden, a park and farm buildings. When Eliza and Forth stayed there they had their own suite of rooms, papered and furnished to suit their own tastes.

There is no doubt at all that Petrie made use of his son-in-law; on occasion he borrowed money from him, and he accepted the loan of Forth's coach for use at Ennery. But Forth did not resent it; on the contrary he greatly enjoyed Petrie's society, and he also respected his judgement. When the lease of 13 Rue St. Georges ended in March 1805 the Forths went to live at Ennery. Forth's Diary conveys an agreeable impression of country life and country pleasures. He and Eliza arrived in time for the great spring wash, when all the household linen, which had been washed and rough-dried during the winter, was laundered in water brought from the river, afterwards to be spread out on the drying grounds, and finally stored away in the linen cupboards. Sometimes the Forths and the Petries walked in the park or the country round it; on other days the Petrie girls and Richard Rettfort went riding. In the evenings there was music or cards. Friends from Paris drove out to dine or stay; neighbours from Pontoise visited or entertained. There were fêtes and dances at Pontoise or Ennery. Eliza's birthday on 2 July, and Forth's on 9 August were both celebrated by a dance (Forth always spelt it *danse* in the French fashion) for all the servants in the house and on the estate.

## 4

Political events are mentioned only very briefly in Forth's Diary. In spring 1804 a series of events occurred which were crucial to the establishment of the Napoleonic régime, but Forth wrote them down after the event, and without comment: 'Moreau au Temple, success to Bonaparte . . . traitor Pichegru taken . . . Monster Georges taken . . . Duc d'Enghien shot as traitor at Vincennes . . . Pichegru hangs himself'. Finally in December, 'Bonaparte crown'd Emperor . . . procession of new Colours, Eagles, in Champ de Mars'.

It was safer for an enemy alien resident in France not to remark on such delicate matters. But it must have been strange for a Briton to live in France while an invasion of England was talked of everywhere and a huge expeditionary force was encamped near Boulogne. In 1805 the Bayeux tapestry was brought to Paris and exhibited to immense crowds in the

Louvre to remind Frenchmen of an earlier successful invasion.
Bookshops displayed caricatures in which English soldiers in
the guise of frogs were cut down one by one by a Frenchman
with a sabre, or King George III was shown jumping the
Channel, and losing his crown in the process, while papers
marked Hanover, Ireland and Malta dropped from his hands.[3]

Although Forth was left to move freely in Paris, he was,
whether he knew it or not, under observation. 'There is not a
family considered worthy of notice', a senior British Embassy
official had written in 1801, 'where one or more of the servants
are not in [Fouché's] pay. It is almost impossible for à foreigner,
and quite so for a foreign minister to procure a servant who is
not a spy on him, indeed this part of [Fouché's] plan is carried
out with as little reserve as to appear likely to defeat its object
by putting people on their guard . . . '[4]

If police spies were so busy at a time when England and
France were at peace, they were busier still when war was
declared. On 27 March 1805 the Minister of Police reported to
Napoleon on Monsieur Forth, an Englishman mixing freely in
society in Paris; whether he had been authorised to do so
Fouché did not know. The report gave a short but well-
informed account of Forth's career since 1776, his connexion
with the Duke of Orleans, and his presence in Paris at the
beginning of the Revolution. The informer thought that Forth
had been there on financial business for the Duke of Orleans,
but it was not impossible that the British government had taken
the opportunity to entrust Forth with some secret mission.
The report concluded: 'Forth let it be known that when he left
Paris he hid 5,000 louis d'or in his study. He has always had
dealings with the notaries, Rouen of Paris, and Barroud of
Lyon, who live in adjoining houses in the Rue Neuve des
Petits Champs. Madame de Genetines, Barroud's sister, was
living in London under Forth's protection. He is an arch-
intriguer, meticulous, and a great talker. Every evening he
makes a point of writing down what he has done during the
day'.[5]

Much of the information on which this report was based
probably came from existing police dossiers, and the remainder
from one of Forth's servants, Joseph, Toussaint or L'Abbé,

perhaps, or one of the others whose engagements or dismissal Forth recorded. It did not amount to much, but it was enough for Fouché; he gave orders that Forth should be kept under observation.

The result was that on 27 May, when Forth was lying ill in bed at Ennery, he received a visit from the Count de Montalivet, the Prefect of the Department of Seine-et-Oise. M. de Montalivet was polite, and did not order Forth off to Verdun. But as soon as Forth was well enough to travel, instead of spending the rest of the summer peacefully at Ennery, he set off to Paris to see Rouen and to put himself right with the authorities. Thereafter he reported regularly to the Mairie of the district in which he was living.

## Chapter Sixteen

### ECLIPSE

#### 1

AUGUST 1805, the month in which Forth reached the age of 61, opened a new phase in his marriage and in his life. His star was in decline, Eliza's in the ascendant.

A strong link with his past was broken on 7 August when Betsy died. Still bound by the intangible connexions which persist between people who have loved each other, he felt her loss deeply. She was buried in the graveyard at Brompton under the name Forth but, unlucky to the last, the name was mis-spelt in the Burial Register.

Forth did not hear the news of Betsy's death for three weeks. He was then in great distress over another death, that of Madame de Genetines's seventeen-year-old daughter, Mimi. Forth had taken an affectionate interest in Mimi ever since her mother brought her to England in 1790 as an émigrée. She had lived with her mother in the house in Oxford Street when Madame de Genetines was under Forth's protection, and he had watched her grow up. He might have expected to enjoy her company for many years; her death was a shock.

As best he could from a distance Forth tried to make arrangements for the support of Betsy's children, especially Betty who was still a minor. His correspondence with the banker, Thomas Hammersley, on the subject provoked a broadside: 'It is impossible for me to conclude a letter to you, for whom I had once such a sincere regard, without a reflection upon the events that are passed. If Mrs. Forth was not your wife, what am I to think of your conduct to me, by your introducing her as such to my wife and daughters? . . . If she was your wife, what am I to think of a ceremony which is said to have passed at Paris,

contrasted with another very serious ceremony ... between
yourself, the Dean of Bristol and me on the 29th April 1802?
One of these positions must be taken, neither of which would
permit me to renew that friendly intercourse with you which I
once cultivated with much pleasure and satisfaction. Both my
wife and I frequently saw the unhappy lady in her decline, and
not long before her death. My wishes for you are that you view
the things that are past with such sentiments as can alone give
you any comfort when your own dissolution approaches,
that your previous conduct to your children may shew that
you have been truly sensible of your own errors.'[1]

The serious ceremony of 29 April was, of course, the service
of reconciliation which Forth had arranged before he left for
Paris in 1802. In alluding to it Hammersley was reminding
him of something which he would have preferred to forget, in
the same way that he had put out of his mind the ambiguous
position in which he and Betsy had lived for so many years.
Hammersley paid lip-service to the convention that a respectably married woman could be contaminated by contact with
one who was not; but it was Forth's abandonment of Betsy and
her children that caused him real indignation. Forth resented
Hammersley's letter, yet one cannot but feel that Hammersley
was in the right.

## 2

Forth heard the news of Betsy's death at a time when he and
Eliza were busy once again moving house. Their new home,
number 10 Rue de la Place Vendôme, unlike the house in the
Rue St. Georges, was within the city boundaries. The street,
now and before the Revolution, known as Rue Louis-le-Grand,
ran north of the Place Vendôme to the Boulevards. At one end
was an entrance to the Mairie of the 2nd Arrondissement over
which Rouen presided; at the other was the Pavillon de Hanovre
in its garden. Forth and Eliza used to attend the concerts there,
and entertained their friends in the public rooms. Nearby, in
the Boulevard d'Antin, were the Chinese Baths which Eliza
frequented from time to time, as the fashion was.

The house itself was spacious enough not only to accommo-
date Eliza, Forth, Richard Rettfort and their servants, but the

entire Petrie family when, as often happened, they came up
from Pontoise to enjoy the amusements of Paris. There was also
room to entertain. During the years since Forth's return to Paris
society had changed much. Napoleon's government had provided a stable foundation on which social life could, and did,
flourish. Forth and Eliza were prepared to play their part,
especially Eliza.

She was now 21. Since her marriage she had developed into
a poised and charming young woman, who was not only pretty
to look at but agreeable in conversation, an ornament at any
entertainment. From the day in January 1806 when Forth
noted 'Eliza's rich gown came home', there was hardly an
evening when she was not invited somewhere: 'Eliza to Rouen's
. . . Eliza to christening dinner and ball at Pérignon's . . . Eliza
to Scherer's, then to Bal Masqué . . . Eliza greatly admired at
Delamarre's ball . . . Eliza much praised at Scherer's'. And on
20 April 1806, supreme distinction, 'Eliza conversed with by
the Emperor at the Court Ball'. This was perhaps the occasion
when, according to a family tradition, Napoleon said that
Eliza's eyes were the most beautiful that he had ever seen.

It seems remarkable that Eliza, an Englishwoman, who had
never even been presented to Napoleon, should have received an
invitation to a Court Ball. But in August of the previous year
Eliza had been present when the city of Paris gave a Ball in
honour of Napoleon: all those who attended it were invited
in return to a Ball at the Tuileries, whether they had been
presented or not. Forth did not accompany Eliza on either
occasion, making it possible for her to appear as the daughter
of Petrie, an ex-representative of the Colony of Tobago, rather
than as the wife of a man about whom, only a few months
earlier, Napoleon had received a confidential report from
Fouché.

It was not only to the Tuileries that Eliza went without
Forth. During his first winter and spring in the Rue de la Place
Vendôme, Forth was so often ill that Eliza had to look elsewhere for someone to accompany her; to her parents if they
were in Paris, if not, to Mrs. Boyd or one of her other married
friends. In his earlier life it had been Forth who went out into
society, and Betsy who stayed at home; Forth did not easily

accept the new situation. He fretted when Eliza was late in returning, and there were scenes: 'Eliza out *five* hours . . . her atrocious behaviour'. But gradually Eliza got her way. Forth became accustomed to see her attend parties without him. He noted her movements in his Diary, and took pleasure in recording the occasions when she was praised and admired. He was not the first man to marry a young and, as he supposed, malleable wife, only to find that she was the dominant partner.

The balls and parties at which Eliza shone took place for the most part at the houses of the bankers and financiers, the generals and administrators, who were at once supporting and exploiting Napoleon's regime; Rougemont, La Sodade, Réal, Madame Scherer. The latter was the widow of a general who had made his name in the Revolutionary wars and the Italian campaigns of the 1790's. At the same time he was supposed to have acquired a fortune by profiteering in military equipment. But when his enemies threatened to accuse him before the Directory, he declared that he would bring down 40 others with him: 'j'ai des pièces', he said. His bluff succeeded, and his widow was left to enjoy his gains, ill-gotten or otherwise.[2]

Another family whose more modest gatherings Eliza and Forth both attended was the Ventenats. They were near neighbours in the same street: 'Eliza over the way', or 'Eliza to Vents': are frequent entries in Forth's Diary. Jean Ventenat was a relation, perhaps the son, of the distinguished botanist who advised the Empress Josephine on the gardens of Malmaison. It was he who wrote the text of *Le Jardin de Malmaison*, now better known for its illustrations by Redouté. Perhaps it was at the Ventenats' house that the Forths met artists and writers such as the painter and engraver, Beljambe, and the poet, Legouvé.

Forth, who had always been hospitable, had planned to return in kind the entertainment offered to Eliza and himself, but this was out of the question during his first season in the Rue de la Place Vendôme; his health was too bad. Besides the recurrent excruciating pain of the stone, he suffered from what he called rheumatism in his head and jaw. Part of the trouble was toothache. Forth's dentist, Bousquet, who had been Surgeon-Dentist to the old princesses, the daughters of Louis

XV, drew some of his teeth, and gave him some relief. But the source of the pain was more serious, although this was not clear until later when Forth began to suffer from nose-bleeding which sometimes lasted for hours. He was also liable, particularly when worried, to gout in his feet; and he was susceptible to colds which led to a 'wheezing cough'. From one or other of all these causes Forth was confined to his room for six weeks between February and May 1806. After an especially sharp bout of pain he sometimes turned to music for comfort: 'touch the violin', he wrote on 19 May 1806.

That month he was sufficiently concerned over his condition to make a new Will. Soon after he married Eliza he had made one giving directions about the disposal of his property in France: now he dealt with his property in England and, bearing in mind Hammersley's reproaches, made provision for Betsy's children. One of his assets was the money which he still hoped to recover from the Prince of Wales. In order to explain his claim he rewrote his *Dikaeology* or *Plea in Defence* as an annex to his Will.

But his time was not yet. In August 1806, just before his 62nd birthday, Forth and Eliza went to stay with the Rouens at Taverny for the opening of the shooting season. Forth was always happy at Taverny. This visit was no exception; for the first time for many months he was 'very merry'. There was a house full of guests, and new ones came and went throughout the Forths' stay. They went riding to nearby villages; attended fêtes and large dinner parties with neighbours; watched donkey races and played billiards. On 17 August Rouen gave a great dinner for the sportsmen: '24 at dinner; 32 at night; dance; music'. When Forth left Taverny he was in better health than he had been for a long time, and ready to embark on a season of entertaining.

That winter was exceptionally gay. Forth was able to accompany Eliza to her balls, and they both entertained lavishly. Apart from dinner parties, Forth gave a billiard party every month, sometimes to as many as 40 or 50 guests. Prizes were offered, and on 2 February 1807 the winner was Madame Baudelaire. Another party caused a slight awkwardness with the Périgons, when one of Forth's servants, who was mending the fire, spilled hot cinders over M. Pérignon.

In January 1807 Eliza began to hold a regular Monday
evening reception. She began modestly on 12 January with a
dozen guests, but at her next evening a fortnight later the
numbers increased. By March her receptions had become a
weekly fixture, which sometimes took the form of a musical
party.

### 3

Such entertaining was expensive. In the early summer of 1807,
when the party-giving season in Paris came to an end, Forth
counted the cost. It soon became obvious that Eliza and he
were living beyond their means. A year or so earlier Forth had
made a new arrangement with Eliza about housekeeping. He
made her a larger allowance, and ceased to keep such a close
watch on household details. But Eliza was a cheerful spender;
she ran up debts which she did not reveal to Forth. He spent
too freely. He liked to entertain on a generous scale, to be able
to comment after one of his parties, 'dinner of 12—very good'.
It was hardly surprising that money began to run out.

Forth was still receiving annual payments on his French
annuity, but he had not yet succeeded in recovering arrears
for the ten years during which France and England were at war.
The French government was reluctant even to admit the
liability. No doubt Forth was able to borrow on his expectations but he was finding it increasingly hard to persuade bankers
to accept the risk.

The political situation was partly to blame. Hitherto Forth
had been able to supplement the income which he received
in France by drawing on his bank in London. He also continued
to receive his pension of £600 on King George III's Secret
Service Fund, and to raise money on it in Paris. In theory
such transactions became illegal when war between France and
England began again in 1803, but in practice it was possible
to avoid the prohibition. The situation changed in November
1807 when Napoleon issued the Berlin Decrees; from that time
any country conquered by France was forbidden to trade with
England. A later Decree ordered any ship of any country
which had traded with England to be seized as a prize.

Financial transactions through other countries became not only difficult but dangerous.

It was now that Forth felt the loss of Trochereau, who died in January 1805, and was no longer there to provide the support and good advice on which Forth had depended for so many years. Perregaux's bank was less helpful than it had been. Perregaux himself was ill, and his partner, Laffitte, was so very much involved with Napoleon's government that he was most unwilling to do anything which might offend it. Forth spent many hours in discouraging financial discussions with bankers and notaries. On 4 May 1807 he fell behind with the rent, and a Bill was posted on the door of 10 Rue de la Place Vendôme. He was feeling all the rigours of the clause in his Marriage Contract that made him responsible for all the household expenses, whether his revenue was sufficient or not.

In June Forth and Eliza went as usual to Ennery for the Ennery fête. They found the Petries were also worried about money. For some time Mr. Petrie had been receiving an annual allowance of 6,000 francs as a former Deputy of the Island of Tobago: it was paid by the Minister of the Navy and Colonies, who in his turn was to recoup himself from the revenues of Tobago.[3] The allowance, though probably supplemented by money borrowed on his other expectations, was quite insufficient to support Petrie and his family. He decided to send the elder girls out to India to stay with his brother, now Governor of Madras: with luck they would find husbands there. In September he and Mrs. Petrie set out for England by way of Rotterdam, leaving the younger girls behind. They and their faithful governess lodged with Forth and Eliza, an increase in the household which made it impossible to save money by moving to a smaller house.

As the winter approached Forth's troubles increased. At about the same time that he heard of the publication of the Berlin Decrees he was told that his landlord would not renew his lease, and his bankers wrote from London that there was difficulty over letting his house in Manchester Square. Small wonder that he wrote in his Diary, 'much afflicted'.

4

Financial worries were not his only afflictions. Inevitably Forth's various ailments complicated his married life and his hopes of begetting a child. Frequent references to changing his bed or sleeping upstairs make it plain that this side of his marriage was far from satisfying. The strain on both Forth and Eliza was considerable. It was the cause of many unpleasant scenes: 'Eliza's unpardonable language', Forth wrote on one occasion; and once, when Eliza behaved, according to Forth, like a violent termagant, he was obliged to call in Mrs. Petrie to make peace.

Nevertheless in June 1807 Eliza was pregnant at last.

With a child on the way, Eliza did not feel inclined for entertaining when the Forths returned to Paris in the autumn. When society reassembled in November *les lundis de Madame Forth* were no longer to be found in the social calendar. Nor did Forth issue any invitations to billiard parties. They dined with and received only their intimates, the Rouens, Boyds and Ventenats. This considerably reduced household expenses, and made it easier to economize. The servants, about whose 'insolence' Forth had several times complained the previous year, were placed on board wages.

Eliza's pregnancy proceeded normally. Only a sharp bout of fever in November gave cause for anxiety. On 11 February 1808, after fourteen hours of labour, she gave birth to a son. 'Eliza in labour at 10', Forth wrote on 10 February; and the following day, 'Eliza in labour till 2 p.m. of a boy; all well . . . dine; see Eliza and child'. The next day he sent out 56 *faire-parts* to let all his friends know of the birth of his son. His pride and satisfaction can be imagined.

Parenthood removed much of the strain in the relationship between Forth and his wife. Whether Eliza gradually became attached to Forth it is impossible to say, but at least they now had a common interest, and someone else to plan for. In doing so they came closer than ever before. When Eliza and the child, whom they decided to call Frederick, were in the country, Forth wrote or received a letter from Eliza every day.

Without a scene or any recrimination, he paid the debts which
Eliza had run up without his knowledge.

When Frederick was four months old Forth gave him a
present. It was the gold snuffbox with Madame Du Barry's
miniature on one side, and an inscription on the other. But
Frederick was too young to appreciate this precious object
which his father had been given by Madame Du Barry in recognition of his efforts to recover her stolen jewels.

Those active days were over. His happiest times were now
passed with Eliza and Frederick. They took a small house in the
country at Villemomble, near Le Raincy, so that Eliza and the
child could have the benefit of country air. Le Raincy was yet
another reminder of Forth's past life. Recently acquired by the
financier, Ouvrard, it had previously been the property of the
Duke of Orleans, and it was there that Forth had gambled
with Orleans and his friends in April 1792. It now developed
gentler associations. He left Villemomble only reluctantly when
it was necessary to go to Paris on business or to consult his
doctors.

At the end of June 1808 the Forths removed from the Rue
de la Place Vendôme to a smaller house, 10 Rue Richer. This
house, Forth's last home, was outside the city boundaries in
what was then a quiet street running between the garden walls
of the large houses in the Rue Bergère and the Rue de l'Enfer.
It is now in the busy, populous quarter of Notre Dame de
Lorette, close to the Folies Bergère.

Although Forth had two houses, the move to the Rue Richer
made it possible to live more simply. Mr. Petrie had returned
to France, at once relieving Forth and Eliza of the duty of
looking after Eliza's young stepsisters, and reducing their
household budget. The reduction was welcome, as Forth was
still finding it difficult to make ends meet. He even raised
money by pawning some of his valuables at the Mont de Piété.
Luckily the banker, Laffitte, was rather more accommodating
than he had been.

In November Forth made a new Will to dispose of his property in France. He left almost all his possessions to Eliza.
He also left her the arrears on his annuity. Arrears on the
annuity which he had originally bought for Betsy were to go to

Richard Rettfort, whc was also to inherit his father's repeater
watch and his clothes. Eliza was urged to care for Richard as
if she was his mother, knowing, Forth wrote, 'the kindness she
has always shown to this beloved child'. To Nat, Forth
bequeathed his and Betsy's portraits, together with a frame
containing four other likenesses: 'one of the late Mrs. Forth,
the mother of my son; another of a lady [possibly Madame
de Genetines] ; the third of the late Duke of Orleans; the fourth
of my great friend, the late William, Earl of Mansfield'. Forth
also gave Nat his repeater by Le Roy; his armorial seal; and a
large pair of gold shoe-buckles, 'at present deposited with
Monsieur and Madame Chansom at Villemomble as a pledge
of the repayment of money which they advanced me to settle
my dear wife's debts'. To his daughter Betty, Forth left a
medallion containing portraits of her mother and her aunt.
By the Will in which he disposed of his English property Forth
had also left her the house in Manchester Square. There was no
bequest to Frederick, who would apparently have to make do
with Madame Du Barry's étui and watch.[4]

Forth's Will shows how little of real value he had to leave.
The income on the annuity on which he and Eliza were living
would cease with his death; recovery of the arrears was highly
speculative. Equally uncertain was the recovery of a sum of
80,000 francs which Forth had lent to the Count and Countess
de Genetines. Eliza would have very little to live on. Forth was
well aware of this. In one clause of his Will he begged his dear
friend, Rouen, kindly 'to continue his friendship to my
beloved wife, to assist her with his counsel and advice on all
questions, and to enable her to profit by this writing which I
declare to be my last Will and Testament'.

## 5

Until the beginning of 1809 Forth was recognizably the same
man who had been Lord Mansfield's Mercury and the Special
Envoy of the British government; the man who organized
the Portsmen, acted as the Duke of Orleans's agent, and raised
money for the Prince of Wales. But gradually the outlines of his
personality are blurred: he is a man, any man, at grips with his
final illness.

His Diary takes the same form as it had done for many years; there are the daily records of the highest and lowest temperatures in centigrade; the times of rising and retiring to bed, and a note to say how he slept. But in the last months the handwriting becomes crabbed, and the entries for the most part describe the dramas of the sickroom, the successful or unsuccessful working of bodily functions which a healthy man takes for granted, and a sick man finds all-absorbing.

Forth's doctors, Dr. Bidou and Dr. Guiot, did their best to help him. Dr. Bidou was an old friend who had treated Forth since he returned to Paris. Dr. Guiot (or Giot) called in only recently, was probably the son of Daniel Guiot, a pioneer of vaccination. There was very little that they could do. The remedies which they applied, the cauteries and the blisters, were often almost as painful as the disease. *Dr. Daharambure's Pectoral*, a patent medicine, gave Forth some relief from an oppression on his chest, but only for a time. An 'oppression' continued to afflict him along with all his other complaints.

Diet was another problem. Forth kept a note of some of the dishes which he tried: stewed apples, oysters, carp, whiting, beef, lamb, jelly, madeira, cocoa, coffee, tea. None of these suited his very much impaired digestion for long. With all the medical resources of today it would by now have been principally a question of killing pain.

If there was no cure for Forth's diseases much could be done to make him more comfortable. His servants, not those who had been insolent, but two newcomers, Julie Tientz and Louise Renaut, nursed him devotedly. Nor is this merely a figure of speech when one remembers that a sickroom in Forth's day was not only without running hot water, but that all water must first be drawn from a pump or well.

Forth was not bedfast. At times he was able to leave his room to dine downstairs and to play cards. He was still able to make his periodic inspections of the house. He was sometimes even well enough to take an airing in Paris or to pay visits to Villemomble. But such efforts left him very weak. In spite of it he continued to write business letters, and receive visits from lawyers and bankers' clerks. He also had more agreeable visitors. Eliza, who was expecting another child, often sat with

him, and brought Frederick to cheer his father. Richard Rettfort and Mr. Petrie dined with him. Another visitor was
Hermine Collard, who was able to show that she remembered
the kindness which Forth and Betsy had showed her when
she was newly orphaned many years ago.

By April 1809 Forth was in almost constant pain. He
continued to fight it, but it was obvious that he had not long
to live. On 17 April he took his last airing in Paris. Two days
later he complained that he felt very sleepy. For the next two
days it was the same. On Sunday 23 April he made the last
complete entry in the Diary which he had kept for 36 years:
'accounts; sick and sleepy all day; no dinner'. Next day he
began: 'easier; write —— ' but from those words the entry
trailed away unfinished. He died on 28 April.

In his Will Forth not only left directions about his funeral
and burial, he had actually made arrangements with an under-
taker, M. Nodin of the Rue d'Antin. He had originally intended
to be buried at Taverny; he loved the place so much that
Rouen had promised him a vault there. But regulations making
the movement of corpses more complicated caused Forth to
change his plans. He arranged to be buried in the old cemetery
of Montmartre. He wished his funeral to be decent, but as
simple and economical as possible. Dr. Nathaniel Smith was to
read the Burial Service, and Forth hoped that Mr. Petrie and
Richard Rettfort would be present.[5]

It is fitting that the body of Forth, this Parisian by adoption,
should be laid to rest in his own favourite Montmartre Quarter.
It was there that he and Betsy had set up house in the first
glorious days of his official appointment, and it was there in
very different circumstances that he ended his life.

# POSTSCRIPT

Eliza, with another child on the way, was left in serious financial straits, just as Forth had feared that she would be. She eventually solved her problem by marrying Rouen's son, the Prefect Rouen des Mallets. He brought up Frederick, and adopted Forth's posthumous son, Alexandre. Frederick founded a family in England, Alexandre in France. Descendants of both are alive today. The English branch still preserves as a curio a Certificate showing what they might have expected to receive at compound interest if George, Prince of Wales, had paid his debt in full.

# NOTES

# THE FORTH MSS

The papers referred to in the Notes as the Forth MSS are those still in the possession of Forth's great-great-grandson Captain Nevill de Rouen Forth. They fall into the following main categories:

*1. Diaries:*

    (a)   30 Sep. 1777 to 13 Aug. 1778 (with a few gaps);

    (b)   1 Jan. 1802 to 23 Apr. 1809.

A fragment of the Diary for 1791 is printed in the notes to Claude St. André, *Madame Du Barry*, 1909 edition.

The entries in (a) are very full, and include some conversations reported in dialogue form. The entries in (b) are very concise, only one line per double page for each day. Broadly speaking, facts are noted on the right-hand page, and comments on the left. A note of letters sent and received foots each page.

*2. Memoir:*

A narration of events concerning the princes' loan; it includes:

    (a)   narrative of transactions that took place between 1789 and 1791;

    (b)   correspondence during the years 1789 and 1799, some of which is also printed in A. Aspinall, *Correspondence of George Prince of Wales;*

    (c)   narrative of the later events connected with the loan, linking the correspondence in (b).

(a), (b) and (c) together make up the document which Forth called his *Dikaeology* or *Plea in Defence*, or more simply, the *Memoir*. As it stands, it is not the original document. Four copies, printed by émigré priests (see Chapter Thirteen), were destroyed by Forth, but he preserved the original, which he amended and kept with his English Will (see an Affidavit filed with Forth's Will in the Probate Registry). But after Forth's death, his grandson produced a printed version of the *Memoir*, and destroyed the original. It is this printed version which is in Captain Forth's possession. Apart from a few mistakes due to a misreading of Forth's handwriting this version seems to be accurate; where the letters in the *Memoir* and *Aspinall* coincide, they also correspond.

*3. Account Book 1972*:
This also contains a pencilled note of a gambling session at Le Raincy, April 1792.

*4. Various correspondence and documents:*
These are for the most part contained in numbered envelopes. They are a very miscellaneous collection; many letters and papers have been destroyed or disappeared in the course of years. Almost nothing has survived for the first half of Forth's life.

Some of the Duke of Orleans's letters to Forth were published by Amédée Britsch, see note 1 to Chapter One and note 3 to Chapter Eight below. A number of Forth's letters to Orleans are among the papers recently deposited in the Archives Nationales, Paris, *Catalogue* 'Louis Philippe, l'homme et le roi, 1773–1850', 1974. At the time of writing they were not open to students.

*Abbreviations used to denote other manuscript collections:*

| | |
|---|---|
| PRO | Public Record Office, London. |
| BL | Manuscript Room, British Library, London. |
| AE | Archives du Ministère des affaires étrangères, Paris. |
| Bibl. Nat. | Bibliothèque Nationale, Paris. |
| Arch. Nat. | Archives Nationales, Paris. |
| Arch. Dep. | Archives départementales, Lyons, and Versailles. |
| Sim., | Archivo General de Simancas, Valladolid. |

## Chapter One

1. Forth's grandfather, another Samuel, was Captain Lieutenant in Wolseley's Regiment of Horse, and served as ADC to Marshal Schomberg at the battle of the Boyne. He was High Sheriff of County Longford in 1704. Forth's two paternal uncles served in Nevill's Dragoons. His father's first wife was Mary Creighton whose family was related to the Earl of Erne. Forth's brother Samuel was Chairman of Sessions and Assistant Barrister for County Meath and Commissioner in Bankruptcy.

Most of the information on Forth's early life is derived from material in the possession of his descendants. But some is based on biographical details given by Amédée Britsch in an article in *Revue d'histoire diplomatique*, vol. 43, 'Lettres de Chartres à Nathaniel Parker Forth', cited as *Hist. Dipl.* Britsch had access to papers that belonged to Forth's French descendants. Unluckily these papers were destroyed by enemy action in the 1939–45 War. I cannot discover why Forth should have been born at Ludlow Castle. According to information kindly given by the Shropshire County Archivist there were some private residents in the Castle precincts, and it may explain why Forth's baptism does not appear in the Baptismal Register of Ludlow Parish Church.

2. In a letter to William Pitt the Younger, Chatham papers, PRO 38/8, vol. LXXXVI. ff. 236–7, Forth describes General Parker as his uncle. The relationship was not so close; possibly Forth used the word in the French sense of a first cousin once removed. On Robert (later Sir Robert) Herries see Herbert Lüthy, *La banque protestante en France* (cited as Lüthy), vol. 2, chap. IV, 4, pp; 654–3, the Carolingian international, and Index entries under Herries. Other information is in Sir William Forbes, *Memoirs of a Banking House*, London and Edinburgh, 1860.

3. Walpole to Rev. William Cole, 28 Feb. 1766; to Anne Pitt, 1 and 7 Mar. 1766; to John Crawford, 6 Mar. 1766; and to Augustus Selwyn, 7 Mar. 1766; ed. M. Toynbee, *Letters of Horace Walpole*, Oxford 1903–5, vol. 6.

4. Charles Butler, *Reminiscences*, London 1822, chap. 7, p. 86, mentions that 'Mr. Forth, who attended Lord Stormont's Embassy, knows something of Junius'.

5. I can find no other reference to the mission to Madrid.

6. In the Knight papers in the British Library, Add. MS. f. 150, there is a mention of a boy; an earlier letter, ff. 103–5, refers to 'young children', suggesting that there were other children besides the boy (who was brought up by Lord Luxborough). There is no specific mention of a daughter, but there are very few letters in the collection for 1759, the year of Betsy's birth. For what it is worth, Betsy's Christian names, Elizabeth and Dorothy, are both names in the Child family. If Betsy was the daughter of Josiah Child, her ill health might be an inherited tendency to consumption from which Child died. Such ifs and ans are not proof. More significant is the background of cross-Channel banking and speculation common to the Knights, the Childs and Forth. There is also the fact

that a Knight, whose Christian name is not mentioned, was a member of Forth's intelligence network. The bank of Selwin and Foley, which was that of Josiah Child and his wife, was one with which Forth had dealings.

7. Stormont to North, and to Weymouth, 11 Feb. 1777, Scone MSS, Box 45.

8. Stormont to Weymouth, 3 March 1777, Scone MSS, Box 47.

9. ibid.

*Chapter Two*

1. Maurepas's remarks about Stormont are in Forth's Diary, entries for 7 Oct. 1777 and 11 Feb. 1778. Stormont's own descriptions of his volubility are in his Dispatches to Weymouth, 25 Apr. and 6 Aug. 1777, PRO SP. 78/302, f. 114, and /303, f. 311. On Maurepas's literary activities see A. Picciola, 'L'activité littéraire de Maurepas' in *Dixhuitième siècle*, revue no. 3, 1971.

2. For North's views on Forth, see North to George III, 29 Mar. 1777, ed. Sir John Fortescue, *Correspondence of King George III*, London 1928, cited as *Fortescue*, vol. 3, letter 1979. Lieutenant Colonel Smith's letter is in the Auckland papers, BL Add. MS. 34413, ff. 353-4.

3. George III to North, 17 Aug. 1777, ed. W. Bodham Donne, *Correspondence of King George III and Lord North*, London 1867, vol. 2, letter 408.

4. North to George III, 29 Mar. 1777, cit. sup. and George III to North, 29 Mar. 1777, *Fortescue*, vol. 3, letter 1980.

5. I cannot find a copy of the letter accrediting Forth to Maurepas in the Public Record Office, but it is quoted by Britsch, *Hist. Dipl.* A comment by Forth, apparently on the document, remarked that it was signed by North and the two Secretaries of State after dinner on 23 Feb. 1777.

6. Stormont to Weymouth, 9 Apr. 1777, PRO SP. 78/302, f. 37.

7. Aranda to Floridablanca, 26 Aug. 1777, Sim. E. lego. 4611, No. 1110. If Stormont had not already known and trusted Forth he might have felt the same. During the 1939-45 War Winant, the United States Ambassador to London, complained that when Averell Harriman was posted to London as President Roosevelt's Special Representative he was by-passed, and not performing the work proper to an ambassador.

8. Quoted, Henri Doniol, *Histoire de la participation de la France à l'établissement des Etats Unis*, Paris 1886, cited as *Doniol*, vol. 1, pp. 1-4, and 243.

9. Beaumarchais to Vergennes, 16 Feb. 1777, AE CP. Ang. 521, f. 293.

10. Same to same, 11 Apr. 1777, AE CP. Ang. 522, f. 397-8.

11. For the Hôtel de Deux-Ponts during the occupation of the Duke and his wife, see E. Stollreicher, *Rokoko und Revolution, Lebenserrinnerungen des Joh. Christ. v. Mannlich*, Berlin 1923.

12. Fullarton's ownership of the *Rake's Progress* is mentioned by Frank Hermann, *The English as Collectors*, London 1972. The Pavillon Bouëxière is described in Jacques Hillairet, *Dictionnaire historique des rues de Paris* under Place Adolphe Max. There is a plan of the Pavillon in Michel Gallet, *Domestic Architecture in Paris in the 18th century*. The Jeans were a masonic family; see Henry Sadleir, *Thomas Dunkerley and his Life and Letters*, London 1891. Dr. Gem was the maternal uncle of William Huskisson; see ed. Lewis Melville, *The Huskisson Papers*, London 1931.

13. Diary 13 and 14 Feb. 1778.

14. There is a plan of the *petits appartements* at this date in Gérald van der Kemp, *Versailles, les petits appartements*.

15. Diary 4 Oct. 1777.

16. ibid. 7 and 8 Oct. 1777. According to the entry for 9 Oct. Herries offered Forth a share of the profits, but he refused it. Herries and Jeans arranged that Betsy should be given £100, and as much yearly for as long as Herries was allowed to administer the contract.

17. Stormont to Weymouth, 3 Mar. 1777, Scone MSS, Box 47.

18. North to Stormont, 1 Apr. 1777, Scone MSS, Box 50.

19. This account of the negotiations in April 1777 is based on Aranda to Floridablanca, 27 Sep. 1777, Sim. E. lego. 4612, No. 1134; on Stormont's Dispatches to Weymouth, PRO SP. 78/302; and a copy of Forth's instructions preserved in the Forth MSS. This is not dated but the context makes it clear that it refers to these negotiations.

20. Stormont to Weymouth, 23 Jun. 1777, PRO SP. 78/302, f. 403.

21. Same to same, 9 Aug. 1777, PRO SP. 78/303, f. 356.

22. The account of these negotiations is based on Aranda to Floridablanca, 26 Aug. 1777, Sim. E. lego. 4611, Nos. 1109 and 1110; on Stormont's Dispatches to Weymouth, especially those of 9, 13 and 20 Aug. 1777, *loc. cit.* ff. 357-8, 360, 367, 372-3, 388, 401.

23. Noailles to Vergennes, 4 and 7 Sep. 1777, AE CP. Ang. 524, ff. 166-7.

## Chapter Three

Unless otherwise indicated the direct quotations in this chapter are from Forth's Diary.

1. Maurice Toesca, *Les Grandes Heures de Fontainebleau*, Paris 1943, p. 179.

2. Mercy Argenteau to Maria Theresa, Nov. 1777, quoted Toesca, *op. cit.* p. 179.

3. Diary, 17 Oct. 1777.

4. ibid., 4 Nov. 1777.

5. ibid., 24 Oct. 1777.

6. ibid., 22 Oct. 1777.

7. The dates of the race meetings were 13 and 25 Oct. and 6 and 10 Nov. Comus was perhaps one of the famous Comus line.

8. Forth hunted with Chartres on 30 Oct. and 9 Nov.

9. Lord Herbert describes Voyer d'Argenson's stables, which he visited on 25 Apr. 1780, see *Henry, Elizabeth and George*, ed. Earl of Pembroke, London 1939. Herbert also dined at the Club on 9 May.

10. On Chartres's bets see Amédée Britsch, *La Jeunesse de Philippe Egalité*, Paris 1926 (cited as *Britsch*), chap. 4, p. 113. His reputation for winning his bets is mentioned by Lord Stormont in a Dispatch, 6 Aug. 1777, PRO SP. 78/303, and also by Auguste Ducoin, *Etudes révolution-naires*, Paris 1845, 'Philippe d'Orléans Egalité', chap. 1, p. 9.

11. On Chartres's Masonic connexions see *Britsch*, chap. 7, pp. 229-57. After the restoration of the Bourbons Chartres's Masonic connexions were supposed to have contributed to his revolutionary ideas. On this and other mythic views of the Craft, see J. M. Roberts, *The Mythology of the Secret Societies*, London 1972.

12. The usual contribution for a man was 1 louis, and for a woman 1 écu of 6 livres; Charles Kunstler, 'Louis XVI et Marie Antoinette à Versailles' in *Versailles au fil de ses Jours, Historia hors série* 4, 1967, p. 132.

## Chapter Four

Unless otherwise indicated the direct quotations in this chapter are from Forth's Diary.

1. The names were: Chevalier de Montgrand; Le Texier; Parkins or Parkyns MacMahon; Préandau; Serre de Latour: Théveneau de Morande. See Paul Robiquet, *Théveneau de Morande, étude sur le 18ᵉ siècle*, Paris 1882, chap. 2, pp. 55-60.

2. In his biography of Linguet, *Un avocat journaliste au 18ᵉ siècle*, Paris 1895, Jean Cruppi says that Linguet was the author of the Libel on Marie Antoinette. It is true that Linguet's letters to Maurepas in 1777 (in the archives of the Ministère des Affairs Etrangères) threaten to reveal many embarrassing secrets, but I think one must distinguish between the *Aiguillonnade* which Linguet certainly wrote, and the pamphlet *La reine des Welches et sa surintendante*, which I believe to be by Morande. In a letter to Noailles, 1 Apr. 1777, AE CP; Ang. 522, F. 294, in which Linguet summarizes his proposed publication, he does not mention any scandal about the Queen. It is not until the good name of the Royal Family is threatened that Maurepas becomes worried. Previously he showed no concern, and indeed had been subscribing, under another name, to Linguet's paper, AE CP. Ang. 522, f. 51 bis. In June 1777 Vergennes received an advertisement for *La Reine des Welches*, and at that point he and Maurepas become really concerned. In writing to Noailles, 7 June 1777, AE CP. Ang. 523, ff. 217-18, Vergennes distinguishes between libels on Ministers, i.e. the *Aiguillonnade*, and on the Royal Family. So far as can be judged, *La Reine des Welches* is more in Morande's style than in Linguet's.

3. Brissot gives an instance of Morande's memory; ed. M. de Lescure, *Mémoires de Brissot*, Paris 1877, pp. 295-6.

4. D'Eon describes his first contact with Morande in some detail in a letter to the Count de Broglie, 13 Jul. 1773, AE CP. Ang. 502, ff. 177-9. The gossip about d'Eon's sex seems to have begun in about 1769, the year of Morande's arrival in London. Morande was a witness in at least one of the lawsuits concerned with bets about d'Eon's sex. One of Beaumarchais's letters to d'Eon begins, Mademoiselle, though it is unlikely that anyone so astute as Beaumarchais believed that d'Eon was a woman. It seems very likely that Morande told Beaumarchais d'Eon's secret. The difference in price which d'Eon had been proposing to offer for the pamphlet, and the price which Morande and Beaumarchais obtained, suggests the possession of a strong bargaining counter; d'Eon to Broglie, 15 Jul. 1773, AE CP. Ang. 502, ff. 182-3. The Agreement between the banker Van Neck and Morande is in AE CP. 508, ff. 197-200.

5. Beaumarchais's mission is described in Cynthia Coxe, *The real Figaro*, London 1961. Beaumarchais's own account is in ed. Brian N. Morton, *Beaumarchais, Correspondence*, Paris 1969, vol. 2, letters 275-85, while the Austrian and German official views are given in the notes on pp; 75-7, 85-8 and 99-102.

6. The chronology of Forth's and Quin's activities in connexion with the Libel is given in Forth's note of his expenses, Forth to Maurepas, 20 Feb. 1778, AE CP. Ang. 528, f. 389.

7. Stormont to North, 3 Dec. 1777 and 6 Jan. 1778, Scone MSS, Box 45.

8. Forth to Le Cler, 16 Jan. 1778, AE CP. Ang. 528, f. 116-117.

9. Forth to Maurepas, 16 Jan. 1778, enclosure ibid. f. 118.

10. Same to same, 16 Jan. 1778, ibid. enclosures, ff. 92-5.

11. Note of expenses, cit sup.

12. *Revue d'Histoire Diplomatique*, vol. 42, 1925, Jehan de Witte, 'L'Abbé Véry et son Journal', entry for Jan. 1778, pp. 144-5.

13. Forth to Maurepas, 30 Jan. 1778, AE CP. Ang. 528, ff. 202-3; and Forth's Diary, 30 Jan. 1778.

14. Forth to Le Cler, and to Maurepas, 6 Feb. 1778, AE CP. Ang. 528, ff. 275-6.

15. Le Noir to Maurepas, 7 Feb. 1778, ibid. ff. 279.

16. Forth's Diary, 11 Feb. 1778.

17. ibid., 18 and 22 Feb.

18. Forth to Le Cler, and to Maurepas, 20 Feb. 1778, AE CP. Ang. 528, ff. 387-8.


### Chapter Five

Unless otherwise indicated the direct quotations in this chapter are from Forth's Diary.

1. Diary 5 Dec. 1777.

2. ibid; 10 Dec., and Stormont to Weymouth, 11 Dec. 1777, PRO SP. 78/305, f. 196.

3. Same to same, 28 Dec. 1777, PRO SP. 78/305, ff. 264-5.

4. Diary 4 Jan. 1778.

5. Auckland papers, BL Add. MS. 34415, ff. 55-6. Vergennes to Montmorin, 16 Jan. 1778, AE CP. Esp. 588, f. 23.

6. Diary 10 Jan. 1778.

7. ibid. 12 Jan. 1778.

8. Forth's account of his meeting with the Ministers and his subsequent comments occur in the Diary entries for 26 to 28 Jan.

9. Diary 30 Jan. 1778.

10. Charles Butler, *Reminiscences*, London 1822, 11, pp. 131 and 139.

11. Among the dispatches describing conversations with Mansfield are Noailles to Vergennes, 3 Feb. 1778, AE CP. Ang. 527, ff. 274-8, and 26 Jan. 1777, AE CP. Ang. 521, f. 94.

12. Reynach's threat to Mansfield is related in Forth's Diary, entries Jan. 13 to 18, 20, 23, 26, 28 to 19; and in AE CP. Ang. 528, ff. 97-8, 116-117; 136-7. Reynach (or Reinach) was apparently involved in a complicated set of relationships that connected him with Tort, formerly secretary to the Count de Guines when he was Ambassador in London; Bourdieu of the bank of Bourdieu and Chollet; and Goat (La Chévre) the smuggler. Speculation, the tobacco farm and contraband all played a part in the relationship, but precisely how, it is very hard to say. Tort was a principal in the scandal that developed when the Count de Guines was supposed to have speculated in the English funds when war nearly broke out over the Falkland Islands in 1771. He speculated heavily, for Guines, according to himself, for his own account, according to Guines. Tort was disgraced, and for years had been trying to justify himself; Reynach claimed to be acting as his intermediary with the French government; Goat was carrying their correspondence. In one of his letters Tort alleges that Beaumarchais kept his secretary Francy informed when ships sailed to America with contraband in which Beaumarchais was not interested. Francy, through Goat, informed his brother Morande in London; Morande laid an information, and when the ship was confiscated they all shared in the prize. Tort alleged that Forth was in some way involved in the scheme. See Tort to Chevalier Péans, 6 Jun. 1777, AE CP. Ang. 523, f. 203; and Reynach to Tort, 3 July 1777, *loc. cit.* f. 361. The allegations are unsupported by proof, but they are unpleasant enough to suggest that Reynach could stir some very muddy waters which might well damage Forth's reputation.

13. Taaffe is not identified but he may have been Theobald Taaffe, a former M.P.

## Chapter Six

Unless otherwise indicated the direct quotations in this chapter are from Forth's Diary.

1. Forth's Diary, 8 Feb. 1778. Other references to the intelligence network are to be found in entries on 9, 19, 21-23 Feb.; 1, 8-12, 14-15, 17, 19, 28 Mar.; and 1 Apr.

2. ibid., 20 Feb. 1778; Count Creutz, 15 and 27 Feb.; Le Noir, 9 Mar.; Necker, 7 Mar.: *Gerusalemme liberata*, 16 Feb.

3. 8 Mar. 1778.

4. Forth to Maurepas, 22 Feb. 1778, AE CP. Ang. 528, ff. 405-6.

5. *Revue d'Histoire Diplomatique*, 1925, vol. 42, Jehan de Witte, 'L'Abbé Véry et son Journal', entry for 22 Feb. 1778.

6. Maurepas to Noailles, 28 Feb. 1778, AE CP. Ang. 528, f. 481, and Noailles to Maurepas, 10 Mar. 1778, CP. Ang. 527, ff. 356.

7. Report of Agent de Police Buhot, 17 Mar. 1778, AE CP. Ang. 529, ff. 143-6.

8. Lord Stormont's difficulties with the Countess de Forbach, AE CP. Ang. 529, ff. 200, 205, 208.

9. Forth's Diary, 18 Mar. 1778. This entry includes the conversation with Vergennes.

10. Forth's Diary, 17 and 20 Mar. 1778.

11. Greenwich 35 MS. 0287, quoted in David Spinney, *Rodney*, London 1969.

12. Forth to Vergennes and to Maurepas, 30 Mar. 1778, AE CP. Ang. 529, ff. 253 and 260.

## Chapter Seven

Unless otherwise indicated the quotations in this chapter are from Forth's Diary.

1. On the Gang see Hector Bolitho and Derek Peel, *The Drummonds of Charing Cross*, London 1967, chap. 4, pp. 60-6.

2. On the Catch Club see Percy A. Scholes, *The Great Dr. Burney*, Oxford 1947, vol. 2, chap. 57, pp. 180-1.

3. Ed. John Beresford, *Parson Woodforde's Diary*, O.U.P. 1924, entries for 9 Feb. and 16 June 1787.

4. There is no explicit account of the functioning of Forth's intelligence system. My summary is mainly based on a number of entries in his Diary. There are comments on O'Gorman and Goat in the archives of the French Ministère des Affairs Etrangères.

5. Diary 17 May, 'Go after man about Brest fleet'; and 21 May, 'Adam's letter'.

6. King to North, 13 December 1777, *Fortescue*, vol. 3, No. 2102, p. 510.

7. Boswell, *Laird of Auchinleck, 1778-1782*, ed. J. W. Reed and T. A. Pottle, Yale 1977, entry 1779. 'Jones the chaplain' is evidently Jeans. I am grateful to Mr. John Brooke for pointing out this reference.

8. AE CP. Ang. 527, ff. 332-41. It would have been interesting to know if Forth's system was ever used to deceive the enemy, the function which one great expert on espionage (Sir John Masterman, *The Double-Cross System*) has described as the main purpose of an intelligence system. One such attempt to deceive the enemy was the Montagu Fox mission in 1780, see Ronald Seth, *The Spy in Silk Breeches*, London 1968. Forth's Diary for this date has not survived, but it can at least be said that he was acquainted with Swinton who played a considerable part in the mission, and that a Fox, not otherwise identified, is mentioned in the Diary for the year 1777-8. The Foxes of Foxcroft, intermarried with the Forths and with the Edgeworths of Edgeworthstown, were fairly near neighbours in County Longford.

## *Chapter Eight*

1. Forth's statement of income, including his pension is among his papers (see Chapter 11). His pension appears in the Secret Service accounts. I owe information on this and on the etiquette governing such payments, to the kindness of Mr. John Brooke.'

2. Forth to Stormont, 25 Oct. 1779, Scone MSS, Box 52. Stormont's answer has not survived, but his comments are written at the bottom of Forth's letter.

3. Chartres's letters to Forth are printed in the Appendix to an article by Amédée Britsch in *Revue d'histoire diplomatique*, vol. 43, 'Lettres de Louis-Philippe-Joseph d'Orléans, duc de Chartres, à Nathaniel Parker Forth', pp. 124-70, cited as *Hist. Dipl.* The letters concerned with Pamela are numbered 3-8, 3 Oct. 1779; 15 Oct. 1779; 13 Dec. 1779; 17 Feb. 1780; 18. Apr. 1780; 16 May 1780.

4. Information about Pamela's birth is to be found in J. G. Alger's article on Lady Pamela Fitzgerald in D.N.B.: it is based on information collected in the Island of Fogo from a descendant of the Syms. It is likely that since Fogo was a centre for the seal fishery, the Syms family were connected with that trade. Robert Southey in a letter to Caroline Bowles, 11 Dec. 1821, says that he heard Pamela's history in Christchurch, Hampshire, and he mentions that the business was negotiated by a clergyman named 'Jones'. I am also grateful for information supplied by the Rev. G. Fitzgerald who, in the 1930's, knew some descendants of the Brixeys, Pamela's stepbrothers and sisters. They firmly believed that Mary Syms had been secretly married to Chartres at Lisbon. Since Chartres never went there this is out of the question, but the child may have been fathered by a Portuguese of good family. The Brixey family knew that Pamela was not the daughter of William Brixey.

5. *Hist. Dipl.* letter 11, Chartres to Forth, 27 June 1781.

6. Madame de Genlis's letter, 1 Dec. 1785, is quoted by Britsch in *Le correspondant,.* 10 Apr. 1913, vol. 251, 'Madame Lafarge et Louis-Philippe, avec les lettres inédites de Louis-Philippe-Joseph d'Orléans et Madame de Genlis'. A certified copy of the Indenture of apprenticeship, 8 Jan. 1784, with Forth's transfer of responsibility to Madame de Genlis, 3 Feb. 1784, is quoted in full in Lucy Ellis and Joseph Turquan, *La belle Paméla*, London 1924.

7. *Hist. Dipl.* letter 57, Madame de Genlis to Forth, 12 Oct. 1785; same to same, 1 Dec. 1785 *cit. sup.*

8. Letters relating to the second little girl, *Hist. Dipl.* letter 15, 26 Jul. 1782; letter 23, 10 Nov. 1782; letter 25, 4 Jan. 1783.

9. *Mémoires d'Alexandre Dumas*, Paris 1863, vol. 1, chap. 32, pp. 245–9. One of Hermine's daughters married an artillery officer named Cappelle, and was the mother of Madame Lafarge.

## Chapter Nine

1. *Hist. Dipl.* letter 22, 4 Oct. 1782; letter 8, 16 May 1780. The portraits which Chartres sent Forth for engraving were by Myris; they were (1) Madame de Genlis, and (2) Madame de Genlis with her own daughters, Chartres's twin daughters and Pamela. The engraver chosen by Forth was Valentine Green. When the elder of the twins died Green was asked to alter the composition on lines suggested by Myris; letter 21, Sept. 1782. Chartres readily agreed that the engravings could be sold for the benefit of the artist; letter 19, 18 Aug. 1782. When Chartres was painted by Reynolds he gave Reynolds permission to have the portrait engraved; the engraver in this case was John Raphael Smith. An un-named artist of Forth's acquaintance was allowed to make a head and shoulders copy; if this was successful Chartres was prepared to allow him to make a full-length copy; letter 56, 27 Aug. 1785.

2. ibid., letter 10, 2 Jun. 1781; letter 9, 15 Nov. 1780.

3. North to George III, 29 Jul. 1780, *Fortescue*, vol. 5, No. 3111; George III to North, 30 Jul. 1780, ibid. No. 3113. It was Thomas Walpole who followed up Maurepas's approach; see Richard B. Morris, *The Peacemakers*, New York 1965, chap. 5, pp. 94–7. Morris describes Forth as a dissolute, loose-tongued Englishman, and a notorious madcap, and he also refers to him as 'the high-living, heavy-drinking spy'. He has evidently taken his impressions from Vergennes' correspondence with the French Ambassador at Madrid, and Aranda's letters to Floridablanca. I have explained why I believe these impressions to have been misleading.

4. *Hist. Dipl.* letter 6, 12 Feb. 1782.

5. Ed. Arneth and Flammermont, *Correspondence secrète du Comte Mercy Argenteau avec l'Empereur Joseph II et le Prince Kaunitz*, Paris 1889,

vol. 1, letter 57, Mercy Argenteau to Joseph II, 12 Apr. 1782 and note; letter 58, Mercy Argenteau to Kaunitz, 12 Apr. 1782. See also Doniol, vol. 5, pp. 40-1.

6. *Hist. Dipl.* letter 43, Chartres to Forth, 26 Jul. 1784.

7. ibid., letter 14, Chartres to Betsy, 2 Aug. 1782; letter 15, Chartres to Forth, 12 Jul. 1782. The first instalment of the service was sent to Chartres from the factory at Sèvres on 20 Sept. 1783, letter 22, *n.* 1. Chartres was the first to receive a service of this type: see Aileen Dawson, 'The Eden Service', *Apollo*, Apr. 1980, p. 297, *n.* 6. See also Svend Ericson, *The Porcelain at Waddesdon.*

8. *Hist. Dipl.* letter 15, 26 Jul. 1784.

9. ibid., letter 18, 15 Aug. 1782; letter 20, 25 Aug. 1782.

10. ibid., letter 20, 25 Aug. 1782; letter 19, 18 Aug. 1782.

11. ibid., letter 47, 31 Jan. 1785; letter 37, 2 Apr. 1784; letter 45, 15 Dec. 1784.

12. Ed. A. Aspinall, *Correspondence of George Prince of Wales*, vol. 1, letter 76, pp. 107-8; letter 78, p. 110. Ed. Earl of Bessborough, *Georgiana Duchess of Devonshire*, London 1953, chap. 5, p. 61.

13. *Hist. Dipl.* letter 56, 27 Aug. 1785 and note; letter 58, 14 Oct. 1785 and note.

14. Chartres's development of the Palais Royal is described in *Britsch*, chap. 9, pp. 311-47 and Pierre d'Espezel, *Le Palais Royal*, Paris 1936, chaps. 7 and 8. Some of his money-raising schemes are referred to in letters to Forth, *Hist. Dipl.* letter 43, 26 Jul. 1784; letter 44, Sept. 1784; and Ducrest to Forth, letter 33, 14 Aug. 1783.

15. Forth to Vergennes, 29 sept. 1783, typescript copy in Forth papers of an original in the Bibl. Nat.

16. *Hist. Dipl.* letter 35, Madame de Genlis to Betsy, 22 Feb. 1784; letters 38 and 39, Madame de Genlis to Forth, Apr. 1784; letter 41, spring 1784.

17. For a detailed study of Orleans's administration of his inheritance see Beatrice F. Hyslop, *L'apanage de Philippe-Egalité*, Société des études Robespierristes 1955. The alkali bleach process developed for Orleans by Nicholas Leblanc at Saint Denis was adapted by the Tennant family at St. Rollox, see Nancy Crathorne, *Tennant's Stalk*, London 1973.

18. On the Rouen family see Vicomte Révérend, *Armorial du Premier Empire*, vol. 4; on his notarial practice see *Régistres des offices et pratiques des Notaires de Paris*, 1786, in the Bibliothèque Historique de la ville de Paris; and *Lüthy*, chap. 2, B.4, p. 303; On Baroud see J. Bouchary, *Les Manieurs d'argent à Paris à la fin du 18ᵉ siècle*, and *Lüthy*, chap. 4, s. 3, pp. 513-5, 528, 542-3n, 555-6, 625, 691.

19. On the 'trente immortelles de Genève, see *Lüthy*, vol. 2, chap. 4, s. 3, pp. 465 *et seq.*

20. For the vicissitudes of the French East India Company see *Lüthy*, *op. cit.* chap. 4, ss. 1 and 2, and s. 4, pp. 673-85.

21. Ledoux's plan for Hosten, BN Est. Ha. 71a. pl. 183 and 178, is reproduced in the Catalogue of *Visionary Architects*, University of St.

Thomas, Houston, 1968. Henry Holland visited Paris in 1787 and was impressed by the forecourts of the Hôtel Thellusson and of the Hôtel de Condé. Dorothy Stroud, *Henry Holland, his life and work*, London 1966, thinks they may have provided inspiration for the screens in front of Carlton House. See Dorothy Stroud, *op. cit.* for the plans of the Hans Town development. For Bélanger's Roule plans see Jean Stern, *A l'ombre de Sophie Arnould, François-Joseph Bélanger*, Paris 1930, vol. 1, chap. 15.

## Chapter Ten

The narrative in this chapter is based mainly on Forth's *Memoir*; unless otherwise indicated the quotations in this chapter are also from this source.

1. Ed. A. Aspinall, *Correspondence of George Prince of Wales* (cited as *Aspinall*), vol. 1, letter 96, p. 120n. On Weltje see also H. D. Roberts, *A History of the Royal Pavilion, Brighton*, London 1939, pp. 11-13, 18, 22.

2. *Procédure criminelle du Châtelet*, quoted André Castelot, *Le Prince Rouge*, Paris 1961, chap. 7, pp. 164-5.

3. One example is a letter from Dr. James Stevenson of Egham, 13. Feb. 1793, Forth MSS, envelope 58.

## Chapter Eleven

1. Forth MSS, Account Book. This is the only surviving account book. All the information concerning Forth's domestic economy in this chapter is based on this source.

2. Forth MSS, *Paterson's Road Book* 1799. Lists drawn up in earlier years, 1792 and 1795, have been pasted into this book. A further undated list is headed 'for a week's jaunt at any time'.

3. *Généalogie Baroud*, Arch. Dept. Lyon, Fonds Frécon; Further information on Baroud and his family has been taken from Edmond Révérend du Mesnil, *Armorial historique de Bresse . . . et franc-lyonnais*, Lyons 1872, and *Archives historiques et statistiques du Départment du Rhône*, 1830, pp. 26-34.

4. A letter in the Forth MSS, envelope 175, J. G. Harris, Old Palace Yard, Westminster, to Madame des Mallets, 7 Sept. 1819, summarises the provisions of an Assignment, 25 Sept. 1789, and a Declaration of Trust, Dec. 1789, together with a Deed of Separation, 1 Jun. 1793. The date and place of the separation are noted in the Account Book.

5. Emile Dard, *Le général Choderlos de Laclos*, Paris 1936, devotes three chapters to Orleans's mission to London, basing them on material in the archives of the Ministère des Affaires Etrangères.

6. *Aspinall*, vol. 2, letter 484, p. 47.

7. Forth MSS, *Memoir, cit. sup.*

8. André Castelot, *op. cit.*, chap. 7, p. 159. Beatrice F. Hyslop, *op. cit.* gives an account of Orleans's revenue and losses as the result of revolutionary legislation.

9. Pierre d'Espezel, *le Palais Royal*, Paris 1936, chap. 8, pp. 173–7. See also Forth MSS. *Memoir cit. sup.* and *Aspinall*, vol. 2, letter 579, p. 149. William Buchanan, *Memoirs of Painting*, 1824, quoted in Frank Herrmann, *The English as Collectors*, London 1972, pp. 137–8, says that the Italian and French paintings in the Orleans collection were sold by Walckiers to Laborde de Méréville, who later took them to London. A letter from Thomas Moore Slade, purchaser of the Dutch and Flemish paintings, to William Buchanan (Herrmann, *op. cit.* p. 144), says that Orleans lost the paintings to the banker Laborde the elder at billiards. The gaming accounts in the Forth MSS show that certainly on one occasion Walckiers actually played billiards with Orleans, whereas Laborde the elder, who was of an older generation, did not so far as I know frequent Orleans's society. The banking houses of Laborde and Walckiers were however very closely linked financially and personally; Laborde the elder's son, Laborde de Méréville, was a first cousin of Walckiers.

10. Forth MSS, Account Book. A *Rape of the Sabines* by Salviati appears in William Buchanan's Catalogue of the Orleans Collection, *op. cit.* vol. 1, p. 56. It was exhibited at Bryan's Gallery and sold for 34 guineas by auction by Messrs. Peter Cox, Burrell, and Foster in February 1800, ibid. p. 158. It is now in the Bowes Museum.

11. *Lüthy* vol. 2, section 4, pp. 431, 3.

12. Sénart, *Mémoires*, Paris 1821, pp. 10–11.

*Chapter Twelve*

1. Lyon De Symons's family had not been very long settled in England. The ancestor of this particular branch was known as der Wiener. Mozart was given a letter of introduction to the De Symons on one of his visits to England. The family was known for its beautiful manners. I am grateful to Mrs. Stollard and Mrs. Clausen for their help in providing information about their family history.

2. Answer of J. B. Lévet in Chancery suit De Symons *v.* Du Barry, PRO C. 12/1398. This chapter is based mainly on information contained in the Bill and Answers in that suit. For a fuller account of the theft of Madame Du Barry's jewels, and details of the sources used, see Marion Ward, *The Du Barry Inheritance*, Chatto and Windus, 1967.

3. The gift of the snuffbox is mentioned in a note on Forth by the 3rd Earl of Mansfield, Scone MSS, Box 45.

4. Pétition supplémentaire, Sipora Joseph and Godel, Versailles, Arch. Dep. 1 F. 87/18.

5. Forth's *Memoir*.

6. After Madame Du Barry was guillotined Grieve moved into her house and went through her possessions. From a story told by James Henry Duveen, *Collections and Recollections*, London 1935, it looks very much as if Grieve was also concerned in the traffic in stolen jewels which went on during the French Revolution, and that some of Madame Du Barry's jewels found their way into his hands. Amiens, where Grieve was at last arrested, was one of the centres for this illicit trade. For further information on Grieve, see *The Du Barry Inheritance, cit. sup.*

## Chapter Thirteen

1. Forth to Pitt, 20 May 1794, Chatham papers, PRO 38/8, vol. LXXXVI, ff. 236-7.

2. Vera Watson, 'A plot to assassinate Pitt', *History Today*, vol. X, No. 9, Sept. 1960.

3. Forth MSS, envelopes 62, 86, 221.

4. Forth *v.* Morland, PRO C. 38/841.

5. This account occurs in a note by the 3rd Earl of Mansfield headed '1836', Scone MSS, Box 45.

6. Forth to Duke of York, 22 Apr. and 5 Dec. 1799, and Duke of York to Forth, 28 Dec. 1799, quoted in Forth's *Memoir*.

7. Forth to Prince of Wales, 10 Jan. 1800, ibid.

8. The narrative of events in this chapter is based on Forth's *Memoir*, pp. 19-34, supplemented by correspondence in *Aspinall*. Some of the letters printed by Aspinall are also reproduced in the *Memoir*. Direct quotations not otherwise noted are also from this source.

9. Forth to Moira, 27 Apr. 1800, quoted in *Memoir*.

10. Moira to Forth, 27 Apr. 1800, ibid.

11. The meeting on 19 April and Forth's subsequent actions are described in the *Memoir*, pp. 21-22.

12. Moira to Forth, 22 and 23 Jun. 1800, quoted in *Memoir*.

13. Forth to Bicknell, 12 Jul. 1800, *Aspinall*, vol. 4, 1550.

14. *Aspinall*, vol. 4, 1633, 'Memorandum of N.P. Forth, 20 Mar. 1802.

## Chapter Fourteen

Unless otherwise indicated the direct quotations in this chapter are from Forth's Diary.

1. Forth to Col. McMahon, 28 Nov. 1800; and Forth to the Prince of Wales, 14 Nov. 1800, *Aspinall*, vol. 4, 1573, p. 170, and 1571, pp. 167-8.

2. Paul and Martial Pradel de Lamase, *Nouvelles notes intimes d'un émigré (le Chevalier Pradel de Lamase)*, Paris 1914, pp. 239-40.

3. *A Practical Guide during a Journey to Paris 1802*. In describing Paris of the Consulate and early Empire I have drawn heavily for topographical information on Jacques Hillairet, *Dictionnaire historique des rues de Paris*. For other aspects of this period I have used, amongst others, J. G. Lemaistre, *A Rough sketch of modern Paris*, London 1803; *An Englishman in Paris* 1803 (Journal of Bertie Greatheed), ed. J. P. T. Bury and J. C. Barry, London 1953; Duchesse d'Abrantés, *Mémoires*, Paris 1833.

4. A document among the Forth MSS lists the requirements.

5. Some of Messrs. Christopher's and Dupuis's accounts are among the Forth MSS. Customers included Lord Lansdowne and Sir Henry Vane Tempest. The painter Danloux knew Genlis's mistress Tiennette Roussée in London, and heard this story from her, Danloux, *Journal*, ed. Baron Roger Portalis, Société des Bibliophiles français, 1910, p. 122.

6. André Castelot, *Le Prince rouge*, Paris 1961, says that Philippe Egalité was buried in the Cimetière des Errancis. But Hilairet, under Place Prosper Goubaux, gives the opening date of the Cimetière des Errancis as March 1794. It follows that Philippe Egalité, who was guillotined in November 1793, could not have been buried there. According to Hilairet, under Rue d'Anjou, he was buried in the Cimetière de la Madeleine. As a child in the 1830s, Madame d'Armaillé played in the gardens of Monceau, and describes them in *Quand on savait vivre heureux*, Paris 1934, chap. 2, pp. 34–8.

7. Title deeds of Gatton Park, 26 and 27 Feb. 1796, Surrey County Record Office, 216/2/17/1. Biographical information on the Petrie family is to be found in *Correspondence of David Scott*, Camden Society, 3rd Series, vols. LXXV and LXXVI, as well as on the family monuments in Lewisham Parish church.

8. Forth MSS.

9. There are directions about investments in the Impey papers, BM Add. MS. 16259, ff. 63–6; 87–9; 175; and 16260, f. 116. For the activities of the banks of Fizeaux and Grand and Grand and Labhard, see *Lüthy, op. cit.* vol. 2, chap. 3, B. 6. The occasion on which Impey is said to have sat down at table with all the parties in the Calcutta crim. con. proceedings, Madame Grand, her former husband, and Sir Philip Francis, probably occurred at Neuilly. Francis, like Impey, may well have been involved in financial transactions with Georges Grand's bank. Impey's son, in his Memoir of his father, questions the likelihood of this meeting. But given the financial connexion, I think it may well have happened. Talleyrand was said to have been present also.

## Chapter Fifteen

Unless otherwise indicated the direct quotations in this chapter are from Forth's Diary.

1. The Marriage settlement, consisting of an Indenture and Bond, both dated 24 April 1804, are given in full in Bain *v*. Forth Rouen, Bill of Complaint, PRO C. 16/B 36/1865.

2. Ed. Charles Wicoulland, *Récits d'une Tante, Mémoires de la Comtesse de Boigne*, Paris 1907, vol. 1, chap. 11, pp. 200-201.

3. St. Hilaire, *Les petits appartemens de St. Cloud et de la Malmaison*, vol. 2, pp. 11-12 and 25-9.

4. Francis James Jackson to Lord Hawkesbury, 8 Dec. 1801, PRO F.O. 27/61, Separate and Secret.

5. Ernest d'Hauterive, *La Police secrète du Premier Empire*, Bulletins quotidiens addressés par Fouché à l'Empereur 1804-5, Paris 1908, vol. 1, 350, 1090, Bulletin 6 Germinal an XIII, mercredi 27 mars 1805 ($F^7$ 6440 Dos. 9185).

## Chapter Sixteen

Unless otherwise indicated the direct quotations in this chapter are from Forth's Diary.

1. Thomas Hammersley to Forth, 16 Aug. 1805, Forth MSS, envelope 28.

2. Stenger, *La société pendant le Consulat*, vol. 1, p. 29.

3. Decree, 21 Mar. 1806, Forth MSS, envelope 327.

4. A copy of the Will concerned with Forth's property in France is among the Forth MSS. His English Will, 14 May 1806, is in the records of the Prerogative Court, 2 Kent 1625 1006/4 73. The Inventory drawn up at the Rue Richer after Forth's death lists the valuables in pawn at the Mont de Piété, Arch. Nat. Minutier centrale, LXXI, 165, 9 May 1809.

5. According to the Bureau des Cimetières de la Ville de Paris, Forth's name is not in the Registers of those buried in the existing cemetery of Montmartre. But I think it likely that he was buried in one of the older burial grounds of that quarter, as were some of the friends whose funerals he attended. The instructions about his burial in his will are somewhat contradictory, but I believe the sense to be as I have stated.

# INDEX

Adam, William, M.P., 162, 167-9
Allen, Edward, 147-50, 152
Amyand, John, M.P., 55-6, 79-80
Aranda, Pedro Abaraca y Boléa,
    Count d', Spanish ambassador in
    Paris, 15-16, 24-5, 50-1, 61
Aremberg, Louis, Prince d', 144
Argenson see Voyer, Marquis d'
Artois, Charles Philippe, Count d',
    became Charles X, 6, 27-8, 32, 35-
    6, 48, 73, 117
Auckland, 1st Baron see Eden,
    William

Baggs, Philip, Major, 54
Baldwin, William, M.P., 173
Baroud, Claude Odile, 115-6, 141,
    180, 182, 190, 198
Baroud du Soleil, Louis Joseph, 141
Barré, Isaac, M.P., 86
Barrymore, Emily (Stanhope),
    widow of 6th Earl of, 19-20, 37,
    54, 67
Baudelaire, Charles, 195
Baudelaire, Jean François, 195
Baudelaire, Rosalie (Janin), 195, 204
Beaumarchais, Pierre Augustin Caron
    de, 3, 16-18, 40-1, 54, 173, 221n4
Beaumont see Eon, Chevalier d'
Bélanger, François Joseph, 117-8,
    193
Beljambe, Pierre Guillaume Alex-
    andre, 203
Bicknell, Charles, 167-8, 171-2, 174
Biron, Duke de see Lauzun, Armand
    Louis Gontaut, Duke de
Biron, Louis Antoine Gontaut, Duke
    de, Maréchal de France, 50, 66-7,
    76
Bolts, William, 185
Bonaparte see Napoleon I
Boswell, James, became Lord Auchin-
    leck, 87
Bourdieu & Chollet, Messrs., 21, 60,
    222n12

Boyd, Robert, 195
Boyd, Walter, the younger, 117,
    185
Brancas, Duke de see Lauraguais,
    Count de
Brichard, Maitre, 126, 128, 132, 169
Brissot, Jacques Pierre, 39, 128-9
Brixey, William, 97, 224n4
Brummell, William, 79-80
Buffon, Marguerite Françoise
    Bouvier de Cépoy (Agnès),
    Countess de, 142, 144
Buhot, Agent, 72-3
Buller, Sir Francis, Bart., 162
Byron, The Hon. John, Rear Admi-
    ral, 85

Catherlough, Earl of see Knight,
    Robert
Chamier, Anthony, M.P., 79
Chartres, Duke de see Orléans,
    Duke d'
Child, Elizabeth Dorothea (Betsy):
    parentage, 8, 217-8n6; children
    by NPF, 9, 67, 109, 112, 141;
    becomes NPF's mistress, 8; at
    Fontainebleau, 27-9, 35-7; NPF
    dicates letters to, 72; refuses
    snuffbox, 75; looks after Pamela,
    97; looks after Hermine, 100;
    return to Paris, 112-4; treatment
    by Chartres, 107-8; treatment by
    Mme. de Genlis, 113-4; separates
    from NPF, 141-2; moves to Hans
    Place, 159; reconciliation with
    NPF, 178-9, 200-1; final illness
    and death, 200-1, ambiguous
    situation, 8-9, 19-20, 36-7, 80
    companions, 137-8
Child, Henrietta Magdalena (Knight),
    The Hon., 8, 217-8n6
Child, The Hon. Josiah, Lieutenant,
    8, 217-8n6
Christie, James, 143, 147
Christopher, Messrs., 181

Clarence, H.R.H. William, Duke of,
    became William IV, 123-4
Clermont, Frances (Cairnes), wife of
    1st Earl of, 35-7, 86
Clonard, Thomas Sutton, Count, 5,
    117
Compton, Hermine (Hermione),
    became Mme. Collard, 100-2, 182,
    211, 225n9
Creutz, Gustave Philippe, Count, 67

Daguerre, Messrs., 7
Deane, Silas, 52
Defermont des Capelieres, Joseph,
    185
Deffand, Marie Anne (de Vichy
    Chamrond), Marquise du, 72
Delaunay, Denis Joseph, 184
Dervieux, Anne Victoire, 193
De Symons, Lyon, 147-50, 152-3,
    155, 159, 228n1
De Symons, Polly (Goldsmid), 147,
    149
Devonshire, Georgiana (Spencer),
    Duchess of, 128, 142-3
Deux-Ponts (Zweibrücken), Christian,
    Duke de, 18
Drummond, The Hon. Henry, M.P.,
    79
Drummond, The Hon. Robert, 79
Du Barry, Adolphe, Viscount, 36, 54
Du Barry, Jeanne (Bécu or Gomard
    de Vaubernier), Countess, 20, 36-7,
    40-1, 54, 147-56
Ducrest, Charles Louis, Marquis, 109,
    112
Dumas, Alexandre, 102
Dunmore, Charlotte (Stewart), wife
    of 4th Earl of, 37, 67, 76, 78, 80
Dunmore, John Murray, 4th Earl of,
    79-81
Duverney, Joseph Pâris, 17

Eden, William, M.P., became 1st
    Baron Auckland, 83
Elliott, Grace Dalrymple, 144
Eon, Charles Geneviève Louis
    Auguste André Timothée de
    Beaumont, Chevalier d', 39-41,
    221n4
Estaing, Henri, Count d', Admiral, 85

Farquhar, Sir Walter, Bart., 161
Flamarens, Elisabeth Olympe
    Félicité Louise Armande (du
    Vigier), Marquise de, 31
Fitzgerald, Lady Edward see Pamela
Fitzherbert, Mary Anne (Maria)
    Smythe, 121-2, 160
Florida-Blanca, Francisco Antonio
    Monino, Count de, 218-9nn7 &
    19
Fontainebleau, 27-33, 35-6
Forbach, Marianne (Gamache),
    Countess of, 18, 73
Forbes, George, Viscount, became
    5th Earl of Granard, 5-6
Forth, Eliza (Petrie), became
    Baronne Rouen des Mallets:
    meets NPF, 186; engaged to
    NPF, 189-90; marriage settle-
    ment, 191-2; marries NPF, 192;
    early married life, 192-7; dislikes
    housekeeping, 195-6; amuse-
    ments, 201-5; extravagance, 205;
    taste for music, 194, 205; birth
    of Frederick, 207-8; financial
    position, 209; second son, 210;
    marries Rouen des Mallets, 212
Forth, Eliza (Betty), 141-2, 178,
    189-91, 200, 209
Forth, Frederick, 207-12
Forth, Nathaniel Parker (summary):
    ancestry, 1-2, 217nn1 & 2; birth,
    1, 217n1; education, 2; employed
    by Herries, 2-5; established in
    France, 3-5; runs intelligence net-
    work, 4-5, 17, 19, 65-6, 72, 76-7,
    82-8, 223n4, 224n8; races in
    Paris, 5-6; races at Fontainebleau,
    27-8; Betsy his mistress, 8-9;
    friendship with Mansfield, 9-10;
    useful to Stormont, 10-11; intro-
    duced to Maurepas, 10-11;
    appointed Special Envoy, 10-16;
    instructions as, 14-15, 218n5;
    dealings with Beaumarchais, 16-
    18, 54; helps to keep peace, 21-5,
    30-1; with Court at Fontainebleau,
    26-31; meets Chartres, 32-5;
    offends Marie Antoinette, 35-7;
    buys Morande's Libel, 41-9; hears
    news of Saratoga, 50; sounds
    Maurepas, 51-3; carries dispatches,

Forth, Nathaniel Parker (*summary*)
  (cont.)
  53-5; concern for career, 55-8;
  helps Mansfield, 59-64; sees
  Chartres in Paris, 50-1, 65; social
  success, 66-7; false peace rumour,
  67-71; last interview with Maurepas, 73-4; last interview with
  Vergennes, 74-5; letter to Maurepas, 77-8; leaves Paris, 76-8;
  return to London, 79-81; seeks
  government post, 81, 86-7, 94-5;
  talks with North, 83-7; purchases
  for Chartres, 80-1, 103; looks
  for foundlings, Pamela, 96-9;
  looks for foundlings, Hermine,
  100-2; peace feeler, 103-6; sees
  Chartres again, 106-8; finds him
  a house, 108-10; caretakes in
  Portland Place, 109-10; resettles
  in Paris, 112-8; business adviser
  to Orléans, 112, 115; raises
  money for Princes, 123-8; journeys to France in 1789, 124-7,
  132-5; recovers Princes' Bonds,
  130-3; lends Orléans money, 130-
  2, 143; liaison with Mme. de
  Genetines, 140-1, 158-9; separates
  from Betsy, 140-2; sale of Orléans
  pictures, 143-5, 169, 228nn9 & 10;
  raises money for Orléans, 145-6;
  helps Mme. Du Barry, 147-54;
  claims reward, 159; affirms
  loyalty, 157-8; financial losses,
  157-60; Stormont's disfavour,
  159-60; claims on Princes, 153,
  160-74; Memoirs concerning
  claims, 162-3, 173, 204,
  215; argues with D. of York,
  167-70; returns Bonds, 170-1;
  defends reputation, 161-2, 164,
  170-4; threatens lawsuit, 162-4,
  171-4; repaid by Princes, 174;
  return to Paris, 177-82; reconciled to Betsy, 178-9; 200-1;
  claims on Orléans estate, 180-1,
  184-5, 205-6; friendship with
  Petrie, 183-6; courts Eliza, 189-
  90; not a détenu, 187-8; marries
  Eliza, 190-2; early married life,
  192-7; spied on, 198-9; later
  married life, 201-5; economizes,

Forth, Nathaniel Parker (*summary*)
  (cont.)
  205-9; birth of Frederick, 207-8;
  English Will, 204; French Will,
  208-9; final illness, 209-11;
  second son, 210, 212; death and
  burial, 211, 231n5

  ───────────

    accounts, 7, 48-9, 86, 137-9,
  144, 166, 195; beliefs, 7; course
  of relationship with Orléans, 32,
  77, 95, 106-10, 112, 130-2,
  142-3, 145-6, 157, 159; diary, 7,
  10, 198, 210, 215; drinking
  habits, 53-4, 225n3; Freemason,
  34-5; friends, 5-6, 9-10, 19, 33,
  36-7, 79-80, 114-5, 180, 183-6,
  194-5, 203-4; gambling, 33-4,
  54, 144, 225n3; health, broken
  jaw, 132, 140, 161, 172; health,
  stone, 140, 174, 178, 180, 192,
  203; health, 'rheumatic complaints
  47, 55, 61, 72, 161; health weakening, 192, 202-4, 209-11; household expenses, 137-9, 181, 195-
  6, 205-6, 208; income, 4, 14-15,
  94-5, 116, 130-2, 137, 142, 158,
  160, 166, 191-2, 205, 209; profession, stockbroker, 4-5, 14, 61,
  76, 94, 107, 116, 137; profession,
  wine trade, 2-5, 33, 78-9, 181-2;
  houses, England, 7, 62-3, 79-80,
  109-10, 118, 137; houses, France,
  113, 118, 137, 158, 186, 192,
  193-7, 201-6, 208-11; tastes,
  books, 6-7; tastes, furniture, 7,
  80; tastes, horses, 2, 6, 27, 32;
  tastes, music, 7, 80, 140, 178,
  184, 204; travelling equipment,
  139-40
Forth, Nathaniel, Junior, became
  the Rev, 19, 67, 80, 109, 112-3,
  141-2, 160, 178, 190-1, 209
Forth MSS., 215-6
Forth-Rouen, Sophie Elie Alexandre, Baron, 210, 212
Fox, Montagu, 224n8
Francy, Théveneau de, 17-8
Franklin, Benjamin, 12, 50-2, 69
Frederick (de Neuhoff), Colonel,
  133-4

Fullarton, William, M.P., 19, 27, 55, 69-70, 72, 81-2, 86, 219n12

Gem, Dr., 19, 67, 72, 83, 219n12
Genetines, François Régis de Charpin, Count de, 141, 158-9, 179
Genetines, Françoise (Baroud), Countess de, 115, 140-1, 153, 158-9, 177, 179, 182, 190, 196, 198, 200
Genetines, Mimi de, 141, 200
Genlis, Charles Alexis Brulart, Count de, became Marquis de Sillery, 33-4, 54, 78-9, 114, 144, 181-2
Genlis, Stéphanie (Etiennette) Félicité (Ducrest de Saint-Aubin), Countess de, became Marquise de Sillery, 32, 85, 96-102, 109, -113-14, 157, 181-2
Genlis, Pulchérie de, became Countess de Valence, 99-100, 102, 182
George III, 14-16, 24-5, 61, 85, 104, 110-1, 121-4, 142, 157-8, 168
George, Prince of Wales, became George IV, 111-2, 121-4, 127-8, 130-6, 142-3, 153, 160-74, 177
Gibbes, Sir Philip, 55
Gluck, Christoph Willibald, 18
Goat (La Chèvre), 17, 53, 56, 60, 65-6, 71-2, 77, 82, 222n12, 223n4
Gojard, Receiver General of Paris, 137
Grand, Catherine Noelle (Werlée), became Princesse de Talleyrand, 185, 188, 230n9
Grand, Georges, 75, 185, 230n9
Gravier see Vergennes, Count de
Grieve, George, 154-6, 229n6
Guilford, 2nd Earl of see North, Lord
Guines, Adrien Louis, Count de, became Duke de, 222n12

Hammersley, Thomas, 122-4, 130, 163, 200-1
Herries, Sir Robert (Don Roberto), 2-5, 20-1, 60, 72, 85, 117
Hickey, William, 36
Holland, Henry, 117, 159

Hosten, Arnaud, 117, 193, 226n21
Howard, Henry see Suffolk, 12th Earl of
Howe, The Hon. William, Major General, became 5th Viscount, 68
Hunter, John, 140
Huskisson, William, M.P., 219n12

Impey, Sir Elijah, 185, 188, 191-3, 230n9

Jeans, The Rev. Thomas, 19, 20, 43, 45-6, 55-6, 58, 62-3, 73, 76, 81-2, 87, 96-7, 141
Judlin, Alexis, 67, 77
Junius, 6, 60, 217n4

Kinnaird, Charles, 8th Baron, 163-71, 173
Knight, Robert, of Barrels, M.P., became 1st Baron Luxborough and 1st Earl of Catherlough, 8, 217n6
Kerr, John William, 117

Laborde de Méréville, François Joseph, 143, 145, 228n9
Laclos, Pierre Choderlos de, 114-5, 125, 128, 142
Lafayette, Marie Joseph du Motier, Marquis de, 127
Laffitte, Jacques, 206, 208
Lamballe, Marie Thérèse Louise (de Savoie-Carignan), Princesse de, 42
La Motte, Henry Francis, Colonel, 88-9
Lauraguais, Louis Léon Félicité, Count de, became Duke de Brancas, 5-6, 33
Lauzun, Armand Louis de Gontaut, Duke de, became Duke de Biron, 32-3, 78, 125, 144, 157
Layard, Charles Peter, The Rev., became Dean of Bristol, 178
Lecler du Brillet, 20, 31-2, 44, 47-8, 70, 73, 75
Ledoux, Claude Nicolas, 117-8, 193
Legouvé, Gabriel Marie Jean Baptiste, 203
Lenoir, Pierre, 47, 66

Levet, Jean Baptiste, 147-50
Linguet, Nicolas Simon Henri, 39, 220n2
Loughborough, Alexander Wedderburn, 1st Baron, became 1st Earl of Rosslyn, 130
Louis XVI, 20-6, 28-9, 31, 35, 38, 48-9, 51, 70, 94, 126, 157
Louis Philippe, King of the French, 157, 163, 181
Luttersloh, Henry, 88-9
Luxborough, 1st Baron see Knight of Barrels

McMahon, John, Colonel, 172
Mansfield, 2nd Earl of see Stormont, Viscount
Mansfield, David William Murray, 3rd Earl of, 160
Mansfield, Elizabeth (Finch), wife of 1st Earl of, 62
Mansfield, William, 1st Earl of, 9, 16, 44-5, 58-64, 79, 86-7, 153, 170
Marie Antoinette, 26-9, 31-2, 35-8, 41-3, 48-9, 66, 70, 94, 105
Maurepas, Jean Frédéric Phélypeaux, Count de: NPF introduced to, 10-11; asks for NPF as Special Envoy, 10-11; favours NPF, 20-1, 30-2; discusses naval armaments, 22-5; asks NPF to buy Libel, 41-3, 49; prepares Treaty with America, 50-1; discusses La Grue, 57-8; and Reynach, 59-61, 63; American negotiations, 65, 67, 71; alarmed by peace rumour, 68-9; last interview with NPF, 73-5; letter from NPF, 77-8; peace feeler, 104; death, 104; character, 12-13, 51; gratitude to NPF, 47-8; opinions on NPF, 21, 71; opinions on English Ministers, 15-16; opinions on American Independence, 52-3, 70-1
Maurepas (La Vrillière), Countess de, 31
Mayne, Robert, M.P., 52, 67
Mercy-Argenteau, Florimond Claude, Count de, 28

Moira, Francis, 2nd Earl of, became 1st Marquis of Hastings, 162-7, 169-74
Montalivet, Jean Pierre Bachasson, Count de, 199
Morande, Charles Théveneau de, 18, 39-49, 94, 142, 221n4, 222n12
Morande, Elizabeth, 41-2, 49
Morland, William, 167-8, 190
Murray, David see Stormont, Viscount
Murray, William see Mansfield, 1st Earl of
Myris, Sylvestre, 98

Napoleon 1, 179, 186-7, 193, 197, 202, 205
Nassau, Charles Henri Nicolas Otto de, Prince de Nassau-Siegen, 5
Necker, Jacques, 56, 66, 116-7
Noailles, Emmanuel Marie Louis, Marquis de, French ambassador, 16, 22, 25, 43, 71, 88
North, Frederick, Lord, became 2nd Earl of Guilford, 10-11, 14-16, 21, 44, 46, 53, 55-8, 79, 81-7, 94-5, 104-6

O'Gorman, Chevalier, d'Eon's brother-in-law, 82
Orléans, Louis Philippe Joseph, Duke d', formerly Duke de Chartres: meets NPF, 28, 32; friendship with NPF, 33-5, 77, 95, 106-10, 142-3, 146; informs NPF of Saratoga, 50-1; employs NPF, 80-1, 84, 95-101, 103, 108-12, 114-16; conduct at Ushant, 93-4; disliked by Marie Antoinette, 94; Foundlings, Pamela, 96-9; Foundlings, Hermine, 99-101; refuses to lodge NPF in Paris, 105; kindness to Betsy, 107-8; settles in Portland Place, 108-11; English impressions of, 110-11; friendship with Prince of Wales, 111-12; business affairs, 112, 114-5, 124-6, 130-3, 142-6; succeeds father, 114; rebuilds Palais Royal, 114; develops estates, 114-5; revolutionary activities, 125-7, 145-6, 157; mission to England, 126-8,

Orléans, Duke d'
(cont.)
142-3, 169; loans to Princes,
123-7, 130-3; annuity to NPF,
130-2, 137, 158, 161; borrows
from NPF, 130-2, 143; pledges
diamond, 180-1, 192; reduced
income, 143-6; sells Orleans picture, 143-5, 169, 228nn9 & 10;
changed relations with NPF,
142-3, 146, 157; takes name
Egalité, 145; votes for King's
death, 157; guillotined, 158;
burial, 182, 230n6; character,
32-4, 94, 145; Freemason, 34-5,
220n11; Reynolds portrait of,
111-12, 225n1
O'Toole, the brothers, 5

Pamela (Anne Syms), became Lady
Edward Fitzgerald, 96-9, 101-2,
224n4
Panchaud, Isaac, 116-17
Paris: Bastille, 47; Bois de Boulogne,
32; Boulevard de Clichy, 19;
Hôtel de Deux-Ponts, 18-19, 72-
3; Monceau, 126, 182, 230n6;
Montmartre, 19, 186, 194, 211,
231n5; Palais du Luxembourg,
117; Palais-Royal, 32, 34, 105,
114, 125-6, 129, 142-5, 182;
Passy, 50, 52; Pavillon Boüixière,
19, 69-70, 219n12; Rue Blanche,
186, 192-3; Rue de la Chaussée
d'Antin, 19, 113; Rue Neuve des
Augustins, 18; Rue Neuve des
Capucines, 186; Rue Neuve des
Mathurins, 113; Rue Neuve des
Petits Champs, 115, 198; Rue de
la Place Vendôme, 201-3, 206,
208; Rue de Richelieu, 113, 115,
117; Rue Richer, 208; Rue Saint
Georges, 193-4, 201; Rue St.
Honoré, 118, 137, 158; Rue de
Varennes, 50; Rue de la Victoire,
193-4; Rue Vieille du Temple, 17
Parker, The Hon. George, Lieut.
General, 2, 217n2
Pepys, Sir Lucas, Bart., 88
Pérignon, Pierre, 194-5, 202, 204
Perregaux, Jean Frédéric, 180, 187-
8, 192-3, 206

Petrie, Anne Harvey (Nancy),
became Mrs. Thomas William
Taylor, 186
Petrie, Eliza see Forth, Eliza
Petrie, Eliza (Vesey), 186, 189,
196-7, 202, 206
Petrie, John, M.P., 178, 183-92,
194, 196-7, 202, 206, 208, 211
Phélypeaux see Maurepas, Count de
Pitt, William, the younger, 157-8
Poirier, Messrs., 7
Pontoise, 196-7, 199, 202, 206
Porta, Giuseppe, called Salviati, 144
Portland, William Henry Cavendish
Bentinck, 3rd Duke of, 134
Pulteney, William, M.P., 67

Queensberry, William, 4th Duke of,
128, 153
Quin, Forth's valet, 24, 38, 41-2,
46, 48-9, 67

Race-horses, Cantator, 111; Caddet,
32; Comus, 32; Eclipse, 33; Gim-
crack, 33; Glowworm, 33; Life-
line, 5-6; Marske, 33; Mexico, 33;
Noir et tout Noir, 5-6; Top-
Gallant, 33
Raincy, le, 144, 208-10
Ransom, Morland & Hammersley,
Bankers, 135, 143, 150, 152,
156, 166-70
Rettfort, Richard, 158, 177, 189-
91, 197, 201, 209, 211
Reynach, Count de, 59-63, 222n12
Reynolds, Sir Joshua, 111-2, 225n1
Robinson, John, M.P., 46, 56, 79-
81, 83, 87
Rodney, Sir George Brydges, Vice
Admiral, 66, 72, 76-7
Rodriguez Hortalez & Co. 17
Rouen des Mallets, Alexandre Jean
Denis, became Baron, 194, 212
Rouen des Mallets, Baronne see
Forth, Eliza
Rouen, Denis André, Maître,
became Baron, 115, 126, 147,
180-2, 186-7, 192-4, 198-9, 201,
204, 209, 211-2

St. Germains, Viscount de, 129
St. Leger, Anthony, Col. 128, 153

Salviati *see* Porta, Giuseppe

Sandwich, John Montagu, 4th Earl of, 80

Saratoga, 50

Scherer, Madame, wife of Barthélemis Louis Joseph, 202-3

Scott, David, M.P., 116, 178, 183-4

Sénar, Gabriel Jerôme, 146

Sèvres, 107-8

Shée, Henri, became Count d'Alton, 184-5

Sillery, Marquis de *see* Genlis, Count de

Sillery, Marquise de *see* Genlis, Countess de

Slade, Thomas Moore, 143-4, 228n9

Smith, Lieut. Colonel, 14

Smith, Nathaniel, The Rev., 192, 211

Smith, Richard, Brig. General, M.P., 36-7, 54

Sonde, Tort de la *see* Tort

Stanley, Hans, M.P., 46

Stormont, David Murray, 7th Viscount, became 2nd Earl of Mansfield: NPF introduced to, 9-11; supports NPF's appointment as Envoy, 10-15, 21, 24; Embassy residence, 18, 19; uses NPF to negotiate, 21-5; at Fontainebleau, 26-7, 30; sends NPF to London, 42-3; hears news of Saratoga, 50-1; despondent, 65, 67; recalled, 72-3; later career, 81, 95, 104; estranged from NPF, 160; character, 12-13; opinion of Maurepas, 24, 51-2; opinion of NPF, 11, 21-3

Stormont, Louisa (Cathcart), wife of 7th Viscount, became *suo jure* Countess of Mansfield, 18-19, 35-7, 160

Suffolk, Henry Howard, 12th Earl of, 15, 44, 55-8, 79, 81, 87, 95

Sutton, Thomas *see* Clonard

Swinton, Samuel, Captain R.N., 44, 84

Syms, Anne *see* Pamela

Syms, Mary, Mrs. William Brixey, 97-9

Taaffe, ?Theobald, M.P., 62-3, 222n13

Talleyrand, Charles Maurice de Talleyrand-Périgord, became Prince de Bénévent, 125, 184-5, 230n9

Taverny, 180, 182, 204, 211

Thynne, Thomas *see* Weymouth, 3rd Viscount

Tickell, Richard, 87

Tort de la Sonde, 222n12

Ventenat, Jean, 203

Vergennes, Charles Gravier, Count de, 16-18, 22, 25-7, 50, 53-4, 74-5, 77, 88, 105-6, 113

Versailles, 20-1, 23, 25-6, 42-3, 48, 51, 53, 65, 70, 73-5, 77, 105, 125-6, 153

Voyer, Marc René de Voyer de Paulmy d'Argenson, Marquis de, 33, 66-7

Walckiers, Edouard Dominique Sébastien de, 144-5, 228n9

Walpole, Horace, became 4th Earl of Orford, 6

Wedderburn *see* Loughborough, 1st Baron

Weltje, Louis, 111, 122

Wentworth, Paul, 52, 67

Weymouth, Thomas Thynne, 3rd Viscount, became 1st Marquess of Bath, 10-11, 15, 55-8, 72, 79

Wilkes, John, M.P., 87

Woodforde, James, the Rev. (Parson Woodforde), 82

York, H.R.H. Frederick Augustus, Duke of, 123-4, 127, 130-1, 133-6, 143, 158, 160-4, 166-74